"My birthday's next month. I've told Joey: 'Shove the sables and rubies. It's an autographed copy of *O' NEW JERSEY* for me.'"
—**Cindy Adams,** *New York Post*

"Robert Heide and John Gilman are in the vanguard of popular culture specialists. Their *O' NEW JERSEY* is indispensable."
—**Patricia Leigh Brown,** *New York Times*

"This book will amuse and amaze you!"
—**Michele Howe,** *Newark Star-Ledger*

"These guys know their onions."
—**Leonard Maltin,** *Entertainment Tonight*

"Heide and Gilman have told the story of New Jersey—an exciting, vibrant, friendly place I am proud to call home. I hope their work will entice travelers to come to New Jersey and enjoy, from Sussex County to Cape May, all we have to offer—especially our people."
—**Bill Bradley**

"An eclectic travelogue taking the weekend adventurer to a pop-culture odyssey from High Point to Sandy Hook to Cape May. From Sandra Dee to submarine sandwiches, from saltwater taffy to Bruce Springsteen, the state's famous and firsts are all remembered."
—**Gail Pendleton,** *New Jersey Herald*

"There's a lot to like about *O' NEW JERSEY*, a pocket-size guidebook to the Garden State. Much of it comes in the form of photos—Joe's Diamond diner in Kearny, with its king-size coffee cup on the roof; the Black Cat Tavern in Absecon, where a giant neon cat stands guard; Kurt Laemmel's Pork Store in Hoboken, with architecture right out of 'Plasticville,' and, almost worth the price of the book alone, a wonderful old MGM still of Connie Francis, fetching behind her flaring eyebrows, fur wrap, and rocket beehive. If you're looking to explore New Jersey, get in your car and get going with your copy of *O' NEW JERSEY*."
—*Asbury Park Press*

"Go buy this book!"
—**Mark Simone,** *WNEW* Radio

"A gem . . . its pages are chocked with wit, humor, and solid research."
—*Library Journal*

O' New Jersey

Day Tripping, Back Roads, Eateries, and Funky Adventures

Robert Heide

John Gilman

O' New Jersey

Day Tripping, Back Roads, Eateries, and Funky Adventures

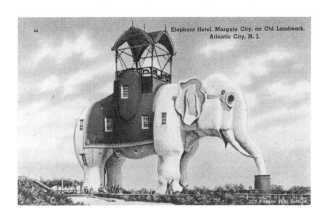

Robert Heide and John Gilman

St. Martin's Griffin ❧ New York

Design by Maura Fadden Rosenthal

Library of Congress Cataloging-in-Publication Data

Heide, Robert.
  O' New Jersey / Robert Heide and John Gilman.
    p. cm.
  ISBN 0-312-18147-7
  1. New Jersey—Guidebooks. I. Gilman, John.
  II. Title.
  F132.3.H47 1998
  917.4904'43—dc20
                  92-2607

First St. Martin's Griffin Edition: April 1998

10 9 8 7 6 5 4 3 2 1

Acknowledgments

· ·

Christine Todd Whitman, Maria Maruca, William La Rosa, Madeline Hoffer, the *Newark Star Ledger*, Cindy Adams, Don Horn, Randy Garber, the New Jersey Federation of Women's Clubs, Scott Rodas and the Ocean County Library—Tom's River, John Bitici, Bill Agnellino, Hoop, Bill Nicholas, Bill Marmaras, Vincent Sorrentino, Robert M. La Torre, Mary Barretta, William Gordon, George Point, Craig Schneider, Kevin Shea, Jim Hans, Hoboken historian and founder of the Hoboken Historical Museum, Vicki Gold Levi, author of *Atlantic City—100 Years of Ocean Madness* and founder of the Atlantic City Historical Museum, former U.S. senator Bill Bradley, Michael F. Hurley—Archdiocese of Newark, the Fitzgerald family, Jim, Andrée, Farrar, Zoe, and James Jr., Peter Camarrano, Priscilla Camarrano, Carol and Kenny Tooker, Gail and Michael Coulter, Susan Hansen, Lucille Luckel, Robert and Alma Broedel and their twin daughters Barbara Baranyay and Beverly Caldora, Robert Young, Timothy Bissell, Jeanne Tyler, Pat and Ken Tecza, Harold Lane, Jerry Pagano, Ric Cuneo, Michelle Kelly, John Reid Currie, Wendy Lipkind, Alexandra Anderson-Spivey, Jock Spivey, Ann and Walter Heitke, Laura Negele, Linda Jonasch Artalie, Ada Schwab, Peggy Miller, Dolores Borowski, Norma and Richard Edgar, Cheryl Daly, Art Generas, Allan Siegel, Bubbles Ricardo, Gillian Goll, Margaret Wilcox, Earl Sague, Michael and Suzanne Wallis (*Route 66*), Paul Lieber, Gwen Victor, Jacque-Lynn Colton, Lise-Beth Talbot, Betty "Bascha" Lipton, Larry Myers, Eric Krebs, John Hammond, Steve O'Donnell, Douglas Coupland, Joe Franklin, Gary Phillips, Paco Underhill, Ann Harris, Fran Jay, Marvin Silverstein, John and Gertrude Koch, Jim and Suzanne Glen, Jeffrey Geiger, Tim Goetz, Steve Gould, Nancy Keller, Jimmy Fouratt, Irwin Chusid (WFMU—East Orange), Tom Kitts, Kenneth Anger, Phil Cohen, Rita Brue Stanziani, Irene Stella, Mr. and Mrs. Wightman, Chris Weidner, Alex Kuczynski, Adele and George Speare of Mother Hubbard's, Wren D'Antonio, Rachel Woodruff, Hong Qing Ling, Luisa McCune, Mel Camuso Renick, Florence Dremel Brown, William Singer, Lois Hausmann, Larry "The Blade" Sorrentino, and Bette "Miss Long Branch of 1945" and "Angel" Jack Coe.

Asbury Park neon.

"Sandra Dee" (Alexandra Zuck) of Bayonne, the eternal teenager, with her electric toaster.

Contents

Foreword   1
Greetings from New Jersey   5
Hoboken Day Trip   10
Hoboken—An Old-Time Town   15
Paterson Day Trip   20
The Diner Experience—Let's Have Another Cup of Coffee
   and Let's Have Another Piece of Pie   23
Diner Day Trip—"Lost" Diner Tour: The Dime-Store Kids
   in New Jersey   27
Newark Day Trip—Cherry Blossom Time in Newark   35
Newark/Bloomfield   40
Montclair/Upper Montclair   47
South Mountain Reservation Day Trip   54
Millburn—Short Hills Shopping Mall, Pal's Cabin, Eagle
   Rock Reservation, and Highlawn Pavilion   57
Irvington Time Travel—A "Memory-Image" by
   Robert Heide   61
Union Day Trip   66
Union, Maplewood, and South Orange Village   68
Great Swamp/Jockey Hollow Day Trip   70
Morris County—Madison—Morristown—Mendham   73
Chester/Long Valley Day Trip   77
Doris Duke's Gardens Day Trip   80
High Posh: Somerville—Far Hills   83
Princeton Day Trip   86
Jersey Country: Hopewell—Flemington—Neshanic Station   90
Lambertville Day Trip   93
Lambertville Antiques—Washington Crossing   97
Trenton   99
Camden's Campbell's Soup   102
Southwestern Farm Country—Burlington, Bordentown,
   Mount Holly, Timbuctoo, Clementon, Swedesboro,
   Mullica Hill, Glassboro, Salem, Bridgeton,
   and Vineland   106
Delaware Water Gap Day Trip   114
Northern Mountains and Lakes—Bergen, Passaic,
   and Sussex Counties   117
High Point Day Trip   122
"Hello From The Jersey Shore"—Notes on Road, Ferry,
   and Train Travel   126
Sandy Hook Day Trip—Via Keyport and Keansburg   129
North Shore—Atlantic Highlands to Deal   131
Monmouth County Side Trips   134

Ocean Grove Day Trip   136
North Shore—Asbury Park to Bay Head   140
Seaside Heights Day Trip   150
Island Beach to Island Heights   156
The Legend of the Jersey Devil   161
Lakewood to Lake Rova to Forked River   164
Long Beach Island and "Old Barney"   169
Old Route 9 Day Trip—From Barnegat to Oyster Creek   171
Pine Barrens Day Trip—and the Carranza Memorial   176
Atlantic City Day Trip   179
Fun and Games in Atlantic City   183
Old Atlantic City   189
Ocean City Day Trip   194
Corson's Inlet to Wildwood-by-the-Sea   199
Cape May Day Trip   201
Postscript—Travelers' Advisory   206
Index   209
Journey Notes   219
About the Authors   225

Three New Jersey maps, left to right: Gulf, 1935, Tydol Flying A., 1944 and a New Jersey Esso (now Exxon). These maps were given free to motorists.

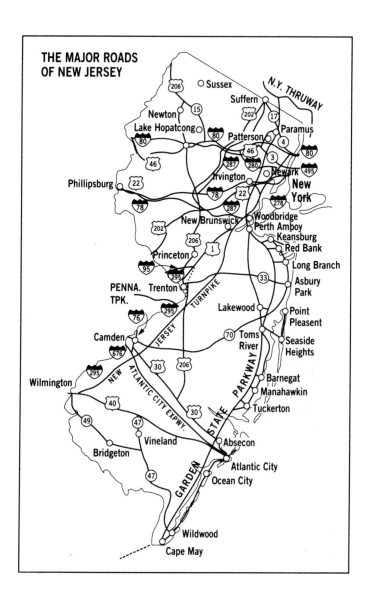

THE MAJOR ROADS
OF NEW JERSEY

A glowing symbol of New Jersey is the Edison Tower, located in Menlo Park.

O' New Jersey

Day Tripping, Back Roads,
Eateries, and Funky
Adventures

Foreword

You go over this fence marked PRIVATE,
through this gate marked DO NOT ENTER,
to a lake that has a sign: DO NOT FISH.
You know, that's the best place for fishin'.

Stan Laurel to Oliver Hardy
in *The Dancing Masters*, 1943.

O' NEW JERSEY introduces the traveler to interesting places to go and journeys to take in a state that many now refer to as "New York's California"—let's face it—it's got everything. For many years now we have chosen to escape the built-up tensions and stress of life in Manhattan by getting into the car, turning on the ignition, and driving through the Holland or Lincoln Tunnel or over the splendid George Washington Bridge, directly into the land of New Jersey. Just-two-guys-on-the-road has been our theme for many happy adventures; and this guidebook sets out to identify and map out for the reader—be they from New York City, Jersey City, Philadelphia, or Los Angeles—the best places to go, explore, and where to experience some good on-the-road food, Jersey style.

For convenience purposes we readily suggest the use of the Garden State Parkway, the New Jersey Turnpike, or the big Highways 78, 80, 280, or 287, but always keeping in mind that the back roads or old two-lane highways (like Route 1-9) are the most scenic and interesting. Our suggestion is that once you reach a destination, you either park the car and take a walk or drive the back road, stopping frequently to see what's there. Our motto is: "Joy is a backroad adventure." Many of the places in this guide are accessible by public transportation via bus or train. Sometimes it is fun to leave the car home. We also include some of the best "Jersey joints"—bars, diners, pizza hangouts, and a selection of some of the very best restaurants in the state. If it takes awhile to get there, or you just want to relax somewhere and not be in a hurry, stay overnight at a motel, hotel, bed and breakfast, or country inn, sprinkled for your convenience throughout the book.

You don't need to go to Zagreb, Vladivostok, Shanghai, or Havana—or even to Kalamazoo, Altoona, or Cucamonga. It's all here, right in your own backyard, in New Jersey. Though there is no Paris, New Jersey, there is a Berlin and a Timbuctoo; and either of these, both in South Jersey, would make for an exciting, do-it-yourself destination and adventure. While you're out there hunt-

"Invaders from New Jersey" T-shirt.

ing, you'll find that the state is going through a renaissance of its own.

Newark is a good example: At the annual Conference of Mayors in San Diego on June 17, 1991, Newark was chosen from among 117 cities as "America's most livable." The designation was conferred on Newark not for intrinsic livability but for "purposeful actions in developing programs that promote livability," says Kay Scrimger of the Conference of Mayors. Newark, the city that has survived a mass of problems from race riots to massive unemployment, was also designated an All-America City by the National Civic League in 1991. Awards are coming in, too, for a recycling program that uses tires in making pavement for roads. Low- and moderate-income housing for hundreds is completed, the first movie theater in 50 years has been built, the first shopping center in 20 years is in operation, the downtown corporations have put large amounts of money into new building construction—the New Jersey Performing Arts Center, rivaling New York City's Lincoln Center, opened with great fanfare in 1997. This book will point the way to Newark and Rahway, to Cape May and High Point, but it is also hoped that it will become a blueprint for personal discovery—that the reader will find his or her own niche using *O' New Jersey* as a guide.

ROBERT HEIDE
JOHN GILMAN

TRAFFIC EMERGING IN N. Y. FROM HOLLAND TUNNEL

Courtesy Port of New York Authority

HOLLAND VEHICULAR TUNNEL, NEW YORK CITY,

One of the main connections between New Jersey and New York is the Holland Tunnel. During Opening Day ceremonies, on November 12, 1927, 20,000 people walked under the Hudson River for the first and last time; at midnight the first car drove through, making the trip in eight minutes. Top: Postcard showing cars emerging from the Holland Tunnel, published by the May Rose Company, 1950s. Bottom: Earliest traffic in what was referred to as the Holland Vehicular Tunnel, 1929 postcard.

Greetings from New Jersey

New Jersey, one of the 13 original states, is just 8,224 square miles, small when compared to most other states; but it is a brilliant microcosm of America. It offers in its grandiose manner skiing, beaches, mountains, lush farmland, swamps, metropolitan landscapes, suburbs, ethnic enclaves, forests, and factories—in short, New Jersey, the land of forgotten time, offers everything. Historic Colonial country farmhouses and beautiful Victorian towns are also integrated into the landscape of the state. There are vast tracts of mountainous forests, pinelands and lakes and a beautiful coastal shore region where you can relax away from the fast lane. There are as well interesting and historical industrialized urban cities that are fun to discover and explore.

The Jersey Bounce

If you don't feel so hot
Go out to some Jersey spot
And whether you're hep or not
The Jersey Bounce will make you swing.

Pine Barrens author John McPhee has referred to New Jersey as a composite of all the other states, and John Cunningham, a New Jersey historian, has written that the incredible variety—the mountain ranges, the vital cities, farmlands, and wonderful white-sand beaches, each of them well defined, unique and nationally known—is the key to the understanding of what attracts both residents and tourists to New Jersey. The secret is out: New Jersey is a wondrous state, a great place either to live or to visit, be it an extended vacation in summertime, or a day trip or weekend at any time of the year.

◆

Jersey Is No Joke!

In the past, New Jersey jokes were a part of the standard repertoire of the old-time vaudevillians who liked to make cracks about "playing Hoboken," and even today's national television comedians or talk-show hosts have only to mention "Joisey" to get an instant laugh. Example: When drafting the Declaration of Independence one of our forefathers offered the proposition that the British keep New Jersey. Because the state is situated between two major American cities, Philadelphia and New York, and is astride the main transportation routes of the East, it has sometimes mistakenly been thought of only as a pathway from Philadelphia to

Manhattan. This concept began with statesman, inventor, and punster Ben Franklin, who enjoyed making jokes about New Jersey, likening it to "a barrel tapped at both ends." It was Ben Franklin who first wrote about "devils" lurking in the South Jersey pine barrens. Although this was meant to be "filler" in a newspaper article during a summer lull, people took it literally, and thus one aspect of the famous "Jersey Devil" legend was born. The idea of speeding through New Jersey as quickly as possible was concretely reinforced in 1952 when the New Jersey Turnpike first opened, giving travelers from all over the country and the world a clear view of a vast inner industrial belt.

New Jersey has a history filled with political corruption from "Boss" Hague, the ex-mayor of Jersey City who amassed a fortune of $8 million on an annual salary of $7,500, to Harrison A. Williams, the New Jersey Abscam senator. These scandals have also contributed fuel for more ongoing Jersey jokes. There has also been much reported—and much more rumored—about mobster rule and crime syndicates sprinkled throughout the state, adding further confusion to this funhouse Jersey jigsaw puzzle.

In recent years, however, according to a report from the Eagleton Institute of Politics at Rutgers University, there is evidence of a growing sense of pride in the state. Half of the New Jersey residents polled said they thought New Jersey was a better place to live when compared with most other states, including neighboring states. Eighty percent of the respondents rated New Jersey as an excellent place to live and to vacation. Rock singer Bruce Springsteen, regarded as the country's most admired "working class hero songster" has, according to "The guy from Jersey" Joe Piscopo, a native New Jersey comedian, completely overturned the Jersey joke. "It's like Polish jokes," Mr. Piscopo said, "they're not funny anymore because the Pope is such a dynamite guy. And now, with the advent of Springsteen, Jersey jokes just don't work."

> Question: What is a Jersey jaunt?
>
> Answer: A jaunt is a short journey made just for pleasure. Jersey is a state of mind.

The 15-mile-wide corridor across New Jersey, called the "industrial belt" has always been a target for jokesters in the past. Jersey is rich for the taking; pottery and steel from Trenton, the brickworks of Perth Amboy, the locomotive industry in Paterson, textiles from Passaic, diverse manufactures in Newark, heavy machinery from Jersey City. Most of the population, too, is jammed into this corridor between New York and Philadelphia, making it one of the most densely settled sections in the country. By contrast, the rest of Jersey geography, both above and below this notorious belt, is pastoral, covered with beautiful streams and sparkling lakes, gentle rolling hills and valleys, 127 miles of pristine coast-

line from Sandy Hook to Cape May, the largest wilderness area on
the East Coast, the famous New Jersey Pine Barrens, thousands of
acres of fertile farmland south and west of the Pine Barrens
stretching to the Delaware River, and vast marshes and estuaries
on the east side of the Barrens.

New Jersey is proud of its history. Descriptive bronze plaques
abound everywhere in every little park, on every prominent rock,
on farmhouses and often even in the middle of a forest region.
George Washington and his army spent over a quarter of the Revolutionary War in New Jersey, giving rise to the oft-repeated
phrase "George Washington Slept Here." When overnight guests
check into one of the state's many country inns, small hotels or
roadside lodgings, they often find this "G.W.S.H." proclamation,
intended as a humorous pun, embroidered or handwritten, in the
frame hung on the wall over their old-fashioned, creaky bed. In
fact, Jack Benny and Ann Sheridan starred in the classic comedy
film about country inns, *George Washington Slept Here* (1942).
    Atlantic City is famous for its glamorous resort-town past, the
Miss America contest, and of course, gambling. Hoboken is famous for the Clam Broth House and Frank Sinatra. Jersey cranberries from bogs in the Pine Barrens are consumed all over the
country, and the Jersey tomato is the best grown anywhere. Architectural wonders abound, such as Thomas Edison's Menlo Park
"lightbulb" memorial and the wonderful Pulaski Skyway, which
soars over the Jersey meadows. Jersey "firsts" are legion (see list),
and include the invention and production of the moving picture
(on the Palisades at Fort Lee).
    A fun-filled exploration of New Jersey, using this book as a
guide, will hopefully put you into the camp of some of the enthu-
siastic celebrities who seem to enjoy talking up the Garden State.
These include: Bruce Springsteen, Joe Pesci, Jimmy Roselli,
Whitney Houston, Dionne Warwick, Olympia Dukakis, Jerry
Lewis, Sandra Dee, Connie Francis, Vivian Blaine, Doris Duke,
Allen Ginsberg, Joyce Carol Oates, Ed Koch, Philip Roth, Anne
Morrow Lindberg, Jack Nicholson, Alan Alda, Meryl Streep,
Michael J. Pollard, John Travolta, Celeste Holm, Susan Saran-
don, Melba Moore, Amiri Baraka (aka LeRoi Jones), and General
Norman H. Schwarzkopf.

◆

New Jersey Facts

The state flag, adopted in 1896, is buff with the state seal embla-
zoned in blue on its center. The colors were selected by George
Washington and reflect the insignia of the state's Dutch settlers.

The state motto is: "Liberty and Prosperity" (this appears on the
state seal and the state flag.)

The state flower: the purple violet, adopted in 1913.
The state bird: the eastern goldfinch, also adopted in 1913.
The state animal: the horse, designated in 1977.
The state insect: the honeybee, named in 1974.
The state tree: the red oak, designated in 1950.

Among the 50 states, New Jersey is 1st in average value of farm-lands and buildings per acre, 4th in per capita income, 8th in value of goods added by manufacture, 9th in population (7,904,200), 29th in gross income per farm, and 46th in size (7,836 square miles).

Some New Jersey "firsts" include:
The first celluloid, invented by John Wesley Hyatt at Newark in 1870.
The first phonograph, made by Thomas A. Edison at Menlo Park in 1877.
The first submarine, built in 1878 by John Holland of Passaic County, and now exhibited in the Pacific Museum at Paterson.
The first motion picture, developed by Thomas Edison at Menlo Park in 1889.
The first incandescent lamp, made by Thomas A. Edison at Menlo Park in 1879.
The first log cabin, built in Swedesboro in the 1640s.
First brewery in America, in Hoboken, 1642.
First steam engine in America, brought from England in 1753.
First steam locomotive, built by Colonel John Stevens of Hoboken in 1824.
First boardwalk in the world, built in 1870 at Atlantic City.
First American flag from an American loom, made at Paterson by John Rule.
First Colt revolver, developed in Paterson in 1836.

"I Love New Jersey" souvenir pinback button.

First "condensed" soup in America, cooked and canned in Camden County in 1897.

First saltwater taffy, produced at the Jersey shore in the 1870s.

First cultivated blueberries, marketed by Elizabeth White of Whitesbog in 1916.

First town to be lighted by electricity, Roselle.

First organized baseball game, played in Hoboken in 1846.

First intercollegiate football game, played in New Brunswick, between Rutgers and Princeton, on November 6, 1869,

First Miss America, chosen in Atlantic City in 1921.

First Indian reservation, established August 29, 1758, at an appropriated tract in Burlington County.

First ferry service in the world, operating between Hoboken and Manhattan in 1811.

First road sheet asphalt pavement, laid in Newark in 1870.

First national historical park, created at Morristown in 1933.

First drive-in movie theater built on a 10-acre plot in Camden County in 1933.

ONE DAY OUTINGS

SPRING EDITION

JERSEY CENTRAL
RAILROAD

Hoboken Day Trip

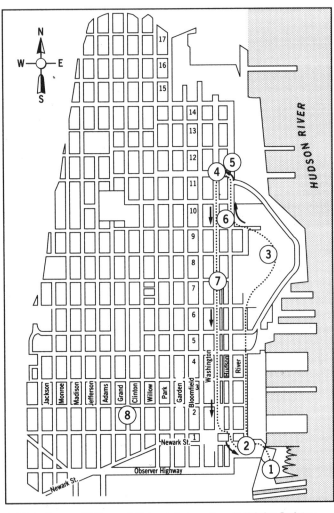

1. Erie Lackawanna Station
2. Clam Broth House
3. Castle Point
4. Helmer's Restaurant
5. Maxwell's
6. Elysian Fields
7. Hoboken Bookstore
8. Leo's Grandevous
Restaurant

Just south of the Lincoln Tunnel and just north of the Holland Tunnel exits in New Jersey, adjacent to the Pulaski Skyway and a spur of the New Jersey Turnpike, lies the old city of Hoboken. In the good old days New Yorkers took rowboats across the Hudson River for afternoon and evening walks in the tree-shaded Elysian Fields of Hoboken. It was the Germans who gravitated to Hoboken in the 1840s (the Irish went to Jersey City to work on the railroads and canals; the Scotch to work in the mills in Harrison and Kearny; the Swiss to West New York and Union City's embroidery industry) and the German beer gardens and gay Oktoberfests there became legendary. Today the PATH (Port Authority Trans-Hudson) trains whisk passengers from Macy's in Herald Square, from the World Trade Center in lower Manhattan, from Journal Square in Jersey City, and from Newark's Pennsylvania Station to Hoboken in less than 30 minutes. The ultramodern PATH system is a cheap, efficient, and pleasant means of travel. Your first big surprise is when you emerge from the PATH into the splendid beaux arts Erie Lackawanna Train Terminal situated atop the Hoboken waterfront. New Jersey Transit trains heading west into New Jersey depart every few minutes from the open-air boarding platforms, and the Hoboken–Battery Park City ferry service is steps away from track 15 at the far end of the station. The recently restored landmark train station, a registered State and National Historic Site, was designed by Kenneth Murchison and built in 1907. It features a brilliant terrazzo floor, Tiffany glass ceiling, and is entirely clad in rich copper work turned luminous green with oxidation.

When leaving the train station the first and the best place to go is straight to the famous (since 1899) **Clam Broth House** at 38 Newark Street, two blocks away. You can't miss it because of the three-story-high red neon hand on the roof with a finger pointing down. The sprawling tavern-restaurant is decorated with pictures of the famous who have eaten there, from Frank Sinatra's mother and father (a Hoboken fire captain under Mayor DeSapio) to Frank Sinatra himself, Jimmy Roselli, Tony Bennett, Liza Minnelli, Brooke Shields, various rock-and-roll groups and . . . well, you'll just have to go and discover yourself. Avail yourself of the traditional free hot clam broth in the old seaman's barroom or a beer and a seafood appetizer, then check out the Clam Broth House's extensive Italian/seafood menu that includes the delectable Fisherman's Delight platter, steamed clams, lobster, clams on the half-shell and giant Alaskan crab legs. This large family-style restaurant is open every day.

Original neon sign from the Clam Broth House in Hoboken.

For authentic Mexican food **Los Dos Compadres Restaurant** at 302 First Street—(201) 653-0540 is worth the side trip. Order up their flautas/fried tacos at $1.50 each, or tortas, quesadillas, chalupas, huevos rancheros, salsa de huevo, huevos a la Mexicana for starters; main courses include *carne asada con arroz y frijoles* at $6.95 and *enchiladas de mole con pollo o queso arroz y frijoles* at $7.50. Your hosts are Evencio Varela and Eutiquio Figueroa.

As you stroll up River Street you will pass on your right what was once the home of North German Lloyd and Holland-America shipping, and the major site for the filming of *On the Waterfront* (1954) which utilized Hoboken townspeople in the cast. Halfway up River Street you can either walk through **Stevens Park,** which is fronted by a manicured little league baseball field, or take the low road, a waterfront avenue called "Frank Sinatra Drive." The high road, however, takes you up to **Stevens Gatehouse,** built of serpentine rock in 1859 as the home of the woman who tended cows for the Stevens estate, the oldest building on the Stevens 55-acre campus. Walk up through the Gatehouse onto the campus where you will find yourself on an outcropping of rock referred to in the log of Henry Hudson's second voyage on the *Half Moon* in 1609. This is where the Stevens family's "castle" was located until the present-day institute structure was built in 1959. Castle Point observatory terrace features a cannon dating from the Civil War and what is probably the most spectacular view of the entire Manhattan and Hudson skyline from the George Washington Bridge to the Verrazano Narrows and beyond. Turning left and walking upriver you cross a yellow brick street with stately homes formerly lived in by Maxwell House Coffee executives. Turn right down the yellow brick road and you will pass through **Elysian Park,** a remnant of Hoboken's famous Elysian fields. The immense red-and-blue-neon Maxwell House "Good to the Last Drop" coffee cup sign cast a glow over the area at night before the factory closed and the sign was dismantled. When the lights went out Manhat-

An intense Marlon Brando takes a cigarette break during the filming of On the Waterfront, *directed by Elia Kazan and filmed entirely in Hoboken.*

The magnificent view of the Hudson River and Manhattan Island from Castle Point at Stevens Institute of Technology in Hoboken.

tanites mourned, particularly Greenwich Villagers who missed the often discernible smell of coffee wafting across the Hudson River.

Walking out from Elysian Park you'll find yourself at Washington and 11th Streets where a plaque, donated by the Hoboken Industry and Business Association in 1984, commemorates the famous Elysian Fields ballgame of June 19, 1846, the first of its kind in the world. By this time you may probably need some sustenance and **Helmer's German Restaurant** at 1036 Washington Street, only steps from the bronze baseball plaque, will fill the bill. Established at the turn of the century, this highly polished, wood-paneled, exceptionally comfortable restaurant and bar offers a really satisfying dining experience. Sitting in one of the commodious upholstered booths is like taking a voyage on an Art Deco ocean liner like the S.S. *Bremen.* The varied Helmer's menu includes traditional German dishes like Wiener schnitzel or sauerbraten with side dishes of red cabbage and homemade potato dumplings. Hackbraten is a delicious German meat loaf made with veal, pork, beef, and other secret ingredients. Norman Lueders, a commanding presence, dispenses an endless variety of German beers and wines. To secure one of the booths, designed originally for large people who enjoy long dinners, it is best to call in advance at (201) 963-3333. Open at 11:30 A.M. until 10 P.M.; Friday and Saturday until 11 P.M.; closed Sundays. Just across the street from Helmer's is the legendary **Maxwell's** (1039 Washington at 11th), an early haven for college rockers like R.E.M. and Sonic Youth. Steve Fallon, owner of Hand Mad, started the place in 1978 and presented the cutting edge of advance popular music groups like This Is It, Flying Saucer, Jive Tribe, The Jesus Lizard, The Loveless, Flat Old World, The Mummies, The Toasters, and Dog Eat Dog. If these last two groups make you hungry, Maxwell's serves a full menu from chili con carne ($3.95) to Burger Maxwell (choice of mozzarella, Swiss or colby cheese served with fries—$5.75) to "daily fresh specials"

The Beaux Arts Erie-Lackawanna railroad terminal, located along the Hudson.

like meat loaf dinner with mashed potatoes and vegetable ($9) and black linguine with bay scallops in marinara sauce ($9). A wide selection of tap and bottled beers and premium wines is also offered at Maxwell's, which is open late. Call for the latest industrial rock music schedule; (201) 798-4064.

Hoboken

. . . .

An Old-Time Town

Hoboken is just across the Hudson River from New York's Greenwich Village, and like people who live in the Village, Hobokenites have a great deal of pride in local history and landmark buildings. They happily take time to point out historic sites or tell stories about local characters like Hetty Green, the infamous miser who amassed a fortune on the stock market but who chose to live in a cheap walk-up on Washington Street. Despite her wealth she constantly complained to whoever would listen about the nickel bus fare.

It is no coincidence that Hoboken became known as a mile square gin mill in the years before, during, and after Prohibition. America's first brewery was established there in 1642; and a surge of German immigrants opened up festive beer gardens in the Elysian Fields. Today there is at least one bar per block in "Hoboghan Hackingh" or "Land of the Tobacco Pipe" which is what the Lenape Indians called this area before the Dutch bought it out from under them for a few blankets and some bright trading beads. Colonel John Stevens, who invented the first steam locomotive in 1825, hit pay dirt back in 1784 when he managed to purchase the entire mile-square area for $90,000. He laid out the plan for the "new" city of Hoboken in 1804. In 1870 the Stevens family founded the Stevens Institute of Technology, recognized as one of the great engineering schools in the world.

The first "open challenge" baseball game, organized just for the occasion, is said to have occurred in Hoboken on June 19, 1846, between the Knickerbockers and the New Yorks. It is generally conceded that until this match America's favorite sport was not seriously regarded at all.

For 100 years, between 1850 and 1950, Hoboken flourished as a great shipping and railroad town; but as factories shut down in the 1950s and 1960s and moved elsewhere, all of this business came to a virtual standstill. My-T-Fine Pudding, Cocomalt, Log Cabin Syrup, Newman Leather, and other factories are now converted into commercial lofts, art studios, and residential spaces. The classic 1954 Academy Award–winning film *On the Waterfront*, directed by Elia Kazan and starring Marlon Brando, Eva Marie Saint, and Karl Malden, depicts the heyday of the shipping industry in a Hoboken that is no more. Frank Sinatra, the singer known as the "Chairman of the Board" who belts out "New York, New York," is a hero in Hoboken, the town in which he was born and raised. Not long ago, amidst the protest of a group of students at Stevens, Sinatra was given an honorary degree. His response to the jeering bunch was "I hope you'll have to listen to my voice forever." The skinny kid who became "the voice" in the 1940s still carries a chip on his shoulder over the tough times he endured growing up on the wrong side of the tracks in Hoboken.

Hoboken is an unusual place to go to. It is isolated from the rest of the world and yet at the same time it's right in the middle of it. The city was originally a tidal swamp, separated from the mainland of New Jersey by the rocky cliffs of the Palisades to the west, the Hudson River to the east, and the vast trainyards of the Erie Lackawanna to the south. When you're there, you're really there. To get the right feel, take a bus from the depot next to the 1908 PATH entrance to the end of town (14th Street). Turn around and walk back down Washington Street (it's only 14 blocks to the train station) and experience small-town America with a city ambiance. There are charming stores. Try Steve Fallon's and Arnold La Spina's **Hand Mad** for folk, funk, and fine art at 116 Washington Street—(201) 653-7276, the **Hoboken Bookstore** at 626 Washington Street—(201) 963-7781, **In-Retro Vintage Clothing and Collectibles** at 608 Washington Street, and **Golden Age Books and Comics** at 1200 Washington. A highlight on Washington Street is **Johnny Rockets** (at number 134). This nationwide chain opened one of its pop-culture 1950s-style moderne architectural gems—complete with vintage rock jukebox music which sometimes has happy customers dancing the "Twist" in the aisles with the frantic waiters. Try their great malteds, hefty hamburgers, homemade apple pies, chili by the bowl, BLTs, and other all-American dishes. There are little Cuban and Italian counters and sit-down restaurants, chic watering holes, and even haute cuisine for the younger "in" crowds, old-fashioned ice cream parlors (try **Schnackenbergs** at 1110 Washington Street), bakeries, newspaper and magazine shops, friendly and relaxed people on the street, and a generally pleasant overall atmosphere. For a better view of all this—and the spectacular Hoboken sunsets—get some new specs or shades at **Myoptics,** 121 Washington Street. Call (201) 420-0644 for an appointment.

A good place for a nightcap is the **Elysian Fields** at 1001 Washington Street (corner of 10th Street)—yes, another place where scenes from *On the Waterfront* were filmed. This little bar has a nautical motif and retains the full flavor of the 1930s, right down to its stoutly loyal customers, its unusual handcarved one of a kind bust of Charlie McCarthy (on the tiled wall leading to the "bilge" room downstairs) and the "ladies" backroom decorated with spectacular handcarved plaster animals cavorting all over the ceilings and walls. There is nothing to eat here, just potato chips and pickled slim jims, but it's a lively place most evenings and worth a visit to soak up local atmosphere. Weekends there are live blues bands. The **Brass Rail** at 135 Washington Street (corner of 2nd Street) is

On the set of the 1940s RKO Radio short The House I Live In, *Frank meets a group of youngsters.*

another landmark bar with a beautiful oil mural depicting Hoboken's history. The place attracts a friendly local crowd, while upstairs a moderately expensive but first-rate French restaurant features bubbling onion soup, spicy garlic sausage, steak Diane, and pheasant and duck dishes. Open from Tuesday to Saturday for lunch and dinner until 10 P.M., Sundays till 9 P.M. — call (201) 659-7074 for reservations.

As far as history is concerned, you can visit the **J.J. Astor House** at 128–133 Washington Street (near an original Lenape Indian settlement site), 107 Washington, Ms. Hetty Green's old place, or 601 Bloomfield Street (one block south of Washington) where songwriter Stephen Foster lived in 1854. At First and Washington Streets is the **Hoboken City Hall,** another registered State and National Historic Site built in red brick in 1881 and enlarged in white brick and brown stone in 1911. This is where the **Hoboken Historical Society** (write Hoboken Historical Museum, P.O. Box 707, Hoboken, NJ 07030, for a sample newsletter) features changing exhibitions of Hoboken history. For stunning laser-color copies of authentic antique Hoboken ephemera, call Hoboken historian extraordinaire Jim Hans for an appointment at (201) 653-7392 or write P.O. Box M-1220, Hoboken, NJ 07030. Burly bohemian Jim and his attractive and exotic wife Beverly, and their cheerful daughter Polly always suggest offbeat walks and interesting tidbits of information, like the exact location of Francis Albert Sinatra's birthplace at 415 Monroe Street (mysteriously torn down; now it is just a brick wall concealing a vacant lot) and his boyhood-teenage home at 841 Garden Street (still standing). For unpretentious dining Jim recommends **Carmelita's Café** at 121 Washington Street, (201) 798-2657. This is the place for genuine Mexican food to go. Take a quesadilla or Carmelita's special burrito filled

Butcher Hans Holst at Kurt Laemmel's Pork Store on Hudson Street, Hoboken.

with pork, red chile, and cactus to one of Hoboken's parks for an alfresco picnic.

Stop at **Laemmel's Pork Store** at 102 Hudson Street before leaving Hoboken for home, for quality German meats, and **Carlo's City Hall Bake Shop** for a homemade-style cruller and piping hot Maxwell House coffee. A must on any Hoboken tour is a stop at **Leo's Grandevous Restaurant,** 200 Grand Street at 2nd, (201) 659-9467 for a viewing of the Frank Sinatra "hall of fame" exhibition, which includes permanent framed photos of Frank with Major Bowes (when Frank was a member of the "Hoboken Four"), Frank with Governor Thomas Kean and Ronald Reagan (at St. Ann's Annual Feast), Frank with the Hoboken police captain, Frank with the fire chief, Frank with the key to the city, and Frank's high school diploma (a copy). Leo's (since 1939), is only a few blocks from Sinatra's boyhood home and several of the employees as well as many of the patrons remember him fondly. Leo's has got everything: good bar pizzas, salads, minestrone, pasta, chicken, meat, and shrimp dishes with prices that are right. Chicken marsala is $9.95, shrimp parmigiana is $9.75, veal franchese is $8.00. Pasta ranges from $4.50 (spaghetti, ziti, or shells) to $8.00 for spinach ravioli alfredo with prosciutto. Shrimp cocktails are $6.00 and antipasto, from small to giant, is $5.75 to $9.00. A regular Leo's salad is excellent for $3.75. Bar pies start at $1.60 for mozzarella, to $4.00 for double crust, to $6.50—for everything!

Carlo's City Hall Bake Shop in Hoboken on Washington Street, just across from City Hall.

There are, of course, meatless Friday specials, including stuffed calamari, eggplant, and filet sandwiches. Chianti Rufino ($7.75 the half bottle, $15.00 full) is served either at "room temperature" or "chilled." There is an excellent bar where you're bound to meet someone with reminiscences of Frank Sinatra or Jimmy Roselli (another local favorite and frequent visitor) and more than likely you will be tended by the original founder Leo DiTerlizzi, or one of his successors, Nicholas DePalma or Sergio DeNichilo. Leo's is open for lunch from 11:30 A.M. to 2 P.M. Monday through Friday; from 5 until 11 P.M. for dinner. Saturday hours are 5 P.M. to 11 P.M. and Sunday the place is open from 4 until 10 P.M.

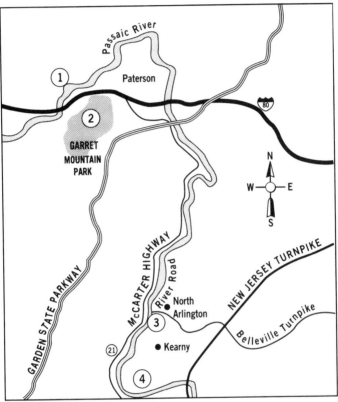

1. Paterson Falls
2. Lambert Castle
3. Stewart's Root Beer
4. Argyle Restaurant

One of the most outré cities in New Jersey is the industrial city of Paterson. Great poems have unravelled from the pens of Allen Ginsberg, who grew up there, and William Carlos Williams, who practiced there as a doctor and poet, dedicated to this old city of hills, valleys, rivers, and factories. In Williams's poem "The Wanderer" a crazed old hag who reminds him of his grandmother instructs the young man who wants to write poetry:

> Go! she said, and I hurried shivering out into the deserted streets of Paterson.

The city comes to life in a visual evocation from Williams's "The Poor" from his *Collected Poems: 1921–31*:

It's the anarchy of poverty
delights me, the old
yellow wooden house indented
among the new brick tenements . . .
Chimneys, roofs, fences of
wood and metal in an unfenced
age and enclosing next to
nothing at all . . .

How to get to Paterson: To approach the Great Falls, in the center of the city, take the Bergen-Passaic Expressway (Route 80) and exit on Main Street. From the Garden State Parkway, take exit 154, which leads into Main Street. Route 46 also crosses Main. Follow the signs to the Great Falls.

One of the splendid sites to see in Paterson are the famous **Great Falls** of the Passaic River, a natural wonder in the Watchung Mountains with a 77-foot waterfall. During the Revolutionary War, Alexander Hamilton helped to create the Society for Establishing Useful Manufactures to harness the Falls as an energy source. A system of man-made channels was built to provide power to operate cotton, silk, and other industrial mills that are now a part of a National Historic District. This is the only industrial district in the nation designated a National Historic Landmark (by President Gerald Ford in 1976). There are 49 mills still standing in the 119-acre historic district that produced 80 percent of America's locomotives by 1880, and where in 1927 the Wright Aeronautical Company built the engine used in Charles Lindbergh's plane *The Spirit of St. Louis.* Renovations on the **Paterson Museum,** on the corner of Market and Spruce Streets, in the heart of Paterson's Great Falls historic district, were completed in 1990. The museum, housed in the Rogers Locomotive Erecting Shop, contains the shell of the original 14-foot submarine invented by John P. Holland in 1878, as well as his second submarine (30 feet long) built in 1881. There is also an excellent mineral display and exhibits of the silk and cotton industries of industrial Paterson. The museum is open Tuesday through Friday from 10 A.M. to 4 P.M., Saturday and Sunday from 12:30 to 4:30 P.M. Just west of Paterson is the **Garret Mountain Reservation** and **Lambert Castle,** built in 1893 of brown-and-gray stone, by silk mill baron Catholina Lambert. Garret Mountain Reservation is a 570-acre woodland park on a 502-foot-high plateau with picnic groves and fishing ponds (open all year). Lambert Castle (open Wednesday to Sunday from 1 to 4 P.M.), now a museum of the Passaic County Historical Society, is noted for its rich interiors, paintings and antique collections. Call (201) 881-2761 for further information.

There is a Great Falls Festival every Labor Day weekend, and in recent years the Flying Wallendas and Philippe Petit (who traversed the twin towers of the World Trade Center) have walked

over the Falls on tightropes. There is a strange and mysterious commingling of the past and present in the old towns of Paterson, Passaic, Rutherford, North Arlington, Kearny, and Harrison, all in New Jersey's notorious "industrial belt" and just a short distance from Newark. Drive back from the Falls along Main Avenue through Passaic to River Road. Driving south along River Road, turn left at the Belleville Turnpike, crossing the Passaic River into North Arlington, a distance of less than 10 miles from Paterson. Just over the river, at the intersection of River Road and the Belleville Turnpike, you have your choice of two of America's traditional eateries: the 24-hour **North Arlington Diner,** (201) 998-6262, that has specials like manicotti-parmigiana, corned beef and cabbage, and Italian sausage with linguine, or the Kearny **Stewart's Root Beer Drive-In,** just across the road, which has been specializing in hot dogs and frosted mugs of Stewart's Root Beer for over forty years. Either place, it's a great spot for a rest. After eating, try a walk in **River Bank Park** for a closeup view of the Passaic. If you're in the mood for something a little more exotic, drive up the Belleville Turnpike to the top of the hill and turn right on Kearny Avenue. Drive south to Bergen Avenue. Here, in the immaculate middle-class town of Kearny, which was originally settled by Scottish immigrants, you can dine as they did in the old country at the wonderful **Argyle Restaurant**—212 Kearny Avenue, (201) 991-3900. Fish and chips is the main order of the day; usually codfish with (french) fries, which comes with crisp coleslaw for $10.07. This is a meal in itself, but the baked tomato at $1.35 rounds it out. Other specialties are Scottish meat pies, fried chicken, or shrimp and scallops. For those in the know (and for the adventurous), the black pudding, made with meat and spices and mixed in blood, with chips and coleslaw is the ticket. An ice cream or shortbread dessert will finish the repast. The Argyle includes a charming Scotland shop where you can take home Scottish jams, shortbreads in tins, canned goods, candies, and other specialty items. Men's Scotch plaid ties, scarves, kerchiefs, or a stuffed Scottie might make for a nice gift for a friend. Hours are Tuesday through Sunday from 11:30 A.M. to 8:30 P.M. Friday until 9 P.M.

A 1938 booklet die cut in the shape of a White Castle restaurant.

The trip to fascinating, historic Paterson Falls, and to dinner at the Argyle may be made at any time of year. The mighty Falls are as beautiful in winter as they are in summer. The portions that are frozen over in wintertime become giant icicles.

The Diner Experience

· ·

Let's Have Another Cup of Coffee and Let's Have Another Piece of Pie

The roadside diner as we know it today is derived from the horse-drawn lunch wagons of the late 1880s and 1890s. In 1872 in Providence, Rhode Island, one of the first of these, Pioneer Lunch, served a ham sandwich, a boiled egg, and a piece of pie for 5¢. Setting a tradition, the Pioneer baked bread and pies on the premises, including blueberry, apple, cherry, mince, squash, huckleberry, and cranberry pies. The first walk-ins—wagons without wheels—in New Jersey were the Quick Lunch and the Stalwart, in Clifton and Plainfield, respectively. Often open all night and in dilapidated areas, they gained a reputation as rough-and-tumble rowdy houses. After the turn of the century when trolleys and electric streetcars came into play, abandoned and used cars were purchased and refurbished by enterprising restaurateurs.

Separate entrances were made for women, with signs proclaiming LADIES INVITED or LADIES WELCOME. The diner was ubiquitous—manufactured by a dozen companies, such as the Fodero Dining Car Company, On-Site, Silk City, Bixler, Comac, Manno, Mountain View, Swingle, and the big three: Patrick J. Tierney in New York, Worcester Lunch Car and Carriage Manufacturing Company of Worcester, Massachusetts, and the Jerry O'Mahoney

Joe's Diamond diner with coffee cup tower, once part of the White Clock System, Belleville Turnpike, Kearny.

The White Rose diner in Roselle serves hamburgers and eggs to customers 24 hours a day.

Company in Elizabeth, New Jersey. Today three companies manufacture diners in New Jersey—Kullman Industries, Inc. (since 1927) in Avenel, Sunrise Diner Manufacturers in Carteret, and Paramount Modular Concepts in Oakland.

The dining car of a train was the inspiration behind the idea of parking an actual railroad car on a plot of land and turning it into a diner that served up steaks, eggs, and homemade pies. Diner design evolved rapidly from the wooden, wagonlike diners of the roaring twenties to the sleek, streamlined moderne style of the Depression Era 1930s, the 1940s and 1950s. Everything from toasters and refrigerators to cars, radios, and locomotives were streamlined. This modernist style seemed perfect for a fast-paced, fast-food demand, and the numbers of diners increased as more and more people bought automobiles and more paved roads were built across America. These attractive food emporiums ultimately utilized stainless steel, glass blocks, mirrored ceilings, chromium fixtures, shiny tiles, neon signs and with leatherette or Naugahyde booths, recessed lumalite, Formica countertops, and blue or peach mirror decorative detail added up to an easy-to-maintain establishment. The same industrial designers who created trains, ships, and automobiles also came up with the perfect machine-age diner, some of them called Streamliner, Pullman, Moderne, Zeppelin, or just the word "Diner" preceded by the owner's name—Joe's, Pat's, Gus's, Freddy's, or Katie's on the enameled metal front or on a huge neonized sign atop the roof. By the late 1950s some diners began to look like huge rocketships with extreme peaks, exaggerated overhangs, and giant tail-fin archways incorporated into an overall zigzag architectural concept. By the 1960s and 1970s they were no longer stylish, streamlined, and practical places, but instead had become huge plush-deluxe

White Diamond dinette on Route 27 in Linden.

restaurants overly filled up with oddball gaudy crystal or wood and metal "pirate-ship"–style chandeliers, rococco brass bins inhabited by dusty plastic plants, and featuring menus offering a bewildering selection from frozen-patty-style hamburgers, hot dogs, and eggs to fancy shrimp cocktails and lobster fra diavolo. Often a cocktail bar was added, serving up old-fashioneds, Manhattans (made with blended whiskies), or martinis.

With the awareness of a diner culture due to the super-realist paintings of John Baeder, books on diners, and diner periodicals like *Roadside*, the original concept of what a real diner is has come full circle. This does not prevent some enlightened diner owners from remodeling and refurbishing a classic goodie into an eyesore and thus turning the whole affair into an unpleasant Mediterranean hodgepodge dining experience. But take heart, a retro movement is afoot. Known for its elegant Art Deco designs of the 1930s, Kullman Industries is manufacturing a new series of classic Blue Comet diners at their factory in Avenel. The aerodynamic angular and curvilinear stainless-steel diner is once again in demand; and having a successful revival. At the same time many vintage diners from the "golden age" are being sold off and trucked out of state or shipped to foreign countries (the Excellent Diner of Westfield now resides in Germany and the Shortstop Dinette of Belleville is in a shopping mall in Cleveland), where they stand as curio-centerpieces to help promote buying in the big chainstores.

Yet, amazingly, many diners are still to be discovered by the side of the road, a highway, or on back-city streets where a weary traveler can stop for a cruller, a piece of pie, waffles, pancakes, a hamburger and a milkshake, or perhaps a big meat loaf special with mashed potatoes all covered with gobs of gravy and served up

The unfranchised White Castle System since 1921.

with canned corn, peas, or string beans and a tall side of white, rye, or whole wheat bread. Put your money in a Seeburg box, drink a cup of coffee, and listen to Elvis, Sinatra, the Inkspots, Glenn Miller, Bruce Springsteen, Patsy Cline, or the latest top ten. Usually the waiter-gals and high-hat cooks are friendly, tell jokes to customers, and create that necessary sense of a home away from home. Some diners continue to bake their own pies and pastries—and take pride in serving wholesome, fresh, American-style dinners. New Jersey is pop-culture diner country—and these hangouts are open late, many around-the-clock. Today full-scale diners and smaller dinettes, new and old, attract interesting and sometimes wacky characters like Bible-thumping religious fanatics or leather-clad "Born to Run" bike boys, fast-lane truckers, and honky-tonk girls; and when traveling, as on a train, conversation is usually easy to engage. The diner has been at the heart of the American experience throughout the twentieth century. Unlike downtown single-screen movie theaters, old-fashioned ice-cream parlors, or five-and-ten-cent stores (all practically gone), the diner is still a place to hang out, have a motorcycle or car meet, have fun and good eats!

DINER FOOTNOTE: If you see a lonely guy or gal nursing a cup of coffee in a diner booth while staring into space and if the record on the jukebox happens to be a nostalgia-hit like "Eddie, My Love," "Earth Angel," or "Twilight Time," just give out a cheery "hello." That's called "diner-friendly"—and if they don't offer a "hello" back, well, we know you'll understand that it's okay to just "live and let live" and remember—it's the reality of the donut, the steaming hot cup of coffee, the piece of lemon meringue pie, and the toasted BLT with mayo—that really matters in Dinerland. Hungry, anyone? Order up. Chase away those blues—in a New Jersey diner.

Diner Day Trip

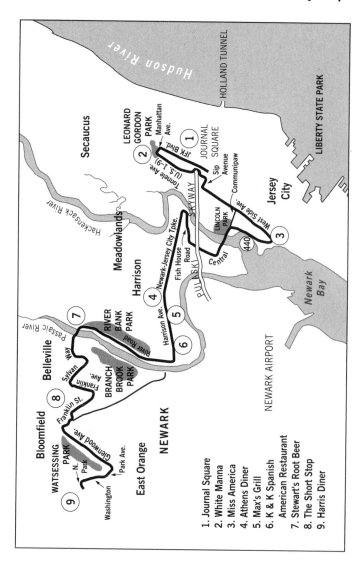

1. Journal Square
2. White Manna
3. Miss America
4. Athens Diner
5. Max's Grill
6. K & K Spanish American Restaurant
7. Stewart's Root Beer
8. The Short Stop
9. Harris Diner

Get in your car, van, or on your motorbike and join the "Dime-Store Kids" (the authors) for a diner tour in New Jersey's beautiful industrial belt. We guarantee a gastric pop-architectural and fun-filled adventure to those who are open to the idea of just plain folks and the enjoyment of a cheap hearty meal. We start off at **Journal Square** in Jersey City, New Jersey's second largest city.

This original circular White Manna has been on Highway 1-9 in Jersey City since 1946. The owner is Mario Costa Jr., who worked in the diner during high school and college, saved his money, and bought it from the original owner, who himself had bought it as a prefab at the New York World's Fair in 1939.

The sights to see here include the enormous **Stanley Theater** and the **Loews of Jersey City,** both built in 1928. The Stanley has been restored as a temple by the Jehovah's Witnesses and is an "atmospheric" theater in the Spanish/Alhambra–Valentino Hollywood style. The interior has elaborate stained-glass sconces, Moorish chandeliers, marble columns, and a "moving cloud" ceiling. Next to Radio City, the Stanley with 4,500 seats was one of the largest of the great movie palaces. Less ornate, the Loews was designed by Rapp and Rapp and featured a "Morton Wonder" theater organ. The Morton organ is gone now slated for replacement in plans for restoration of the 3,200-seat theater.

Drive north up Kennedy Boulevard to Leonard Gordon Park— featuring a turn-of-the-century bandshell, two huge stone buffaloes and a bear with a breathtaking view of the western slopes of the Palisades and the Meadowlands. Turn left by the Park on Manhattan Avenue and coast down the hill to the **White Manna,** 470 Tonnelle Avenue (Route 1-9), owned by Mario Costa Jr., a New Jersey and New York fight manager. Mario worked in the diner during high school and college and bought it from the original owner, who bought it at the 1939 New York World's Fair, where it was on display with another identical prefab fast-food eatery that wound up on Route 1-9 in Elizabeth. Several years ago this latter one disappeared one night and no one has ever seen it since.

Go down Tonnelle (Highway 1-9 South) through the Tonnelle Traffic Circle. Continue on Tonnelle to Sip—make a right on Sip and zip down to West Side Avenue. Turn left on West Side and drive on down to the **Miss America Diner.** This beautiful streamlined diner, 322 West Side Avenue, (201) 333-5468, owned by Tom Carlis and Sam Galatas, was built in 1939 and has been in its present location since 1944. Their motto: "The old-fashioned diner with the home-style cooking." Backtrack a few blocks north and turn left on Communipaw Avenue, which takes you past Lincoln Park and onto the old Lincoln Highway (1-9 South). Half a mile past the Hackensack River Bridge, exit at Central Avenue East, Kearny. Turn right at the Fish House Road intersection, following Fish House to the Route 7 West Belleville exit ramp on the right. On Route 7 West, bear left following signs for Harrison. This will become Harrison Avenue. The sights along the way include the PSE&G Generating Plant, a view of the magnificent Pulaski Sky-

Vanishing diners—this one, a relic of the 1939–1940 New York World's Fair, disappeared mysteriously a few years ago from its location near the Rahway State Prison.

Interior of the vanished 1939 diner, Route 1-9.

Max's Diner, 731 Harrison Avenue, Harrison. O'Mahoney built ca. 1927, its original railroad wheels still in place, the exterior is maroon-and-deep-cream baked enamel with wood trim.

way (1928)—at seven miles, the longest viaduct in the world—the moderne-style Coca-Cola bottling plant, and the bulk-mail facility of the U.S. Post Office. The **Athens Diner,** 1002 Harrison Avenue, Kearny, was manufactured by Fodero Dining Car Company in New Jersey. The **K & K Spanish-American Restaurant,** 424 Harrison Avenue, Harrison, used to be called the China Town and before that it was a classic diner. Check it out—this could be exotic diner food at its best. Harrison's shining light is **Max's Grill** at 731 Harrison Avenue, (201) 483-2012, built in 1927 by the O'Mahony Diner Company. Often painted by renowned diner artist John Baeder, Max's Grill, though not a registered historic landmark, is a diner not be be missed by connoisseurs. Barrel-roofed and with a maroon-and-cream porcelain-enamel exterior and with deco-style lettering that says LADIES INVITED and MAX'S GRILL, the diner now serves Spanish-Portuguese food. A Portuguese shell steak dinner costs $8, and eggs, potatoes, and toast are $1.50. Max's closes every day from 2 to 4 A.M. but is open at all other times. To get to Max's in a hurry, take exit 15W off the New Jersey Turnpike into downtown Harrison. The PATH train makes a stop here also for diner aficionados on foot.

Leaving Max's continue over Harrison Avenue to Passaic Avenue in East Newark. Turn right and drive north on River Road alongside River Bank Park and turn left onto the Belleville Turnpike. This intersection offers **Stewart's Root Beer** on one side of the road and the **North Arlington Diner** on the other. Cross the Passaic River into Belleville up to Washington Avenue. Take a left to Sylvan, which meanders west between Belleville Park and Newark's Branch Brook Park. Drive to Franklin Avenue and turn left. Go to Franklin Street and turn right. Continue out to the **Short Stop Diner,** 315 Franklin Street, Bloomfield. This 18-seat Kullman-Manno-built diner (1955) is the last of five. There was one in Plainfield, two in Newark, and one in Belleville (now in Cleveland). The Short Stop's eggs in the skillet, he-man rib stickers, and coffee are the best in the world (see page 45 for more details on the Short Stop).

The Short Stop's red, blue, green, yellow, and orange diagonal stripes shimmer in the distance as you drive away left over to Bloomfield Avenue. Turn left onto Glenwood Avenue and drive

Jersey Springsteen–style diner regular leaves the Short Stop Diner in Bloomfield after wolfing down famous "Eggs in a Skillet" breakfast.

alongside Watsessing Park to Park Avenue. At Park turn right and right again on Washington Street. At the "point" of Washington and North Park, just a few blocks from Main Street, East Orange, is the **Harris Diner,** 21 North Park, (201) 675-9703, built in 1952 by the O'Mahoney Dining Car Company and owned since 1958 by Bill Nicholas and Bill Marmaras. This is a large stainless-steel-and-chrome diner that rates the very highest for original decor and food. It is well-lit with indirect recessed lighting, has a mirrored ceiling, and individual jukeboxes at each Formica-topped table, offering the Mills Brothers and Tommy Dorsey alongside Frank Sinatra and Bruce Springsteen. Connie Francis singing "Who's Sorry Now," alas, is nowhere to be found. The Formica, chrome, steel-and-tile interior of this diner is perfect and is kept immaculate. The Harris Diner waitresses are themselves out of another era, and the food is mighty fine indeed. Try the famous Black Angus Steak Sandwich or a special Harris Diner Dagwood "Sputnik," which—it is promised—"is out of this world." There are many egg specialties for late-night or early breakfast, as well as triple-decker sandwiches, fried seafood, Reubens, and homemade, thick Belgian waffles served with Log Cabin syrup or La Salle ice cream. The Harris Diner, with its friendly atmosphere, is open 24 hours every day. End of tour.

◆

More Jersey Diners

Take your own diner tour. The **White Manna** in Hackensack, 358 River Street, (201) 342-0914, is a good example of the 1930s streamlining concept in early eatery chains. This building could almost qualify for the Smithsonian Institute with its glass blocks and chromed metal front. The **Melrose Diner,** previously located in East Windsor (about 12 miles east of Trenton), is the one that ended up in the National Archives in Washington, D.C. The Hackensack White Manna was also a futuristic architectural feature at the 1939–1940 New York World's Fair. Later it was purchased and transported to its present site, where brothers Ofer and Ronnie Cohen serve up hamburgers smothered in onions and de-

Menu from the Harris Diner, showing the streamlined stainless-steel-and-chromium diner that serves good food at 21 North Park and Washington Streets in East Orange.

licious ice cream shakes. Open Monday through Saturday from 7 A.M. to 6 P.M., Sunday only until 4 P.M.

The **Summit Diner,** (908) 277-3256, is on Summit Avenue at One Union Place, across the road from the New Jersey Transit Morristown Branch Summit Railroad Station. Legend has it that Ernest Hemingway used to stop off here. This is another spot where the food is cheap and the dinner portions truck-drivin' big. Try the Summit Diner meat loaf. A heavy, hearty meal! This 1929 Depression-era diner is still 80 percent original and it is an Edward Hopper painting come to life. The place may be an anachronism at the end of the twentieth century, but it is a gem to be treasured by all.

In addition to the **White Castles,** which are everywhere, and the **White Mannas** in Jersey City and Hackensack, many early chain

A typical view from a diner counter stool.

eateries still survive in New Jersey, offering up atmosphere and good eats, including the **White Rose** System in Roselle, Linden, and Highland Park, the **White Circle** System in Bloomfield, the **White Star Diners** in Plainfield and Elizabeth, the **White Diamonds** in Linden and Clark, and the **Blue Diamond** in Pomona. Other old-fashioned treats are the orange-painted **Stewart's Root Beer Drive-in** restaurants, which feature carhops and cartray attachments. Usually they are freshly enameled orange and lit with yellow bug lights. The service is friendly and courteous—and the ice-cold mug of root beet and a Stewart's hot dog is good stuff.

There are over 600 diners in New Jersey, more than in any other state. A careful selection of some of the good ones includes the following: **Newark Avenue Diner** and **Tunnel Diner** in Jersey City, the **Liberty** in North Brunswick, the **Americana** in East Windsor, the **Truck Stop Diner** in Kearny, the **Avenel** and **Premium Diners** on Route 1-9 in Avenel, the **Egg Platter Diner** in Paterson, **Chappy's** in Paterson, the **Queen Elizabeth** on Route 1-9 near Newark Airport, the **Bendix Diner** on Highway 17 and Williams Street in Hasbrouck Heights, **Tops** in Bayonne, **Kless's Diner** in Irvington, **Betsy Ross** in Elizabeth, the **Mark Twain** and **Huck Finn diners** in Union, the **Tom Sawyer** in Ridgewood, the **Dumont Crystal,** the **Teamsters** in Fairfield, the **Clairmont** in Clifton, the **Freehold Grille,** and **Tick Tock Diner** on Route 3 in Clifton (built in the "classic" style in 1994 by Kullman), the **Lido Diner** in the center of Route 22 in Springfield, the **State Diner** in West Orange, the **Park Diner** in Montclair, the **Franklin, Boonton, Bound Brook,** and **Washington diners,** the **Colonial** in Lyndhurst, the **Crossroads** in Bridgeville, **Toms** in Ledgewood, **Linda's** in Sussex, **Sue and Bernie's Diner** in Belvedere, **Key City Diner** on Route 22W, Phillipsburg, and the **Five Star,** Route 206, and the **New Royal,** 3331 Route 22E, both in Branchville.

Down the shore, in the Pine Barrens and in southwest New Jersey's vast farm belt, diners are a mainstay. Some of these include the **Peterpank Diner** in Sayreville, the **White Crystal Diner** in Atlantic Highlands, the **Roadside Diner** in Wall Township, the **Riverview** in Belmar, **Joe's Chadwick Diner** in Chadwick Beach (operated by Joseph B. Gillies, grandson of Captain Joe Basile, who was the bandleader at New Jersey's famed Olympic Park), **Bay Avenue Diner** in Manahawkin, **Captain John's Mr. Breakfast** in Surf City and **Moustache Bill's Diner** at Barnegat Light, both on Long Beach Island, the **Olympic Diner** in Pleasantville, the **Point in Somers Point,** the **Wildwood** and **Big Ernie's** in Wildwood, the **Shore** in Rio Grande, **54 Diner** in Buena, **Angie's Bridgeton Grille, Salem Oak Diner** in Salem, **Mastoris Diner** in Bordentown, **Hammonton Diner** in Hammonton, **Time Out** in Tuckahoe, the **Liberty** in Clayton, **Angelo's Diner** in Glassboro, the **Elgin Diner** in Camden, the **Club Diner** in Bellmawr, and the **Mount Laurel Diner** in Mount Laurel.

If you don't find one of these diners at the location listed, drive on to the next one. Diners sometimes disappear mysteriously, right off the face of a map. For the latest Jersey diner updates, send for a copy of *Roadside Magazine* (Coffee Cup Publications, P.O. Box 652, West Side Station, Worcester, MA 01602), published by Randolph J. Garbin, who keeps abreast of diner renovations and sales and other news of interest to roadside enthusiasts.

Tunnel Diner in Jersey City outside the Holland Tunnel. Open 24 hours a day, the vintage diner displays a great neon sign, and has a pink, blue, and chromium 1950s interior.

Newark Day Trip

Cherry Blossom Time in Newark

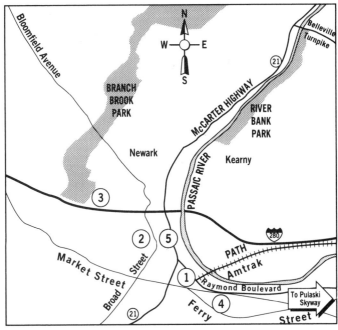

1. Penn Station
2. Newark Museum
3. Newark Cathedral
4. Portuguese Restaurants
5. New Jersey Performing Arts Center

Penn Station in downtown Newark is a good starting point for this city day trip. It is "the end of the line" of the PATH commuter train from New York, Hoboken, and Jersey City. If you come by car over the Pulaski Skyway into Newark or from south or north on Highway 1-9, all roads lead into downtown Newark and Penn Station. Buses from all locations also head in and out of this station to suburban cities and towns. You can park the car in one of the many lots near the station.

The monumental station itself is an Art Deco masterpiece. Completed in 1933, it was designed by Stanford White and features faces of lions and statues of spread-winged eagles on its limestone facade, while the interior, completely restored by New Jersey Transit, who bought it from Amtrak in 1984, has beautiful bronze ceiling fixtures with astrological signs of the zodiac, glass deco globes, and transportation-theme wall medallions. Outside the station, bordered by Market Street, the McCarter Highway, and Raymond

A terrazzo mural in the lobby of the Bell Telephone Company in downtown Newark.

Boulevard, walk (or drive) up Market Street past the old **Newark Paramount Theater** to Broad Street, Newark's famous crossroads. Continue on Market Street to the old **L. Bamberger's Department Store** (closed in 1992); throughout downtown Newark original 1920s and 1930s storefronts still exist, their facades clad in vitreous glass or sheets of terra cotta. Newark is the home of the **Prudential Insurance Company** and it maintains several office buildings downtown. On the 13th floor of the **Gibraltar Building** at 153 Halsey Street, near the bank, is the **Prudential Museum,** filled with company memorabilia and early Newarkiana. A main attraction is the Tiffany stained-glass window of the Rock of Gibraltar (the Prudential's trademark symbol) that was originally created by Maitland Armstrong for the Panama Pacific International Exposition held in San Francisco in 1915. While strolling in the downtown Newark areas, take note of the fine old and new

Greetings from Newark—linen postcard made for the Star Stationery Company of Newark by Tichnor Bros., Inc., circa 1930s.

architectural attractions. A spectacular monument to culture (completed in October, 1997), representing a gigantic leap in faith in the city's future is the **New Jersey Performing Arts Center,** adjacent to Military Park. Providing a permanent home for the New Jersey Symphony Orchestra, it also features artists like Isaac Stern, Wynton Marsalis, and famed dance troups like the American Ballet Theater and the Alvin Ailey American Dance Theater, as well as providing creative arts workshops for children and community groups. Leaving the Arts Complex walk past Military Park to the **Bell Telephone Company,** at 540 Broad Street at Lombardy. This magnificent Art Deco building, designed by the architectural firm of Voorhees, Gmelin and Walker is one of the best examples of an early art deco skyscraper to be found on the East Coast, and is definitely worth a visit. The lobby, with its elaborate and ornate bronze-work grills in deco-floral patterns, tall bronze Egyptian-style torchère lamps and an artful communication-theme terrazzo mural is exhilarating and awe-inspiring. The cast cement relief sculptures, with operators talking on the telephone and callers listening in on the building's facade, must be the ultimate in camp *Deco-Moderne.*

Just across the street from Bell Telephone, through Washington Park, is the **Newark Museum** at 43–49 Washington Street, (201) 596-6550, open throughout the year. After a $21 million reconstruction and renovation project completed in 1990, in which architect Michael Graves integrated four existing museum buildings as well as a five-story building acquired from Newark, into one great cultural complex, the building is a masterpiece. The museum's African and Asian holdings and one of the most extensive Tibetan collections in the Western Hemisphere (there is a complete Buddhist altar as well as paintings, musical instruments, and intricately woven Tibetan costumes) are well known; less known and a must to visit is the Renaissance Revival **Ballantine House,** restored to complete Victorian perfection in the spacious grounds behind the museum's main building. The Ballantine House, built by John Ballantine, the son of the founder of the renowned Newark brewery, built the house in 1885. Now designated a National Historic Landmark, each room offers a glimpse into Victorian excess; the stained-glass window in the library, based on Mr. Ballantine's design, depicts the family name, derived from the Scottish words *bael*, or fire, and *antin*, a worshipper. The window shows a maiden worshipping the sun as incense rises skyward.

Branch Brook Park in Newark is accessible from East Bloomfield Avenue, spur Route 506; from Park Avenue, Route 16. Not to be missed in the spring (usually early April) are the pink, white, and

The spectacular flying-eagle that revolves atop the Anheuser-Busch brewery (maker of King Cobra Premium malt liquor and Budweiser beer) on Highway 1-9 in Newark. This extravagant and artful sign across from the Newark Airport was designed by Jacob Starr of Artkraft Straus.

mauve cherry blossoms opening forth annually in full splendor. There are 2,700 cherry trees in this 2-mile by a quarter-mile-wide section of the park designed by the famous Frederick Law Olmstead. The magical, sweet-smelling cherry blossom display is larger than Washington, D.C.'s. In the winter there is an ice center for ice skating and ski slopes for sledding. Bicycling is permitted, and there is a boating lake.

Following a visit to Branch Brook Park, the hungry traveler in search of excellent cuisine should go back to Penn Station. The **Ironbound District,** so named because it is surrounded by the rattle of the trains that enter Newark, is within walking distance of the station and is the center of Newark's large Portuguese population. Go out the Raymond Plaza East exit from Penn Station, cross the street, walk right one block to Ferry Street and make a left, walking two more blocks past Edison Street and McWhorter Street. Populated by over 35,000 Portuguese immigrants, this mile-square area, surrounded by the factories and manufacturing sections of Newark, is a lively place by day or night and the restaurants, dozens of them, serving piping hot paella, stewed rabbit, and dried salt-cod specialties, are open late. Most of the establishments serve either a marinara (with shellfish) paella or a Valenciana (with sausage) paella, *gambas al ajillo* (shrimp tumbled in an oil–and–red-pepper mixture with diced garlic), sweet sangria and *papo seco* (cornmeal-enriched loaves and rolls). Other dishes include chicken in garlic, clams in green sauce, *mariscada* (the Spanish version of bouillabaisse), which is a stewpot full of lobster, shrimp, clams, mussels, and scallops with a tangy garlic sauce, and garlicky pork chops served with potatoes and rice. Some of the better restaurants include **Fornos of Spain,** 47 Ferry Street, (973) 589-4767; **Roque and Rebelo,** 90 Ferry Street, (973) 589-6588; **Sagres Restaurant,** 71 Ferry Street, (973) 589-4070; **Castelo's Restaurant,** 61 Ferry Street, (973) 589-2929; **Iberia Tavern and Restaurant,** 82–84 Ferry Street, (973) 344-7603; and slightly-off-the-beaten-path **Tony Da Caneca's** at 72 Elm Road, (973) 589-6882, and **O' Poeta Bar and Restaurant,** 97–99 Lang Street. Particularly authentic and charming, O' Poeta is named to honor Portuguese poet Luis de Camoes. The prices and portions at all of these restaurants are unbelievably reasonable by any standards.

Newark is one of the oldest cities in America, and in 1991 it celebrated its 325th year. In 1666 Captain Robert Treat, on a foray from Milford, Connecticut, with a band of New England pilgrims, landed on the shores of the Passaic River at the site of what is now Newark. He had to buy the land from the Indians, paying over 850 fathoms of wampum in addition to axes, coats, guns, pistols, kettles, swords, blankets, beer, breeches, and 20 gallons of liquor. Eleven years later, with an additional payment of 2 guns, 3 coats, and "13 kans of rum," the English settlers acquired deed to land stretching to the top of the Orange Mountain. Quite a real estate bargain! Celebrated persons who lived in or are from Newark include writers Philip Roth, Stephen Crane, Amiri Baraka (formerly LeRoi Jones), Washington Irving, Zane Grey, Allen Ginsberg (born in Newark, raised in Paterson), Nick Tosches, and Dore Schary. Entertainers Whitney Houston, Joe Pesci, Frankie Valli, Eva Marie Saint, Vivian Blaine, Sarah Vaughan, Melba Moore, the Ritz Brothers, and Connie Francis are also from Newark. Whitney Houston is currently active in the revitalization of this great city, investing in new real estate development. Former New York Mayor Ed Koch is from Newark, as was composer Jerome Kern.

Newark's greatest monument is the **Cathedral of the Sacred Heart,** a spectacular French Gothic cathedral, the fifth largest in the nation. The flagship of the Roman Catholic Archdiocese of Newark, at the corner of Clifton and Victoria Avenues, it is noted for its 9,500-pipe organ, its massive gargoyles, and the largest rose window in the Western Hemisphere. Architectural tours are given on the first Sunday each month after noon Mass; at other times you can tour the cathedral yourself. The entrance is at 89 Ridge Street; call (201) 484-4600 for further information.

Another Newark landmark, Newark's 2,800-seat **Symphony Hall** at 1030 Broad Street, hosts year-round programs of plays, concerts, and other performances. Built in 1925 as a Shriner Temple, its sculptured limestone facade is a sight to behold. Call (201) 643-8009 for tickets or (201) 643-4550 to be put on their mailing list. Another fascinating section to visit in Newark, and one that will give you renewed faith in the city's future, is **St. Joseph's Plaza**—a complex that includes a medical clinic, a sandwich shop, a spa, and a restaurant, all housed in the historic 19th century priory at St. Joseph's church. The **Priory Restaurant** features made-to-order waffles, hot-and-cold selections, and other treats—brunch is 9:30 A.M. to 2:30 P.M.; Dinner buffet from 3:30 to 10.

Three New Jersey hometown gals also happen to be international recording stars: Top: The Divine Miss Sarah Vaughan, now buried in a cemetery in Belleville, New Jersey, near her beloved Newark. Middle: Whitney Houston, a major force in the development of new housing in the City of Newark. Bottom: Glamorous Dionne Warwick, native of East Orange, now resides in a posh Newark suburb.

Newark city subway system, WPA tile mural showing men at work, 1935.

This extraordinary "Turkey-Deco" terra-cotta panel was on an industrial building at Washington and Linden Streets in downtown Newark.

Cathedral of the Sacred Heart in Newark.

The Priory Restaurant is just a part of the "New Community," a development corporation founded by Monsignor William J. Linder (a 1991 MacArthur Foundation Award winner), which provides guidance to inner-city residents for housing and jobs, financing for fast-food franchises, a day-care center, and other services. Father Linder was also instrumental in bringing a Pathmark supermarket into Newark, something that had been lacking for two decades. St. Joseph's Plaza is in the University Heights district of Newark at 233 W. Market Street, (973) 242-8012.

According to lifelong resident and historian Michael Immerso, by 1910 Newark's First Ward (a half-mile square between Sixth Avenue and Nassau) was home to the fifth largest Italian population in the country. Immerso claims a 1910 Italian business directory lists 63 grocery stores, 4 macaroni manufacturers, 17 bakeries, 23 shoemakers, 40 barbers, and 88 saloons in the old First Ward. In the 1950s the First Ward's "Little Italy" attracted celebrities like Abbott and Costello and Jayne Mansfield and performers Billie Holiday, Gypsy Rose Lee, and Jackie Gleason, who performed in

Newark's large downtown theaters. After the riots of the 1960s what was left of that teeming population finally fled to the North Ward, out Bloomfield Avenue. Pizza and other Italian restaurants on either side of Bloomfield Avenue are all bound to be authentic, as this vicinity, though it is more spread out than New York City's Italian restaurant section, is now known as Newark's new "Little Italy."

Dickie-Dee Pizza, 380 Bloomfield Avenue, is a favorite of Joe Pesci, who comes in often for a pie with friend Robert De Niro, who likes to hang out on Bloomfield Avenue. The pizza here has been rated number one by many culinary periodicals, and it does not disappoint. Dickie Dee's features one-size of pie which is $7.00. Extras like sausage or pepperoni are $1.25; a slices is also $1.25. Recommended is the Special (everything on it) at $10.55. Pizzas fall into the categories of regular, Sicilian, or deep dish, and there are "gourmet" pizzas like spinach and ricotta that are very tasty indeed. Connoisseurs of "the best" pizza arrive from every-where to have a pizza or a Dickie-Dee antipasto, which includes rolled ham, black olives, and anchovies.

The Belmont Tavern and Restaurant, 12 Bloomfield Avenue, (973) 759-9609, *is actually in* Belleville on the border between Newark and Bloomfield. It is presided over by attractive Helen Churchill, who runs a tight ship. Everything is cooked from scratch, so you must be patient. This is fine Italian food in a small family-style setting. "Stretch's Chicken Savoy" is a specialty cooked in wine and olive oil and Helen's secret spices. Two can enjoy a meal with salad and wine here for about $25. The spaghetti and ziti dishes are also first rate. The tangy sauces are home cooked and fresh whether made with ground meat, cheese, or sausage. This is a bustling, fun place to go. You will not have trouble park-ing your car on a side street here, and like New York's Little Italy, the streets are safe. There is a middle class feeling to the Belmont, and a homey atmosphere. It's a dinner-only place; hours are Mon-day, Wednesday, and Thursday from 5 until 10 P.M.. Friday and Saturday they are open until 11 P.M. Sunday until 9:30 P.M. Closed Tuesday.

Driving up Bloomfield Avenue through Newark's North Ward Italian district, which is immaculately maintained, you will arrive in Bloomfield. A notable stop-off is an old-fashioned–style ice cream parlor called **Holsten's Brookdale Confectionery** that serves its own homemade ice cream and sells quality homemade chocolate candy, all made on the premises. Holsten's is run by Rudy and Ron Stark and specializes in French ice cream cakes and ice cream logs for parties and events, to order. A luncheon-style menu serves a variety of relatively inexpensive American sandwiches, including peanut butter and jelly, which is $1.80.

Artist's rendition of Holsten's Ice Cream Parlor depicted on their menu.

Grilled cheese and tuna is $4.40, double-decker clubs are $4.50 to $5.60, hamburgers are $2.30; and naturally, there is a terrific selection of ice cream sodas—French-style with real whipped cream, $2.50, special sundaes (some with four scoops of ice cream), $5.25, selected from 15 flavors, and malted milkshakes, $3. In summer try a fresh-fruit orange or lemon fizz at $4. **Holsten's,** which also offers eggs and omelettes and delicious coffee, is at 1063 Broad Street at the corner of Watchung Avenue. Store hours are 11 A.M. until 11:30 P.M. and Sundays till 10 P.M. The service and old ice-cream-parlor decor make this a friendly stop, and well worth a trip in itself (973) 338-7901.

On the other side of the coin in Bloomfield—for those who like funky hamburger-and-egg eateries—try the **Short Stop Diner** at 315 Franklin (right off exit 148 of the Garden State Parkway, the second light down off Bloomfield Avenue). This 24-hour miniature stainless-steel, chrome-and-Formica 1950s moderne dinette has ten sit-down chrome-leatherette stools at the counter and seating for eight more facing out the window. Debbie Heath and Kathy Clockedile, the night counterwomen, sling hash and tell ribald jokes at the same time, occasionally invoking the Short Stop's one and only rule—Do Not, repeat, Do Not slide your eggs out of the pan! Eggs at the Short Stop are cooked in an iron skillet in creamery butter over gas heat and put under a broiler to make them extra hot. The chef's specialty is the He-Man Cheese Omelette made with three "Joisey" farm-fresh eggs. These He-Mans are served with American home-fried potatoes, lettuce, tomato, toast, and piping-hot, rich delicious coffee. Another special is the Rib-Sticker, a half-pound of chopped sirloin with fixins'. A good-sized tasty hamburger with onions on a hard roll is hard to beat but the two skillet eggs (served and eaten right off the pan, placed before you on the counter on a wooden board—to save the Formica) is flabbergasting. Add extra for pork roll, bacon, sausages, or ham. BLTs and Taylor ham sandwiches are also on the menu, printed on the board above the grill. The Short Stop proudly serves a few hundred or more customers each day. Nothing satisfies like good American fare with what they call "the town's best cup of coffee."

If, after too many He-Mans or too much good ice cream, you need a walk, there is the lovely **Town Green Historic District** that has 229 Queen Anne, Federal, Greek revival, and Italianate Victorian buildings surrounding it. This is New Jersey's largest "town green" and a self-tour guide pamphlet is available from the **Historical Society of Bloomfield,** 90 Broad Street, Bloomfield 07003. The Historical Society itself is open September through June (Wednesdays from 2 to 4:30 P.M.; Saturdays 11 A.M. to 3 P.M. or by appointment in summer).

Bloomfield is a treasure trove for collectibles, a very good selection of them residing in the shop of **Al Levine** at 292 Glenwood Avenue, (973) 743-5288. Make an appointment with Al in advance, to sell or buy rare coins, precious metals, movie star memorabilia, comics, Big Little Books, and other collectibles. This is where you can finally lay your hands on a rare Buck Rogers or Dick Tracey or Mickey Mouse pop-up book—but watch out for the prices or bring something to trade—they're going for $250 and up these days!

Garden State Parkway, exit 148, at Bloomfield Avenue. Up the hill along Bloomfield Avenue, just before coming to Montclair and as you leave the town of Bloomfield, is Glen Ridge. There are many fine old New Jersey homes to view in this gaslit town; and if you turn left or right off Bloomfield Avenue, the main thoroughfare, you will drive down wonderful tree-lined streets that will immediately give you a feeling of serenity and well-being. One of the great houses here belonged to singer Connie Francis—the "Empress of New Jersey."

The city of Montclair is set on a high ridge of the Watchung Mountains, overlooking the New Jersey and Manhattan megalopolis. West Bloomfield wanted a rail link to New York City and Bloomfield did not so in 1868 the two towns separated, the former

Miss Connie Francis, the "Who's Sorry Now?" girl of Bloomfield, who is often referred to as "The Empress of New Jersey," courtesy of MGM.

The Montclair railroad station at Bloomfield Avenue, which has been turned into a mini mall (top). The famous Hinck Building (above) shopping and office complex, which also houses the Claridge movie theater, and is still functioning to this day. This is 1931, but Montclair continues to be a gracious town that values its past.

renaming itself Montclair. Once you're in town you should park on a side street or in the many metered public parking lots. It is fun to walk up the hill in Montclair, beginning at the old, restored Erie-Lackawanna railroad station designed by William Hull, an architect who perished at the age of 26 on the *Titanic*. Montclair, of course, is accessible by train: Take the Montclair Branch of NJ Transit from Hoboken to Bay Street Station. Bay Street is a block away from the old train station, which is now part of a minimall shopping complex; its great waiting room a fast-food eatery. Several very fine antique stores abound in this elegant old town as well as some interesting bookstores and boutiques.

For fabulous contemporary crafts and gift items, shop at **Dexterity,** 30 Church Street, (973) 746-5370. This extravagant shop features exotic kaleidoscopes, one-of-a-kind jewelry, perfume bottles, boxes, glassware, paperweights, clocks, handbags, dinnerware, and more. Next door the menu changes daily and no reservations are needed at the casually elegant Art Deco **28,** 28 Church Street, open 6 to 10 P.M., Tuesday to Saturday, 5 to 9 P.M. on Sunday. BYOB.

Antique and bookshops are most likely to be open from Tuesday to Saturday with closings at 4 or 5 P.M. Try **Stations West Antiques** on Glen Ridge Avenue (just off Bloomfield in town center), (973) 744-9370, which is chock full of whatnots, pop-culture artifacts, oddities, and bona fide antiques. Two charming ladies, Shirley Shaller and Minna Mandlebaum, operate this co-op shop. Down the hill a few steps is the **Montclair Book Center** at 221 Glen Ridge Avenue, (973) 783-3630, which carries a large selection of books, paperbacks, magazines, and comics. Attached to the Book Center is **Page I Cafe,** where poets and performers read and play. The best New York antique dealers look upon Montclair as a good town to buy in, since many of the shops purchase their goods right out of nearby mansions that periodically have garage sales or estate auctions. Several shops carry crystal, silver, 18th- and 19th-century furniture, oak pieces, wicker sets, rugs, lamps, and other household furnishings, as well as paintings and prints. A Church Street shop called **Beans,** run by Stefan Peters since 1974 (he arrived in Montclair as an actor with the Whole Theater Company, founded by a Montclair celebrity, actress Olympia Dukakis) sells freshly ground coffee, tea, condiments, jellies, honey, and other culinary

gift items; (973) 783-7175. On Bloomfield Avenue there are two fully stocked health food emporiums as well as a well-stocked jazz record store called **Crazy Rhythms. Yesterday Books and Records,** also on Bloomfield, carries unusual boxed sets of 78 r.p.m. records, early and hard to find 33⅓ r.p.m. record albums and an assortment of books, including many collector's items. There is even a fully restored Art Deco beauty parlor with chrome chairs and torchère floor lamps that should be seen for its authentic details; **Park South Beauty Parlor,** 23 South Park, 11 to 6 by appointment; call (973) 744-0022. **Powerhouse Tattoo** at 545 Bloomfield Avenue near Park Street, (973) 744-8788, run by Diane Farris will give you temporary or permanent tattoos; they specialize in custom work, autoclave sterilization and male and female artists are available seven days a week. A local Salvation Army

Tom Morrow showing a 1950s worker's shirt at a vintage clothing shop on Bloomfield Avenue, in Montclair.

Stefan Peters in his gourmet coffee store Beans at 42 Church Street in Montclair.

band often plays on the streets of town, lending an old-time musical biblical air to the gracious surroundings. The 1930s **Trinity
Apartment** buildings, one block off Church, with their bevelled-
crystal glass doors, add to the town center's charm. The entire top
of the hill shopping area, with its brick sidewalks, is centered
around the terra-cotta-clad **Hinck Building** and has an aristo-
cratic feeling about it that bespeaks a slower, easy pace for shoppers or casual strollers. If a movie is in order on your Montclair
sojourn, try the **Claridge** in the Hinck Building, which now
houses three theaters as well as several shops.

A note of historical interest: The Montclair Historical Society
maintains a historic house-museum at the **Israel Crane House** at
110 Orange Road, (201) 744-1796. This 1796 Federal-style mansion depicts the life of the wealthy in Colonial times. The Montclair Junior League offers tours and a cooking demonstration
featuring the use of old utensils, utilizing a fireplace oven and
an old reflector rotisserie. There is a country store on the premises.
Israel Crane House is open Sundays only from 2 to 5 P.M. It is
closed during July and August because no air-conditioning is used.
The **Montclair Art Museum,** South Mountain and Bloomfield
Avenues, (973) 746-5555, has a good permanent collection of
20th-century prints and art, as well as many excellent changing exhibitions. Open Tuesday, Wednesday, and Friday, Saturday from
10 A.M. to 4 P.M.—Thursday and Sunday from 2 to 5 P.M.

A beautiful drive in Upper Montclair is along Mountain Avenue.
Turn right off Bloomfield Avenue if you are driving downhill, left

if you are going up, onto Mountain Avenue. Along this drive you will see the huge mansions with their manicured lawns and landscaped grounds that are the grand homes of many New York and New Jersey corporate executives and millionaires. Eventually you will find yourself in the tiny Upper Montclair hamlet where there is a charming old wooden railroad station, a movie theater called the **Bellevue,** a popular "good time Charlie" restaurant and pub and a handful of interesting shops. Just down the hill is **Applegate Farms** at 616 Grove Street, (973) 744-5900, where you can park and line up at a stand for delicious homemade ice cream served in cones, elaborate cup sundaes, and malted drinks and shakes. Applegate was established in Upper Montclair as a dairy farm in 1848. They began selling homemade ice cream at their roadside stand in 1930. The current owner, Betty Whay, says it has always operated at this location only. "Accept no substitutes," she adds. Hours in spring, summer, and fall are 9 A.M. to 11 P.M. and in winter from 9 A.M. to 10 P.M. There are no booths or tables (perhaps a couple of benches), so you must enjoy your ice cream standing around the farm's parking lot or in your car. There is ample room for parking here. The farm also sells milk, butter, and double-yolk eggs.

A fine place to either dine or spend a weekend in Montclair is the **Marlboro Inn** at 334 Grove Street, (973) 783-3300 or toll-free (800) 446-6020. This intimate manor house on a shaded hillside is like a visit to a country estate. There are 27 beautifully decorated rooms and 9 suites, all retaining the ambience of the 1920s. Rates are from $105 to $180. This includes a continental breakfast. It's a perfect spot for honeymooners or lovebirds in search of a bit of privacy and luxury without the blandness and conformity of the larger motel chains. This first-class hostelry was remodeled from an old Tudor mansion built in 1903. The public dining room with its wood beamed ceilings is a gracious place in which to enjoy a luncheon for two (or more) far away from the urban rush. Sandwiches, salads, and pasta dishes are available as well as lunch and dinner entrees. Call to ask about special Sunday brunches. Homestyle soups as a starter (hot or chilled, depending on the season) are popular. For the luncheon entree you could try a boneless Idaho brook trout with a butter-and-lemon sauce or chicken "à la Marlboro," or try the delicious chilled-and-poached Norwegian salmon filet with a mustard-dill-horseradish-cream sauce. Dinner includes salad and fresh cooked vegetables. Large salads—a meal in themselves—include a wonderful Caesar-and-chicken salad, which is warm chicken tenderloins served on a generous bed of Caesar salad. The large salad specials are a good bargain. Prices for dinners in the evening jump for the trout, and the range for other entrees is $13.50 to $15.50 and you can enjoy their traditional Wiener schnitzel—veal tenderloin medallions with lemon and served with *spaetzle* noodles—a German delight! Breakfast at the Marlboro is particularly pleasant on the sunporch or in good weather on the open patio. Meeting rooms are available here for business conferences.

A nice place to walk is just over the ridge along Bloomfield Avenue in nearby Verona, the next town west. **Verona Park** will be on your left off Bloomfield Avenue on Pleasant Valley Way. This beautifully landscaped park, which actually evokes the feeling of old Verona in Italy, has charming walkways and bridges and surrounds a large lake with wild ducks and chirping frogs. There is a planned exercise regime around the park and you can also rent a boat and row across the lake. Nancy Reagan, when she was known as Anne Frances Robbins, spent her formative childhood years in Verona. This was before she was adopted by her "second" father, Loyal Davis, who made the adoption when Nancy was a teenager. Connie Francis, who moved from Glen Ridge to Verona and finally to Florida, was often seen on the paths and bridge in Verona Park.

Based on recent media polls, the ultraswank show-spot restaurant of New Jersey—**the Manor**—is the most popular dining spot in the state. Ronald and Nancy Reagan, George and Barbara Bush, Richard Nixon, and other celebrities have elected to dine here when in New Jersey. The Manor, hard by the **Montclair Country Club,** at 111 Prospect Avenue, West Orange, (973) 731-2360, in addition to using Limoges china and crystal-and-silver place settings, serves excellent food. Culinary awards include nine consecutive Holiday Awards for Dining Distinction, the National Restaurant Association's Great Menu Award, and the International Geneva Association's Restaurant of the Year Award. Set on 22 acres, the 11-room Regency mansion can accommodate up to 3,000 people a day, 7 days a week. The Villa d'Este waterfall and gardens and the rococo decor and outside twinkle lighting must be seen to be believed. It resembles an EPCOT Center restaurant and is Disney all the way, ostentatious yet grand. If you are looking for an intimate hideaway to meet that other woman or man, the Manor is not the place. But if you want to impress a client, date, uncle, mother, or show your designer clothing off to the world, this is the restaurant in which to be seen center stage. There is dancing under the stars in **Le Dome,** the sophisticated nightclub, Wednesday through Saturday evenings. Buffet meals are specialties at the Manor; luncheon buffet is served in the Manor Room Wednesday from noon to 3 P.M.; lobster buffet is Tuesday to Saturday from 6 until 9:30 P.M. Sunday dinner buffet is from 1 to 8:30 P.M. À la carte luncheon in the Terrace Lounge is served Tuesday to Friday from noon to 3 P.M. À la carte dinner on Sunday is served 3 to 9:30 P.M. Try as a cold appetizer avocado stuffed with seafood ($11), Maine lobster cocktail ($17), or one ounce of Oregon caviar ($16.50) or *osetra caviar* (one ounce) at $34. Hot appetizers

This Depression-era Jersey lampshade was found in the Stations West Antique Shop in Montclair.

that are delicious include grilled farm quail with herbed orzo or Maryland crab cakes. Classic main courses are: filet mignon with truffle sauce, $27; roasted duck with sun-dried black cherry sauce, $24; a special (service for two) at $54 plus tax includes chateaubriand and rack of lamb served with a bouquet of seasonal vegetables. In a mood for seafood, try the Manor's softshell crabs, or roasted lobster stuffed with scallops and shrimp. From the Lincoln Tunnel, take Route 3 West to the Garden State Parkway South, exit 145. Follow signs for 280 West, exit 8B. The Manor is on the left-hand side of the road, straight ahead one mile. You can't miss it.

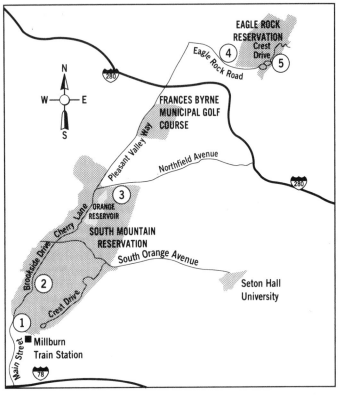

1. Paper Mill Playhouse
2. Elmdale Picnic Tables
3. Turtleback Zoo
4. Pal's Cabin
5. Highlawn Pavilion

South Mountain Reservation, a 2,048-acre preserve bordered by the townships of Millburn, Maplewood, South Orange, and West Orange, situated on the first and second of the three Watchung ridges of New Jersey, affords spectacular views of Newark and Manhattan to the east, less than a half-hour drive away. But once within its wooded, secluded confines, hiking the **Lenape Trail** or picnicking by the side of the upper reaches of the Rahway River, you can forget the hustle and bustle of modern civilization. To preserve the long wall of the Watchung (Lenape Indian for "high hills") ridges, the Essex Park Commission, established in 1895, consulted with the renowned Frederick Law Olmstead, creator of New York's Central Park. The plan conceived by Olmstead comprised 3 reservations and 23 parks, the middle and largest of which is the South Mountain Reservation. Eagle Rock Reservation to the

A vintage rumble-seat Ford parks by the side of the road in the South Mountain Reservation (Millburn area).

north and the Watchung Reservation to the south, across Route 24, together with 2,000-plus green acres in between, throw off enough oxygen to more than offset all the bad effects rising up out of the urban-suburban morass lying below.

To get to South Mountain Reservation, go to the little town of Millburn; Route 78 to Route 24, exit at Route 527 (Millburn Avenue). To get to the Reservation by public transportation, take the Gladstone or Morristown NJ Transit trains from Hoboken or Newark's Penn Station. They all stop at Millburn, right across the street from the Reservation. Millburn sits at the base of the South Mountain Reservation.

Driving, take Brookside Drive, just beyond the railroad tracks, out of Millburn Center, pass the Papermill Playhouse and enter the preserve. The Rahway River, dammed at various spots, flows by the side of the two-lane road. There are several picnic groves along the way, equipped with tables, fireplaces, and garbage cans, and places to park for fishing, wading or walking. Elmdale, the first picnic area, features two large wooden tables and two fireplaces. The little stream separating the parking area from the picnic spot fills with fresh watercress every spring and is a treat to eat. If you're feeling like a hike, cross the road and the river beyond, jump from rock to rock and climb the hill until you reach the broad trail. Used for bicycling, horseback riding, and walking, it meanders for miles through the secluded valley, culminating beneath the Hemlock Falls. Stand under the falls for a wet nature experience, turn around and hike on back to your car. Pack up your picnic things and drive through the reservation, cross Orange Avenue and continue to Brookside Drive. The Orange Reservoir, surrounded by pine trees, will be on your right. When you come to Northfield Avenue, turn right and drive to the **Turtleback Zoo,**

New Jersey's largest. It's located at 560 Northfield Avenue in West Orange. The hours are 10 A.M. to 5 P.M. weekdays and Saturdays in summer, 11 A.M. to 6 P.M. on Sunday. In the winter it's 10 A.M. to 4:30 P.M. daily. There are about 800 animals at this zoo, featuring native New Jersey species including cougars, bobcats, wolves, bears, otters, bison, and deer, as well as birds, fish, reptiles, and amphibians. Call (973) 731-5800 for information on train rides, picnic facilities, etc.

Walking, the **Lenape Trail** begins at the Locust Grove parking lot next to the Millburn train station. Cross the road and enter the woods, following the yellow-marked trail out to the **Oakdale Trail,** marked in red, and return on a different part of the Lenape Trail and the **Cascade Trail,** marked in white. A quarter of an hour from the parking lot you will be at the top of the ridge, opposite historic **Washington Rock.** Here you can see New York City, Newark Airport, and the entire megalopolis. Naturally George Washington slept here, while keeping his eye on the British who were foraging down in the valley. You can continue your hike through the South Mountain Reservation or opt out by hiking *down* a trail leading to the village of South Orange. You can catch the train here also, the advantage being that it's cheaper because you're closer to your departure point (providing that was Hoboken or points east), and also you don't have to double back over territory you've already seen. Another advantage is that it is a much shorter walk this way. As an incentive to keep you going, there are some fun singles bars and restaurants in the village of South Orange. For terrific Italian cuisine and pizza, don't miss **Reservoir Pizzeria & Restaurant** at 106 West South Orange Avenue, (973) 762-9795 and 763-1488.

Millburn

• •

Short Hills Shopping Mall, Pal's Cabin, Eagle Rock
Reservation, and Highlawn Pavilion

To get there: From Route 78 take Route 24 and exit at Route 527 (Millburn Avenue) into Millburn. For Short Hills take Route 24 to the intersection of JFK Parkway.

Millburn and the adjoining town of Short Hills have the charm of old New Jersey Revolutionary towns. "Mill-on-the-burn" comes from the Scotch-Presbyterian people who settled there when the town was first incorporated in 1857. During the industrial revolution, Millburn was known for its cloth mills, sawmills, hat mills, and paper mills. In fact, the beautiful **Papermill Playhouse** on Brookside Drive in Millburn is on a site that served as a paper mill from 1795 to 1926. In 1934 the mill was converted into a theater by Frank Carrington, an actor, and Antoinette Scudder, a patron of the arts, as a home base for their Newark Art Theater. With the help of none other than Eleanor Roosevelt, it has become the oldest continuously operated nonprofit theater in the United States. It became the official state theater of New Jersey in 1972. After a disastrous fire in 1980, it was completely rebuilt, combining the old and the new and featuring glass-enclosed promenades on the second floor, looking out into the South Mountain Reservation, and including a stark-white art gallery and a modern wide fanlike design for the theater itself. The emphasis at this theater is and always has been musical; a staple of operettas from Rudolf Friml to Jerome Kern has been the entertainment since the 1940s, and today there are 26,000 subscribers. The average annual attendance of 250,000 makes it the largest performing arts organization in New Jersey. The box-office telephone number is (973) 376-4343.

Geraldine Page, Rip Torn, and Sandy Dennis in the Papermill Playhouse production of The Little Foxes.

Millburn itself, just down the road from the Playhouse, has an exquisitely landscaped park, perfect for a nice walk in spring during the full floral bloom and an assortment of interesting gourmet shops, boutiques, bakeries, ice cream parlors, coffee shops, and intimate restaurants for before or after the theater are to be found in the village on Main Street and Millburn Avenue. **Buncher's** hardware store is an old-style hardware supplier carrying everything but the kitchen sink—but it is the shopping mall at Short Hills, just over the ridge on Route 24, where it intersects with the JFK Parkway at Chatham, that is a "shopping" must. Some of the major department stores at **The Mall at Short Hills** include **Bloomingdale's, Macy's, Neiman Marcus, Saks Fifth Avenue,** and **Nordstrom.** Some of the fine shops include **Borders Bookshop, Brooks Brothers, Brick Church Pipe Shop, FAO Schwarz Toy Shop, Godiva Chocolatier, Polo/Ralph Lauren, Roots, Saint Laurent, Rive Gauche,** and many others. There are also sit-down restaurants, including **Friendly's, Ruby Tuesday, Houlighan's, Au Bon Pain, Dean & DeLuca,** and **Johnny Rockets.** Hours at the mall are 10 A.M. to 9 P.M.; call (973) 376-7350 for weekend and holiday hours. Speaking of malls, the **Livingston Mall** in nearly Livingston features all the major department stores as well. It is much larger in scope than the Short Hills Mall but it is by no means as unique or intimate. Shopping in New Jersey is not only diversified and pleasant, but cheaper, as you save on taxes on many items.

One of the best restaurants in the area is **Pals Cabin** in West Orange. This famous landmark restaurant first opened as a small roadside refreshment stand–cabin in 1932 serving hamburgers, franks at 10¢, and orange soda for a nickel. By 1934 Martin L. Horn and Bion LeRoy Sale—the two pals—were offering a charcoal broiled steak for 50¢. By 1936 the enterprise grew—in the true American style right in the middle of a Great Depression—into a full-fledged restaurant serving the special steak for 75¢ and a filet mignon for $1. A sirloin choice-cut charbroiled steak was

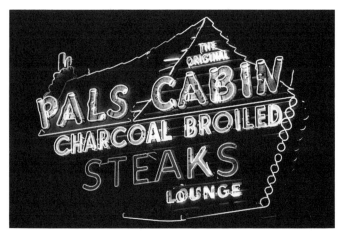

The original Pals Cabin neon sign. Pals opened as a roadside stand in 1932 and still serves excellent food at Prospect and Eagle Rock Avenues in West Orange.

Liberace pounded the ivories in his rise to fame at Pals Cabin in West Orange. His salary: $50 a week. The famous Liberace piano is still on view in the cocktail lounge.

$1.50 and a sirloin for two was $2.90. A broiled half chicken was 85¢, all served with french fried potatoes and a chef's salad served in a wooden bowl. By 1941 the two pals, Marty and Roy, could afford to hire a cocktail pianist named Liberace (yes, the same) who was then paid $50 a week and all he could eat. The two men subsequently opened another restaurant called the **Mayfair Farms**, just a stone's throw from Pals; this is considerably more formal than Pals, however. Pals has three dining areas; a sit-down counter, a bake shop, and a room for special occasions such as birthdays, anniversaries, or catered business meetings (lunch or dinner). The clean, stainless-steel kitchens and brick charcoal grill are wide open for all to see. If you sit in the first dining area, which has comfortable leatherette booths, your picture window view is a gas station across the roadway and cars whizzing by, which seem to suit the delicious charbroiled American fare. The "Winchester Room," decorated with oil paintings of cattle and cattle ranches, is a jacket-and-tie affair, and reservations are accepted there.

The service at Pals is swift and they have the best naturally aged beef in New Jersey. If you are not in the mood for a big steak there are hamburgers, Welsh rarebit, or hot gravied white-meat turkey sandwiches. Pals cold, crisp salads with croutons are still served in a large, wooden bowl and are excellent. A Caesar salad—made right at the table—is also a specialty. Pals does not offer meat or fish that is frozen and does not use artificial tenderizers. Jackie Gleason and Babe Ruth were two guys who were regular customers. Though the two pals are no longer around to enjoy the fun they have created at Pals, the tradition of "good food for good health" is carried on by the Horn family sons Marty Jr. and Don (and their children) who are all earnest about maintaining the top standard set by the founders. Pals has a good wine menu and offers tempting mixed drinks of all varieties. They are open daily from 9 A.M. to 10:30 P.M. Friday and Saturday until midnight. Call (973) 731-4000.

To get to Pals: Located on the corner of Prospect and Eagle Rock Avenues in West Orange, Pals can be approached from the south by driving from Millburn over Brookside Drive (though this road does not change its direction, it does change names: from Brookside Drive to Pleasant Avenue and finally to Valley Way). When you hit Eagle Rock Avenue, turn right and drive to Prospect Avenue. From the metropolitan area exit onto 280 West either from the Turnpike or from the Garden State Parkway. Exit 280 at Prospect Avenue.

Route 280 West (exit Prospect Avenue, left onto Eagle Rock Avenue) will also take you, within minutes from the metro region to **Eagle Rock Reservation,** a gem of the Essex County Parks system. The lookout area here provides the best view anywhere. It also has picnic tables, walking trails, bridle trails, and birdwatching sites. It's a magnificent spot, ideal for giving you a sense of the height of the Watchung ridge and a geographic "feel" for the region. It's also an excellent place for a walk after dinner at Pals. The parks' architects, the Olmstead brothers, said in 1902 that from this spectacular overlook "you see all the intervening country as from a balloon." The Knowles family, who run the Manor Restaurant as well as the Ram's Head Inn in Absecon, opened a new place in 1986 on the site of a pavilion built on the outlook in 1908 as a refreshment stand. The Northern Italian, Mediterranean architecture of **Highlawn Pavilion** blends perfectly with the old restored Florentine pavilion—muted corals, terra-cotta, and deep blue-green colors in the high-ceilinged rooms, a splashing fountain and the riveting view make this a wonderful dining experience—a French rotisserie, wood-burning Italian brick oven and char-grill whet the appetite with specialties including roasted baby chicken, honey-glazed duckling, baked oysters, gourmet pizzas, and grilled veal chops. Telephone to make reservations at Eagle Rock Reservation before the Indians get them all. (The *reservations* that is. Another "Jersey" joke, folks!) Call (973) 731-DINE.

Irvington Time Travel

A "Memory-Image" by Robert Heide

The small town of Irvington (population 60,000) was a wonderful place to grow up in. It had been settled by German immigrants at the turn of the century. My father, Ludwig, had a bakery with a man named Schmaltz in Newark and later got into the tool-and-die-making business manufacturing needles for the Singer Sewing Machine factory in Elizabeth. We lived at 34 Franklin Terrace and then moved to 214 Elmwood Avenue, just two blocks away. Today the neighborhood and the houses my father owned are exactly the same. The orange-brick Second Reform Protestant Church where I went to Christian Endeavor and where I was confirmed is unchanged. My favorite teacher in the fourth grade, Ada Schwab, lived on the block on Elmwood Avenue near where the church stands. The Florence Avenue School seems also to be just as it always was. The majestic Frank Morrell High School that I graduated from in the 1950s looks the same, with its high cement columns in the Greek Revival style. Right in the center of town,

Robert Heide on the steps of the very same house at 34 Franklin Terrace where he lived as a child. The wood-frame house and the neighborhood in Irvington remains virtually unchanged.

on Springfield Avenue, the five-and-dime stores I loved to go into back then are still there. Gone are the old movie theaters, the Sanford, the Liberty, and the Rex. The Castle, listed as an important architectural landmark by the Theater Historical Society, is still intact, however. Merkhin's ice cream parlor, with its wood-paneled booths and stained glass is, alas, no more. Whatever happened to the Wurlitzer jukebox, where as a teenager I first heard Elvis shouting out "You ain't nothin' but a hound dog!"? I used to love to take the Springfield Avenue bus to downtown Newark with my mother, Olga, who couldn't get enough of the great department stores there, mainly Kresge's, Hahne's, and L. Bambergers.

The most famous place in Irvington, though, was Olympic Park, one of the greatest of the old-time amusement parks. It be-

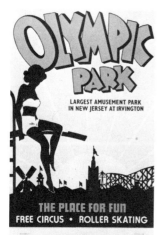

LARGEST AMUSEMENT PARK
IN NEW JERSEY AT IRVINGTON

THE PLACE FOR FUN
FREE CIRCUS • ROLLER SKATING

1943		JANUARY			1943	
SUN	MON	TUE	WED	THU	FRI	SAT
					1	2
3	4	5	6	7	8	9
10	11	12	13	14	15	16
17	18	19	20	21	22	23
24/31	25	26	27	28	29	30

A 1943 souvenir Olympic Park calendar. The graphic was used on gigantic billboards that advertised the same Irvington amusement park.

came the prototype for the Disney theme parks; but they are only a slick imitation of the original. When I talk to many of the New Jerseyans who went to Olympic Park they are usually ecstatic. Some remember Palisades Amusement Park; but all agree that Olympic Park was bigger and better. I considered myself lucky to live only two blocks from the great park that usually opened on Memorial Day and closed right after Labor Day. Trolleys and buses up Springfield Avenue deposited visitors at the magical entrance to the old park that first opened as a tree-shaded beer garden in 1887. The first thing you saw was the white stucco archway; after you paid your entrance fee of 10¢ you passed through to the geyserlike fountain with a revolving rainbow of colored light. To a child, a visit to Olympic Park was like going over the rainbow and landing in Oz. A real brass band led by Captain Joe Basile featured blond singer Bubbles Ricardo. She was a former trapeze artist who lost an arm in a fall from the high wire. The Guenther family, who operated the park on land in both Irvington and Maplewood, built "the world's largest" swimming pool, where many of us learned to swim. There was a sandy beach, a restaurant on the side, and a jukebox for dancing. The pool had an opening-day ceremony on July 4, 1924 and featured that day a star performance by athlete Johnny Weissmuller. The wooden roller coaster, called the "Jack Rabbit," brought screams of sheer terror the minute you hit the first incline, and was a favorite for years with roller-coaster aficionados. Amidst the games of chance, which offered painted plaster Popeyes,

Painted felt Olympic Park souvenir banner.

Newark Sunday Call rotogravure showing girls emerging from the tunnel of love in the Old Mill, Olympic Park, 1942. The blonde is author Heide's cousin Doris Dinger of Flemington.

Lone Rangers, or Betty Boops, were an array of rides like "the Whip," electric "dodgem" cars, "the Caterpillar" (with a green canvas top that opened and closed), "the Tunnel of Love," a giant Ferris wheel, and a spooky and musty walk-through called "the Haunted Castle." There were penny arcades on the midway, a real live circus featuring Hildy's Midget Troupe, some of whom were the Munchkins in the film *The Wizard of Oz*, aerial artists and animal acts; but it is the merry-go-round, with its ancient calliope and beautifully carved wooden horses that will remain as an image in my mind forever. The Guenthers had purchased the carousel with 80 hand-carved horses, 4 chariots, and 3,000 lights in 1928. The horses are now in Disney World, Florida.

My parents would meet many of the members of our large German family in the open beer garden on a summer Saturday night. Great-Aunt Gussie, Aunt Emma, Aunt Alma, Aunt Martha, Aunt Bertha, Uncle Adolph, Uncle Freddy, Uncle Albert, and others would sing along with Bubbles and the orchestra. I remember them singing the songs of World War II—"The White Cliffs of Dover" and "When the Lights Go On Again All Over the World." Bubbles would usually end with a rousing version of "The Star Spangled Banner" while the crowd cheered. Sometimes fireworks would explode in the night sky while she was singing. Now they are all gone; and so is Olympic Park. But the memory lingers on.

Note: The Guenther family decided not to reopen the park for the 1966 season. Today, if you drive by the old site of Olympic Park,

Memory image, Irvington. Top: Author Robert Heide's mother Olga, grandmother Amelia Strafehl, the author himself (center), and sister Evelyn (with flowers) sitting on the steps of the house at 34 Franklin Terrace. Middle: Back row, left to right—Billy Burlew, Richard Edgar, Lois Hausmann, Norma Edgar; front row, left to right—Cousin Georgie Reiman, Robert Heide, Cousin Herbie Reiman, at author's birthday party, all neighborhood kids. Bottom: Robert's parents Ludwig, Olga, and great-uncles Adolph and Louie on the front porch at 34 Franklin Terrace.

on Chancellor Avenue, you will see not shaded tree gardens or glittering lights but drab boxlike buildings that comprise an industrial park. If you listen carefully, though, you might hear the sound of the brass band, the calliope, or the organ from the old roller rink. The great Olympic Park served Newark and its suburban environs from 1887 to 1965, when it was shut down. Area bookstores sell copies of *Smile—A History of Olympic Park* by Alan A. Siegel (New Brunswick, NJ: Rutgers University Press).

The **Old Homestead** in Irvington, just a couple of blocks from the grounds of Olympic Park, still stands at 1133 Stuyvesant Avenue. It is the oldest building in Irvington (1833) and was originally a stagecoach stop. It is the only tavern right next door to a church, the Mount Zion Primitive Baptist Church. Next to the church is

The Old Homestead Restaurant-Tavern, "the only bar next door to a church," in Irvington.

a 1950s drive-in Dairy Queen. The anomalous juxtaposition of these three peculiar places has achieved historical trivia status by several mentions in *Ripley's Believe It Or Not*. Operated for over 20 years by a character named Johnny Metropolitan, it features an Italian-style menu and the restaurant "special" is its famous big-size hot dog. A very jovial barroom, restaurant, and poolroom, the Old Homestead serves excellent sandwiches, German liverwurst, kielbasa, sausage, homemade potato salad, baked clams, and other tavern-style food to be enjoyed with imported beers and other alcoholic beverages. A 28-inch party pizza is $25; $28 to go. You can read the bewildering array of food signs all over the walls either at the bar, which snakes through two rooms, or at the comfortable booths in the dining room. The place is completely decorated with breweriana, a testament to the fact that the Old Homestead has been and still is the first stop for liquor distributors who leave off sample bottles and elaborate liquor, wine, and beer display pieces and advertisements. Dennis Casale, the night bartender for more than 20 years is proud of the displays and always stays open late (until 2 A.M., Friday and Saturday nights until 3) for elbow bending and good conversation. Nearby in Irvington, after the Homestead has closed, you can go to the terrific 1950s-style 24-hour **Kless's Diner** at 1212 Springfield Avenue. Kless's (you can't miss the giant neon sign) has good home cooking and endless steaming cups of hot black coffee. They also offer free home-baked cookies at the cash register, which is a smart alternative to their giant cakes, pies, and pastries.

Union Day Trip

Going into the town of Union is almost like entering the twilight zone, circa 1950. Even the friendly townfolk seem to have come from another time, another place. It has been called the "most typical American town" because of its melting-pot population ratio of Polish, German, Hispanic, Italian, African-American, Asian, and other nationality groups. Presidents come to visit; George Bush in 1989 and Bill Clinton just before his second inauguration in 1996. Road signs proclaim WHAT HELPS YOUTH HELPS UNION. To be sure. This flag-waving town would never be confused with the colorful, predominantly Spanish-speaking town of Union City, on the edge of the Hudson River, just above the Lincoln Tunnel, famous for its raucous nightlife and bars.

(Indeed, Bergenline Avenue, stretching through Union City and West New York, has become a microcosm of Central and South American cultures. There are excellent Cuban and Ecuadorian restaurants, food markets that sell Caribbean products like frozen papaya pulp and bricks of guava paste, upholsterers who specialize in clear-vinyl furniture coverings and shops selling painted plaster Catholic and Santeria saints, many life-size.)

Getting to Union is easy: Route 22 borders Union Township and exits 140 and 142 from the Garden State Parkway lead directly into town. You can also take Highway 78, which has an exit marked Union-Vauxhall. Stuyvesant Avenue is the main street that runs through Union Center.

Park your car and walk down Stuyvesant Avenue, which is a great place to shop. A famous landmark is **Lutz's Pork Store** at 1055 Stuyvesant Avenue, (908) 688-1373. Here you can stock up on the best in homemade bolognas, bloodwursts, liverwursts, potato salad, German rye breads, and German import mustards and pickles to go along with it. Likewise, you will find just up the street, on Morris Avenue, which crosses Stuyvesant, **Gaiser's Pork Store** with its neon pig glowing in the window. This is a large specialty butcher delicatessen of the type that used to be found in the German Yorkville section of Manhattan. Take home some of these goodies for sandwiches and you will not be disappointed. **Union Center,** which has ample and convenient parking was, like many "main streets," in decline until energetic locals protested the encroachment of the shopping mall. Now it is bustling with shops and places to go. All on Stuyvesant Avenue are **Corrigan's Tavern** (a good place to watch the Super Bowl), **Here's The Story—**

A furniture store in the shape of a ship on Route 22 in Union was a nightclub where the big bands played in the 1930s and 1940s. (This building now houses a Wiz electronics center.)

Books and Video, (908) 688-2665, **John & Mary's Luncheonette, Mr. Nino's Pizza and Restaurant, Perkin's Pharmacy, Van Gogh's Ear Cafe, The Blue Ribbon Bakery, Rock-Star Headquarters,** and **Jahn's** (since 1897). Jahn's Old Fashioned Ice Cream Parlor, though rebuilt, is the choice of patrons of the **Union Cinema** after a movie for that special ice cream treat, a banana split, malted milk, or other giant concoction. Around the corner from Jahn's is a cozy place for cocktails and fine food, **Spaeter's** on Rosemont—or hustle over to **Artie's "Club Elmour,"** 1871 Vauxhall Road, (908) 687-7777, for burgers, steak sandwiches, boardwalk pizza, and malted milkshakes, not to mention a terrific liquor bar. Classic rock is provided here every Wednesday, Friday, and Saturday. This place is run by Artie Ehman and C. J. Pierce.

Summit is just a hop, skip, and jump out of Union Center (take Route 82 West—Morris Avenue—to Broad Street), and the charming town center is worth a visit. One of the finest dining experiences anywhere is **Fiorino Ristorante,** 38 Maple Street, (908) 277-1900, Summit. Legendary restaurateur John Bitucci (the former owner of the Minetta Tavern in Greenwich Village) serves first-class Italian dishes in a cozy atmosphere that features artful murals of Italian scenes. Bitucci has assembled his best chef and waiters from Minetta Tavern.

Union, Maplewood, and South Orange Village

One of the highlights of the Union area is the **Connecticut Farms Presbyterian Church** (at Stuyvesant Avenue and Chestnut Street), which was founded in 1730. Visiting the church and the adjacent graveyard, you can imagine General George Washington tromping around as he did during the Revolutionary War when he commandeered the place as a temporary headquarters. The ghosts can make you hungry, so head on out Chestnut Street to the **Galloping Hill Inn** at 325 Chestnut, Union. Situated in a mind-boggling intersection called "Five Points," where five different rural roads cross each other, driving into the parking lot of this drive-in–type place feels oddly like berthing a ship, out of the flow. Order terrific roadside hamburgers, hot dogs, or french fries with special relishes. A small, nostalgic restaurant with sparkling painted red tables and knotty-pine walls lined with antiquarian calendars and yesteryear photos (there are even some old menus from the time when a complete chicken dinner was only 35¢ and coffee a nickel), it is intimate and fun in the family style. Special American meals of stuffed capon or flounder, fried shrimp, or large beef hot dogs and potato salad all cost less than $10. Hours are 10 A.M. to 11 P.M. every day; telephone (908) 686-2683. Still in Union, but over on Springfield Avenue (at Millburn Avenue), is another legendary eatery called **Joe's Famous Pizzeria,** which has been serving up mouth-watering tomato pies, hot dogs, sausages, and such Italian specialties as lasagna, calzone with pizza toppings, and mozzarella sticks since 1948. To take home food, stop in at **Di Pietro Italian Specialty Foods,** 1701 Springfield Avenue, (973) 762-4077, hours 7:30 A.M. to 6 P.M., just across the road from beautiful Maple Crest Park.

To get to the Hamlet of Maplewood, drive over the hill from Maple Crest Park to Valley Road, past the lush golf course and country club, the town library and beautiful Maplewood Memorial Park. Across the road from the top of this park is the Maplewood train station, and the charming hamlet is just beyond. Shops and restaurants line both sides of the curving, hilly Maplewood Avenue. There is a choice of several movies at the **Maplewood Cinema.** Try the **Cafe-Grill Rotisserie** at 165 Maplewood Avenue, which features fifty gourmet flavored coffees, a showcase of dessert sensations, and food with low-fat and low-cholesterol ingredients. **Robin Hutchins Gallery** at 179 Maplewood Avenue, (973) 762-4714, features changing art exhibitions.

Greetings from Union, New Jersey, postcard.

The hilly outlying streets and roads of South Orange are all lit by old-fashioned gaslight—in the higher elevations on the mountain there are astonishing views of Manhattan and the metropolitan region. **Seton Hall University,** famous for its basketball games, is located in South Orange. South Orange Village has a charming railroad station and brick firehouse and tower. Located at the steps to the train on South Orange Avenue is the new 1950s-style retro diner **Blue Moon. Town Hall Deli,** up the street, is sheeted in 1930s black vitreous glass. There are some "Good-time Charlie" and "Stuff Y'er Face" hangouts for the college kids, but the place to go for pan pizza is the **Reservoir Pizzeria & Restaurant** at 106 West South Orange Avenue, (973) 762-9795 and 763-1488. Try one of Tony's immense salads, too! Old-timers remember this place when it was located down next to Newark's old reservoir. A legend then, a legend now.

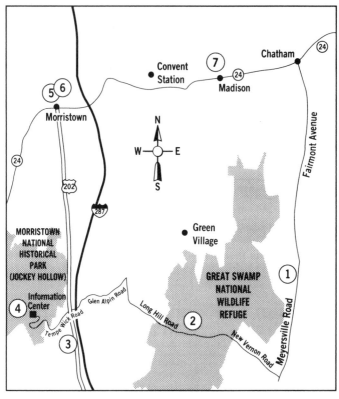

1. Passaic Township Grange
2. Center of the Swamp
3. Minuteman Family Restaurant
4. Wick House
5. August Moon Chinese Restaurant
6. George Washington's Headquarters
7. Museum of Early Crafts and Trades

To get to the **Great Swamp,** located just to the south of the little town of Chatham, take Route 24 off the Garden State Parkway or the Jersey Turnpike. In Chatham, turn left into Fairmont Avenue and drive up the hill until the avenue doglegs onto Meyersville Road. You'll pass a good produce farm on the hill to the left and the **Passaic Township Grange** farther down the road on the right. Here, every Sunday, October through April, from 8 A.M. to 3 P.M., the Grange ladies have a soup tasting and bake-off as well as a good indoor flea market, which attracts a good selection of antique dealers. Call (908) 689-5188 or 647-9727. Beyond the Grange, turn right on New Vernon Road to enter the Great Swamp. Posted signs direct you to various locations inside the Swamp; headquar-

ters is on Pleasant Plains Road. Fifteen thousand years ago a glac-
ier receded across the Passaic Valley, creating a 30-mile-long, 10-
mile-wide lake that gradually drained off to leave behind 7,400
acres of swamp, hardwood forests, marshland and open fields, now
known as the **Great Swamp National Wildlife Refuge.** Ideal to
visit September through May, when there is no humidity or mos-
quitos, the Great Swamp was saved by residents of Morris County
from developers who were planning on turning it into a jetport.

This incredible swamp has 30 species of mammals, 24 of fish, 21
of reptiles, 18 of amphibians, and more than 200 varieties of birds.
Open daily from dawn to dusk, the 3,600-acre core of the refuge
allows no motorized vehicles or equipment, and there are no
man-made structures to block the view. The National Wilderness
Preservation system provides a primitive "outdoor experience" for
the public — 10 miles of trails at the northeast end of White Bridge
Road and Laurel Trail — and 5½ miles of walking trails on the western border as well as a wildlife observation center off Long Hill
Road with a mile of trails and blinds for observing wildlife. To exit
the Great Swamp continue on New Vernon Road, up Long Hill to
Logansville Road. Turn right on Logansville to Glen Alpin Road.
Turn left on Glen Alpin and drive to Route 202 (Mt. Kemble
Avenue). Turn left on 202 and drive south to the 145-acre **Wightman Farm,** owned and operated by the Wightman family since
1923. At the farm's produce store you can pick up fresh cider, apples, homemade doughnuts, jellies, pickles, relishes, smoked hick-
ory bacon and ham. Pumpkins and farm-grown mums are the big
fall specialty.

If you are looking for a lunch stop in the area the **Minuteman
Family Restaurant** on Mt. Kemble Avenue (Route 202) as you
head back toward Jockey Hollow is just the spot. This is a knotty-
pine place with comfortable booths and a relaxed atmosphere.
Under "burger brigades" on the menu you'll find the Ethan Allen,
a burger on a toasted bun with french fries, coleslaw, lettuce, and
tomato. The James Madison is a burger covered with pizza sauce
and mozzarella cheese. The Nathan Hale has Old English cheese
and Russian dressing. There are others including the Ben
Franklin, the John Adams, the John Hancock, the Thomas Paine,
the Thomas Jefferson, and the Alexander Hamilton. The Ichabod
Crane is a diet special, a burger on toast with lettuce and cottage
cheese. Other patriotic American fare includes triple-decker sandwich deals, homemade apple, sour cherry, blueberry, fresh peach,
or strawberry-rhubarb pies. The delicious pies may also be taken
home; but served with Welsh Farms ice cream and Minuteman's
strong coffee, they should be eaten on the spot.

After fueling up at the Minuteman, drive up to Tempe Wick Road
at the traffic light, turn left, and drive through the densely wooded

Wick farmhouse where Tempe Wick hid her favorite horse for three weeks (in her bedroom) to prevent its seizure by the British soldiers during the Revolution. Linen postcard from Tichnor Brothers.

area known as **Jockey Hollow,** part of Morristown National Historical Park. Reconstructed quarters that housed our Revolutionary-era soldiers yield sobering insights into the harsh realities of winter during the Revolution—huts chinked with clay and held together with wooden pegs. There are over 900 wooded acres in this designated wildlife sanctuary, with miles of hiking trails.

The **Wick House** is restored and furnished and set next to a fascinating Colonial kitchen herb garden where something edible seems to grow year-round. Quince, gooseberry, and currant shrubs are prominent in spring. This is a lovely farm site with wooden fences enclosing a pasture and apple orchard where deer and horses gambol in proximity. The Wick House, field headquarters for Washington's Major General Arthur St. Clair during the Revolution, is located in the Jockey Hollow encampment area and has parking, an information center, and rest room facilities. An interesting bit of historical trivia associated with the Wick House during the Revolution is the story of Tempe Wick, a strong-minded farm woman who was the daughter of the owner. Everyone was away and the British soldiers, as usual, were rampaging through the area. Tempe Wick, in order to prevent the seizure of her horse by the British, secreted the animal in her bedroom for three weeks.

The man who slept around—George Washington's Revolutionary War headquarters are in Morristown, but Washington himself apparently camped out all over the state during the war as well as having slept the night in many country inns and farmhouses.

Morris County

Madison—Morristown—Mendham

Worth looking into in the Morris County area, home of the Great Swamp and the Morristown National Historical Park, are the grounds of **Drew University.** Drew University is a Methodist college with a liberal attitude, located in the town of Madison, which is called the "Rose City" (from the turn of the century through the 1950s, Madison was the center of the commercial rose-growing industry), on Route 24. Park the car inside the 186-acre forested campus grounds, which are entered through a stone arch just to the left as you drive west from Madison center. Beautiful plantation-style mansions such as the administration building, Mead Hall, the manor house of the Gibbons family, built in the neoclassic style with Greek revival decor in 1836 and listed on State and National Historic Registers, abound. The New Jersey Shakespeare Festival, a not-for-profit professional (Equity) theater group is in residence at Drew each summer; and they alternate the plays of Shakespeare with modern classics like *Long Day's Journey Into Night* or *A Man For All Seasons.* The town of Madison is sparkling clean, with a 1920s architectural style. It is filled with inexpensive luncheonettes, antique and boutique shops. **Time After Time Clothing From the Past** at 81 Main Street, is run by a vivacious woman named Bette Moore. Bette likes to dress up in vintage silk dresses and 1940s platform pumps. Check out her stock of 1930s, 1940s, and 1950s shirts and jackets for men, and dresses, blouses, undies, hats, and accessories for women. The college crowd keeps the glad rags moving but Bette is constantly restocking. Call (973) 966-6877.

Also on Main Street at Green Village Road is the **Museum of Early Crafts and Trades,** located in a stone church and open daily from 10 A.M. to 5 P.M. and Sunday from 2 to 5 P.M. The museum houses reconstructed shops of the early trades and presents the life of the early settlers in this historical region, with seasonal crafts exhibited at corresponding times of the year.

Drew is not the only college in the Madison area. Farther out on Route 24 is the **Fairleigh Dickinson University Florham–Madison campus,** situated on 187 acres of what was once the 900-acre estate of Florence Vanderbilt Twombly and centered around a 100-room replica of Henry VIII's Hampton Court Palace, designed by Stanford White. Here, as in many other places in New Jersey, the parklike grounds were designed by Frederick Law Olmstead. A few miles west is the **College of St. Elizabeth,** a Catholic college for women at Convent Station. At this spot, still on Route 24, is the **Madison Hotel,** (973) 285-1800, a 195-room hotel run by Motor-Hotel Management Company. **Rod's 1890s Ranch**

House, owned and operated by the Keller family, which also runs the building housing the Madison Hotel, is right next door, serving breakfast, lunch, and dinner and featuring a beautifully decorated (in period) cocktail lounge.

Route 24 rambles on into the business district of Morristown, the shopping center and "hub" for more than 300,000 people in three counties. The town is also on Interstate Highway 287 (north-south) and U.S. Route 202.

Morristown made the iron and gunpowder used in the Revolutionary War and because of this the town was subject to many attempts by the British to capture it. Its high perched location and defensibility made these attempts futile however, and Washington consequently decided to make it his headquarters. There are two major department stores, a half-dozen large office buildings, banks and two movie theaters, several beautiful historic churches, and dozens of retail shops situated around the large town green. During the 1960s small bands of hippies congregated here; now it's more or less a ragtag group of mild-mannered homeless men. At Christmas time the "green" becomes a fantasy of Santa Claus's North Pole headquarters, in honor of the famed cartoonist Thomas Nast, who lived in Morristown and created the character of Santa Claus as we know him today. The town decorates the square with elves' houses, castles, and giant, brightly colored Christmas packages. Santa and his reindeer, crèches of the Madonna and Child and other yuletide exhibits make this a "must stop" for the kiddies during the Christmas season, particularly if there is snow on the ground.

Right off the "green," down the hill on Morris Street and just across the street from Morristown's beautiful train station, is the **August Moon Chinese Restaurant,** owned by Henry Lam, 147 Morris Street, (973) 538-8316. This place is very hard to miss—its 1930s glass-brick facade, lit from behind by rods of colored neon, is covered in pink, red, and blue neon stars and moons; an extraordinary sight and ranking high on the list of the most beautiful pop culture neon in the state of New Jersey. The interior is clean with a simplified modern look—1930s recessed lighting and decorative Chinese plates on the wall. Mr. Colan Iu, "the president" of the whole enterprise, cooks up and serves fried wonton with Chinese mustard and duck sauce and a delicious three-course meal consisting of three-mushroom chicken with abalone mushroom, a specialty, baby corn and snow peas, pork fried rice and the August Moon curry shrimp. Lunch and dinners are reasonable (including the family dinners with choices from group A and group B) and the hours are Monday to Friday, 11 A.M. to 10:30 P.M., Saturday from 11 A.M. to 11:30 P.M. and Sunday from noon to 10:30 P.M. Call to find out the date of their Chinese celebrations, held every two months.

The **Old Book Shop** in Morristown, run by Virginia Faulkner and Chris Wolff, specializes in Americana and New Jersey history. Their total stock of over 30,000 books, on a great variety of subjects, includes several thousand volumes of fiction, many with their original dust jackets intact, as well as maps and a good selection of paper ephemera. From the train station, pass under the tracks to Ridgedale Avenue (near the Gulf station). Turn left on Ridgedale, drive one-half mile to John Street, turn right; they are at 4 John Street. Hours are Monday through Saturday, 10 A.M. to 5:30 P.M., (973) 538-1210.

Twice a year the **Morristown National Guard Armory** hosts a splendid antiques show, which is well worth a visit, if only to view the fine antique wares exhibited by as many as 100 top quality dealers in the lofty premises of the regimental headquarters. Call Wendy Show Management, Westchester Enterprises, Inc., (914) 698-3442, for the exact dates, usually in late January and again in late April.

Morristown is steeped in Revolutionary War history and is quite proud of the restored **Jacob Ford House** (Washington's headquarters during the tough winter of 1779–80) and other preserved and restored historic structures, many of which, it is rumored, George slept in. The Ford House (230 Morris Avenue), built in 1772 and furnished with period pieces, is part of the Morristown National Historic Park that includes Jockey Hollow, the Wick House and Farm, and Fort Nonsense, the latter on a high hill on the western outskirts of town, which has a fine vista. The **Schuyler Hamilton House** (5 Olyphant Road) where Alexander Hamilton met his future wife, Betsy Schuyler, is now the headquarters of the Morristown DAR. **Acorn Hall** (68 Morris Avenue) is a fine example of Victorian Italianate architecture with a beautiful Victorian garden. It is also the headquarters for the Morris County Historical Society, (973) 267-3465, and has a complete Victorian research library.

Washington's Headquarters, Morristown, New Jersey.

Proceeding southwest out of Morristown on Route 24 is Mend-ham, home of the **Black Horse Inn,** opened in the farmhouse of Ebenezer Byram in 1742 and in continuous operation for well over 200 years as a tavern for travelers. A sign at the rear door pro-claims: PURVEYORS: BRING THROUGH THESE DOORS ONLY THE FRESHEST, FINEST TOP QUALITY MERCHANDISE OR BE PREPARED TO TAKE IT BACK! This old inn is open for dinner daily from 5:30 P.M. to 10 P.M. and Sunday from 1 P.M. to 8:30 P.M.; closed Mondays. A popular and more casual place to eat is the **Black Horse Pub** (just behind the main inn), which has a fine old bar decorated with old Lowenbrau casks and kegs, copper kettles, and knotty pine. They serve Bass Ale, Grolsch, and New Amsterdam beers. Call (973) 543-7300 for inn reservations and pub hours. **Sammy's Ye Old Cider Mill Inn** on Route 24, Mendham, (973) 543-7675, has no signs and you wouldn't know it was a place of any kind if it weren't for the Mercedes, Jaguars, Bentleys, Rolls-Royces, and Cadillac Coupe de Villes parked in the back. The simple white farmhouse is the setting for wonderful family-style meals featuring large steaks, thick lamb chops, and 2-pound lobsters, served with com-plete meals. You have to bring your own wine, dress simply but nicely, and be patient while waiting to be served. This is the place that Bill Bradley told us was one of his favorites. There will be "a certain thrill, a prickling of the skin" for lovers of antiquarian books at **Painted Pony Antiques** in Mendham Center (just off Route 24) at 6 Hilltop Road, (973) 543-6484. Two floors of books and antiques are spread throughout five rooms. Presided over by proprietor Steffi Terry, the shop has big, overstuffed chairs for "pondering" in her Dickensian, old-world shop. Hours are Tues-day, 1 to 5 P.M.; Wednesday through Saturday, 11 A.M. to 5 P.M.

Between Chester and Long Valley (see *Chester/Long Valley Day Trip*) on Parker Road, off Route 24, just beyond the grist mill, is the beautiful and mysterious **Hacklebarney State Park,** situated in a gorge along the brooding Black River. There are dozens of picnicking areas with tables and fireplaces with running water and rest room facilities within easy walking distance. There is also very good fishing and hiking. Stop at the Jacobson family farm— **Hacklebarney Farms,** phone (908) 879-6733—established in 1851 on the winding road to the park and stock up on apples, peaches, home-baked goods, and fresh apple cider pressed in their own mill, and sold by the quart and gallon to take along on your picnic. The Jacobsons also give tours of their beautiful farm by appoint-ment.

Chester/Long Valley Day Trip

The historic (1799) township of Chester (west of Mendham) is at the junction of Routes 24 and 206. Settled in 1713, sawmills, grist-mills, and distilleries utilized the industrial possibilities offered by the waters of the Black River. Later woolen mills and iron mines operated here. Today all that remains of this busy past are the peach orchards southwest of town. The bustling town has more than 40 shops and almost a dozen restaurants. The old-style shops, in restored 19th-century buildings, have humorous names like **Chester Drawers, Bare Necessities, Geppeto's Workshop, Party Parrot, Spiced Apple,** and **Pegasus.** Take a peek into the last and browse through the past—there are Mickey Mouse toys, Jerseyana, and other antique goodies for sale including 20th-century pop-culture collectibles, advertising signs, toys, furniture, and Fiesta ware. For vintage and antique clothing, jewelry, and more furniture and collectibles, try Tom & Jacqui Crowe's **The Beauty of Civilization,** 30 Main Street, Suite 6, Chester, (908) 879-2044.

Chester goes all out several times a year with events and celebrations such as the arts and crafts show in the spring, an Oktoberfest, and a Christmas open house. Cabin fever weekends and sidewalk sales and special antique shows abound. And when you get hungry, walk to **Larison's Turkey Farm** on the hill, the largest restaurant in the area, where families can walk across a sloping lawn

One of the many farms in the Long Valley region.

under a spreading oak tree to visit the turkeys, peacocks, ducks, goats, chickens, rabbits, and donkeys in the paddocks or shop for specialty souvenirs in the gift shop. Don't worry: the turkeys in the paddocks are not the ones you'll be eating later. Upstairs in the restaurant, near the rest rooms, are two very unusual rooms fitted in 19th-century style as bedrooms, but filled with dozens of gigantic stuffed bears, deer, raccoons, and other ferocious animals. You can peek in through the windows on the doors. Larison's is known throughout Jersey for heaping bowls of stuffing, mashed potatoes, string beans and lima beans, tureens of gravy, platters of white and dark meat turkey, side dishes of creamed corn, cranberry sauce, olives and pickles, coleslaw—all you can possibly eat—for $14.95. They also have steaks and other items. Hot dinners are served Sundays all day long. Monday through Saturday lunch is served from 11 A.M. to 3 P.M., dinner from 3 to 9 P.M.. Call (908) 879-5521 for reservations.

From the crest of a hill on Route 24 (west of Chester) one looks down upon the length of **Long Valley,** a tributary of the Raritan River running through the center, and the **Schooley Mountains** forming a backdrop to the northwest. Long Valley is a rich farm region (stop at **Ort Farms** just off 24 on Route 625 as you cruise down into the valley) and though the town itself is not much more than a crossroads, it is well worth a long stop for "on foot" investigation. There is a general store that juts over the stream at the back, a gas station, an ancient tavern, and a very good family-style restaurant. The Zion Lutheran Church has a sign out front declaring that Long Valley was originally called German Valley before the First World War. Behind the church is a miniwilderness area with miles of walking paths meandering alongside a fast-moving stream. This is an excellent (and relatively unknown) place for spotting large, rare birds. There is also a dairy and other farm-related operations, including a distributor for delicious Welsh Farms ice cream and milk. There is an ancient cemetery with headstones dating from the late 18th and early 19th centuries, quite open for walking. In the center are the ruins of an old stone church. Back at the **Long Valley Inn** tavern at the crossroads, you will find huge framed sepia-toned photographs of the days of the horse and buggy in German Valley. Have a beer at the tavern and then walk next door to the **Chesapeake Bay Seafood Company,** (908) 876-3922, which serves luncheon daily from noon to 2:30 P.M., dinners Monday through Thursday 5 P.M. to 10 P.M., Friday and Saturday until 11 P.M., Sunday 12 noon to 9 P.M. Entrees run from $9.95 to $21.95 for the stuffed lobster. The fish is fresh from the

Matchbook, Long Valley Inn.

At Ort Farms in Long Valley you can pick your own pumpkin right off the vine at Halloween.

Fulton Street Fish Market in New York and the menu contains fish and chips, Alaskan Dungeness crab legs, and twin lobster tails. Entrees range from crab cakes or crab Wellington to Maryland steamed shrimp and shrimp and scallop scampis. The prices are reasonable and they also serve hamburgers and homemade desserts.

Route 24 takes a northerly turn at Long Valley, and a very steep ascent up Schooley Mountain, before it connects with Route 46 in Warren County. Schooley Mountain has a 2-gas-pump general store with a potbellied stove and penny candies in glass jars (and 100 post office boxes lined up side by side). **Schooley Mountain Park** and the 1½-acre Lake George are located on Camp Washington and Springtown Roads, just off Route 24. There is a unique floating bridge that separates the swimming area from the fishermen and boaters. Swimming on a hot summer day is a pleasure and there are many picnic sites, hiking trails, an amphitheater, and scenic overlooks.

Traveling southwest through Long Valley from Long Valley Center on Route 513, you drive through Lockwood Gorge where **Voorhees State Park** is located. There is a magnificent view of the **Spruce Run State Park** region in the western distance from here. There are picnic facilities and fireplaces. Refresh yourself and drive down the steep road to High Bridge, where Highway 31 will connect you to quick connections at east-west 22 and 78.

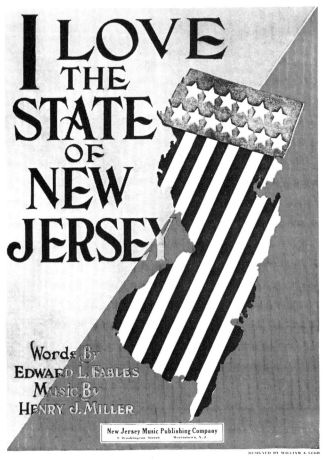

Early 1900s sheet music "I Love the State of New Jersey," words by Edward L. Fables and music by Henry J. Miller, published by the New Jersey Music Publishing Company.

To get there: Take Route 287 South. Exit at 13, Route 206 South, to Somerset Shopping Mall. The **Duke Gardens** are a mile and a quarter south as you head in the direction of Princeton. From midtown Manhattan take the Lincoln Tunnel to the NJ Turnpike to Interstate 78 West. Exit at Pluckemin onto Route 287 South. From lower Manhattan take the Holland Tunnel to the Pulaski

Skyway to I-78 West. From New York City the trip to Somerville should take about one hour. Buses from New York Port Authority leave every day for the estate.

Drive through the great iron gates of the Duke estate and park your car. Once inside you will have that very special feeling of quietude and grace usually offered only to the wealthy and privileged members of society. The 6,000-acre private estate was created out of the low, flat farm country south of Somerville, the county seat of Somerset. Doris Duke's father, James Buchanan Duke, the tobacco and electric-power mogul, spent $10 million in the days when a dollar went a long way, creating a magnificent series of lakes and 25 miles of paved roadways that wind around the lakes, through wooded hills, lagoons, grandiose fountains, waterfalls, cottages, stables, and greenhouses. Doris Duke, the late tobacco heiress and sole owner of the place, kept up the formal greenhouses, originally built for family use, opening them up to the public for the first time in 1964, by appointment only. The gardens are open from October through March, seven afternoons a week, from noon to 4 P.M. Call (908) 722-3700 at least one week prior to making this trip. There is an admission fee of $5. From the parking lot inside the gates a van takes about 10 people through the estate, offering glimpses of manicured meadows and gigantic trees, to the formal gardens. The walk through the garden is never rushed; but you may not wander, take photographs or eat snacks or sandwiches during the tour. Once deposited at the visitor's center, a tour guide will take you through the eleven 19th-century glass-enclosed Victorian hothouses. The entire walk-through with a guide takes about one hour.

The first garden you enter is a very romantic Italian garden filled with rare Italian statuary and fountains. Luxurious plants include birds of paradise, bougainvillea, and mimosa. Stepping through an archway you find yourself in the American Colonial garden featuring clipped hedges, camellia bushes and magnolias, all in an early-American setting. The Edwardian garden beyond houses a vast assortment of rare orchids, palm trees, and rubber plants with extra humidity pumped into the atmosphere. The other gardens that follow are the formal French garden, an English garden, a desert garden featuring giant cacti from the Southwest, a traditional Chinese garden with a mysterious "grotto among the stones," landscaped Japanese gardens, an Indo-Persian garden that contains the atmospheric beauty of the Taj Mahal and its gardens, an African rain forest garden that assimilates the jungle plants one might also find in the Amazon regions of South America, and finally, the Mediterranean semitropical garden.

Once this exotic tour is over and you are brought back to your car you will feel as if you have actually had a miniature trip around the world; a truly enchanting experience. These types of gardens were extremely popular among the wealthy at the turn of the century; but few private ones exist today. Certainly, none of such magnitude. Once outside the great gates and driving around the stone-walled estate on Duke's Parkway, one can appreciate the extent of the late Ms. Duke's personal desire for privacy, as the trees are posted with signs that read, NO TRESPASSING — PROPERTY OF DORIS DUKE. The great mansion itself is hidden from view behind a forest of pine trees. It has over 100 rooms, a huge indoor swimming pool, indoor tennis courts, a theater, and among the many wonders on the grounds is a miniature version of the Black Forest of Germany.

After a visit to the Duke Gardens, take a picnic lunch and drive to **Duke Island Park.** If you are adventurous, in the winter months or early spring, bring along a hot thermos of coffee and another filled with soup. Bring along a pair of ice skates too, because you can ice-skate on the lake during very cold weather at Duke Island Park, upstream from the Duke Farms. It is located on grazing land donated by the Duke Foundation, between two branches of the Raritan River (just off Highway 22 on Old York Road). This large park, just south of North Branch Park (site of the Somerset County fairgrounds) has a loop bike and hiking trail, a fine new boat pavilion, canoeing, rowboating, fishing, and playgrounds. There are large picnic areas for family groups.

If you don't bring your own picnic or winter thermos, you will find plenty of diners and eateries on nearby Routes 202, 206, or on Highway 22 heading east to New York or west to Clinton. The **Lido Diner,** a nifty fifties diner, sits in the middle of Route 22 in Springfield, its tricolor neon sign blinking at motorists speeding both ways on the busy highway. Try it out for atmosphere and coffee on the way home.

Watch out for a roadside oddity in the shape of a dinosaur on Route 9, south of Tom's River. The 1935 Sinclair map features New Jersey roads on one side, and on the other, an artful, all-color recreational map of the United States.

That famous neon sign that reads CLAM BROTH HOUSE, 38 Newark Street, Hoboken.

THE EDISON TOWER
MENLO PARK, NEW JERSEY

The 131-foot Art Deco Edison Memorial Tower, with a massive, glowing fourteen-foot lightbulb at its top, casts a beam of light visible from highways and byways throughout the area. A small Edison Museum is located on the grounds of this unique place, atop a hill off Route 27 in Menlo Park.

Spectacular rocketship neon sign—MOON MOTEL— beckons motorists on the Route 9 motel strip in Lakewood.

Fred's Diner, 188 Stuyvesant Avenue (corner of 18th Avenue), stood next to a gas station in the Vailsburg section of Newark. Proprietor Fred Steinke was also the cook and baked pies on the premises. This 1940s "memory image" snapshot is from the family scrapbook of Evelyn Heitke, who worked as a waitress at the diner.

Classic 1954 pink Plymouth Belvedere convertible parked in front of the Miss America Diner, 322 West End Avenue, Jersey City. This stainless-steel streamliner was manufactured by the Jerry O'Mahoney Company in Elizabeth in the 1950s.

Stainless-steel, blue-enamel, and glass-block Truck Stop Diner on Hackensack Avenue and Scout Street, South Kearny. Owner Sam Kolokithas is always on the premises of this New Jersey-built Kullman diner.

The classic 1929 enamel-fronted Summit Diner, Summit Avenue and Union Place, Summit.

Original wood-panel-and-tile interior of the Summit Diner, which has continued to serve top-notch food from the Depression era right up to the present time. The Summit's extra-thick BLT sandwich was said to be a favorite of Ernest Hemingway, who frequented the joint.

The Jerry O'Mahoney Dining Car Company of Elizabeth built the splendid Harris Diner in 1952. Owned since 1958 by Bill Nicholas and Bill Marmaras, the twenty-four-hour diner is located in East Orange at the point of North Park and Washington Streets.

A 1944 Asbury Park seashore guide features attractive beauty contestant Bette Coe, posing in front of the Convention Hall and the Paramount Theater (both recently restored) at Asbury Park's Boardwalk.

The 1950s Howard Johnson's round, space-port-style restaurant with zigzag roof pictured in this souvenir postcard is on the boardwalk across from the Paramount Theater in Asbury Park. It is still serving fried clams, hamburgers, ice cream sodas, coffee, and cocktails—with an ocean view.

Curteich-Chicago, "C.T. Art Colortone" vintage linen postcard, showing beach girls on a portable merry-go-round at Manasquan.

Seaside Heights Casino Amusement Center at night. The boardwalk and the ocean amusement piers at Seaside boast sensational action rides, games of chance, bars, nightclubs, Berkeley's homemade candies, Johnson's caramel popcorn, Kohr's frozen custard, Marucca's Pizza, and more. Tichnor Bros., Inc., vintage color linen postcard.

"Old Barney"—Barnegat Lighthouse—Long Beach Island. Vintage Tichnor linen postcard.

NEW JERSEY

POINT PLEASANT

This automobile window decal for Point Pleasant Beach could also be used as a luggage sticker. This is from the 1940s.

High Posh

Somerville, county seat of Somerset County, was very respectful and protective of its premier millionairess, Doris Duke, whose 6,000-acre estate, Duke Farms, came closest to being a real "home" for the heiress of the American Tobacco Company. After she inherited $79 million from her father in 1925, 13-year-old Doris, then known as "DeeDee," was hounded by the press and labeled the "richest girl in the world." Tom Valentine and Patrick Mahn, the authors of the book *Daddy's Duchess*, worked as accountants for Ms. Duke and commented thus, "Shall we say—the richest *person* in the world." Her reported wealth, the authors claimed, is only the "tip of the iceberg." Publicity-shy and single (her two marriages, to James Cromwell, and playboy Porfirio Rubirosa, ended in divorce), Doris Duke spent her time in Somerville caring for her extensive collection of Oriental art, studying such alternative lifestyles as yoga and vegetarianism, and keeping up with the horsey social set. A few years before her death she and some friends threw a lavish party for King Farouk at a Far Hills estate, complete with outdoor tents and pavilions and a real live elephant for high-posh society invites only. In her later years, adding to her eccentric image, Doris offered much needed sanctuary at her estate for such beleaguered high-profile celebrities as Betty Hutton, Pee-wee Herman, and Imelda Marcos.

One of Doris Duke's husbands was the playboy Dominican ambassador to Argentina, Porfirio Rubirosa, shown here on his wedding day with a glamorous Doris in the late 1940s.

Jacqueline Kennedy Onassis maintained an estate in Peapack in the fox-hunting countryside of Far Hills.

Morris County, traditionally the home of New Jersey's largest number of millionaires, has given way in modern times to the area a bit farther south known as Far Hills in Somerset County. Route 202 traverses this beautiful section not too far off the beaten track from the late Jacqueline Kennedy Onassis's 10-acre hideaway weekend escape estate in Peapack. Jackie O. bought the estate after renting in the area and staying at the Far Hills estate of Charlotte Ford. Bernardsville, the largest town in this rural area, has long been the center for wealthy estate dwellers who have their Rolls-Royces and Bentleys serviced in the many garage and auto service stations. Far Hills itself, west of Bernardsville, is no more than a small village with a handful of shops and a train station. The population is about 800. One of the best ways to see this rich (scenery-wise) countryside is taking the train. The newly rebuilt and electrified commuter trains on the Morris and Essex Line of New Jersey Transit (out of Hoboken) take you through middle-class communities, open farmlands, and rolling woodland hills to Gladstone, the end of the line, with stops at Bernardsville, Far

WARNING
NO TRESPASSING

THIS IS PRIVATE PROPERTY
**Hunting, Fishing, Trapping or
Tresspassing for Any Purpose is
Prohibited Under Penalty of the Law**

DUKE FARMS
Doris Duke, Owner

PATROLLED

A sign from along the Doris Duke Parkway.

Hills, and Peapack. A good restaurant in Gladstone, the **Brass Penny** at Main Street and Potterville Road, is open seven days a week until 10 P.M., and in addition to its regular reasonable prices, offers a terrific Sunday brunch from 11 A.M. to 3 P.M. As it is only steps away from the train station, you can leisurely lunch, walk around the lovely little town, and take the train back.

It would seem that this is a special train just for millionaires and their families and friends, like the Dillon family (Douglas Dillon was chairman of New York's Metropolitan Museum) who have holdings in the NCR Corporation and other investments worth conservatively $300 to $500 million. The Dillon family has an elegant estate in Far Hills, as does Jane Engelhard, widow of the prototype for James Bond, the main character portrayed in Ian Fleming's *Goldfinger*, Charles Engelhard. Mrs. Engelhard reputedly New Jersey's wealthiest woman, lives at Cragwood, a fantastic Rhine-like turreted castle on a 172-acre estate overlooking the lush hunt country where, as a young girl, Caroline Kennedy was taught the symbolic meaning of the traditional (and bloody) fox-hunt. Newcomers to the sport are smeared with the blood of the dead and mangled fox that is supposed to imbue them with a life-long understanding and appreciation of "the excitement of the kill." Another Far Hills home belongs to the Forbes family, publishers of *Forbes Magazine*. The family also owns a 20,000-acre ranch in Montana, a 260 square-mile ranch in Colorado and New Mexico, a castle in Tangier, and a mansion in London (plus 10 other spectacular homes around the world).

Princeton Day Trip

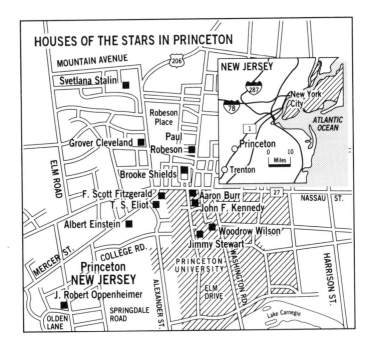

HOUSES OF THE STARS IN PRINCETON

MOUNTAIN AVENUE — 206
NEW JERSEY
Svetlana Stalin
287
New York City
78
ATLANTIC OCEAN
Robeson Place
1
Paul Robeson
Princeton
0 10
Miles
Grover Cleveland ■
Brooke Shields ■
Trenton
ELM ROAD
F. Scott Fitzgerald ■
Aaron Burr
27
NASSAU ST.
T. S. Eliot ■
John F. Kennedy
Albert Einstein ■
Woodrow Wilson
MERCER ST.
COLLEGE RD.
Jimmy Stewart
PRINCETON UNIVERSITY
HARRISON ST.
Princeton NEW JERSEY
ALEXANDER ST.
WASHINGTON RD.
J. Robert Oppenheimer
ELM DRIVE
SPRINGDALE ROAD
Lake Carnegie
OLDEN LANE

To get there: Princeton is at the junctions of Route 206 and Route 27, just a few miles west of Route 1, which traverses this middle section of New Jersey like a straight arrow, from Trenton to New York. The Turnpike is not far; take exit 8 onto 571 West directly onto the campus. Signs along the road will point the way from any direction and from all of the scenic back roads. All autos are barred from the actual campus so once there, park the car and walk. Buses also depart regularly from Port Authority in New York and from other points.

The great Gothic architecture and hallowed halls of Princeton University and the old Revolutionary-style town with its quaint shops and interesting restaurants make Princeton a great place to go on a day trip. The university's many acres are enclosed by stone and iron fences and intricate sidewalk paths are provided for the stroller. Autumn and spring are good times for this day trip. Summer is also a lovely time when the campus is most peaceful and quiet, as there are few students. Princeton is particularly enchanting during and after a snowfall, so if you choose to go in winter it might be fun to do a snow walk.

Whig Hall, built in 1893, designed in marble by A. Page Brown in the ionic style of a Greek temple.

Princeton University was founded in 1754. **Nassau Hall,** in the center of the campus, was built in 1756 and is still in use as university administrative offices. In 1783 the Continental Congress met there. The Gothic **Princeton Chapel** is an architectural wonder and should not be missed. Built in 1928, it is a strange mixture of Gothic gargoyles and Art Deco stained-glass windows. There are fine examples of Greek Revival architecture and an excellent art museum. A map of the campus and the walkways, and Princeton proper, is available at **Maclean House.** The map will also direct you to the former homes of Svetlana Stalin, Paul Robeson, Thomas Mann, Woodrow Wilson, and Albert Einstein, who worked and lived in Princeton (at 112 Mercer Street) for 20 years at the Institute for Advanced Study. If you are interested in the Princeton football games, call (609) 258-3000 for tickets. You might also want to ring up the **Historical Society of Princeton,** (609) 921-6748, for further information or a brochure. There is also the **McCarter Theater,** which mounts professional productions of thoughtful, exciting plays like those of Edward Albee, Tennessee Williams, or Eugene O'Neill—the latter a Princeton attendee. Other writers who were either students or teachers at Princeton include F. Scott Fitzgerald, John O'Hara, Joyce Carol Oates, Philip Roth and former publisher Nelson Doubleday. Some other points of interest on the campus are the Princeton cemetery, with stones dating back to pre-Revolutionary times, and the Firestone Library, which has over three million books. If you want a guided tour with an escort, this is also available by calling (609) 258-3603 for a reservation.

Albert Einstein, shown here with fellow genius Charlie Chaplin, lived at 112 Mercer Street in Princeton. Chaplin married Jersey girl Oona O'Neill, whose mother Agnes Boulton lived in the seaside town of Point Pleasant, New Jersey.

When you are finished with the walk on the grounds and going into the inside of some of the buildings to examine their interiors, you may want to look at some of the shops in town. Antique stores, bookstores, university clothing shops, a Brooks Brothers, and gourmet shops are part of the fun of Princeton. The place to stay in town is the **Nassau Inn** on Palmer Square, just across the street from the main entrance to the campus. The inn, which originated in 1756, moved to its present location in 1937 and has 217 attractive rooms for overnight accommodations in the $170 to $190 and up range. If you are in the mood for a weekend, it is a gracious place in which to stay over. Call (609) 921-7500. The **Greenhouse Restaurant** in the inn serves breakfast and lunch, as does the taproom. The place to dine is **Ichiban** at 66 Witherspoon, (609) 683-8323, which is close to the Princeton Library. Graced by beautiful bamboo gardens, the restaurant serves traditional Japanese tempura noodles, sushi, and teriyaki, with dinners averaging about $15. Lunch Specials are also offered. Hours are Mon-

Brooke Shields, the actress-model, during her student days at Princeton University.

day to Thursday from 11:30 A.M. to 10 P.M., Friday and Saturday until 11 P.M. and Sunday 2:30 P.M. to 10 P.M.

A good inexpensive meal in Princeton can be had at Ruth Alegria's **Mexican Village II** at 42–44 Leigh Avenue, (609) 924-5143, where the food is truly Mexican, fresh, and well prepared. Ruth's mother, Ramona Alegria, who owns the **Mexican Village** at 224 Thompson Street (212) 475-9805, in Greenwich Village, taught her daughter how to prepare the delicious Mexican dishes served at both restaurants including *flautas* (a long, crispy tortilla shaped like a flute) with guacamole and stuffed with melted cheese, chicken or beef; burritos, tamales, tostadas, enchiladas, or tacos served with rice and refried beans, *chile relleno, carne a la tampiqueña, bistek a la Mexicana,* enchiladas *Jalisco* or *chalupas.* The hot Mexican salsa with warmed taco chips served at each table is prepared fresh daily. Also available is *salsa verde* and *salsa mole.* There is also a full range of vegetarian dishes and delicious margaritas and other drinks and Mexican beers. The motto here is: ¡*Comer bien es vivir bien!* (Translation: To eat well is to live well!)

Jersey Country

It's great fun and very relaxing to take drives into the countryside outside Princeton. The following country towns can all be reached by major roads, but "back country" routes are recommended to give you an idea why New Jersey is called "the Garden State."

Hopewell is at the junction of Route 518 and route 569 (about midway between two major roads, Route 1 and Route 202). From Princeton take the Rosedale Road north to the Hopewell–Princeton Road (569) to Hopewell Borough. Hopewell, not to be confused with Stanhope, New Hope, or Hope, was the home of Charles Lindbergh in the 1930s. The famous Lindbergh baby kidnapping was perpetrated by Bruno Hauptmann in Hopewell, though he was tried and convicted in the neighboring county at Flemington. In October 1991 Anna Hauptmann returned to the Union Hotel on Main Street in Flemington for the first time since February 13, 1935, the day her husband was sentenced to death in the electric chair. "From the day he was arrested, he was framed, always framed," she said at a press conference where over 50 years later she still proclaimed his innocence. "It is my duty to fight for my husband as long as I live," she added. Interesting footnote: The lead investigator in the case was New Jersey State Police Superintendent H. Norman Schwarzkopf, father of the commander in the Persian Gulf war, General H. Norman Schwarzkopf. Today Hopewell is antique country, and the **High Button Shoe Antique Center,** on Blackwell Avenue off Broad Street, is an excellent place for browsing and shopping for country antiques. They're open every day until 5 P.M. Also notable for antiquers is the **Hopewell Canning Company** (two blocks off Route 518), a restored factory building housing the **Tomato Factory Antique Center** with 35 shops on two floors, (609) 466-2990. Worth a stop in Hopewell is the **Hopewell Museum** at 28 East Broad Street, considered an excellent small museum, with collections of early costumes, china, and a Native American room containing Navaho handwoven rugs and baskets, as well as stone artifacts and tools made by local Lenape Indians.

Flemington (at the junction of Route 31 and Route 202, or take Route 569 to Route 514 from Hopewell) is another great old farming town and tourist attraction not far from Princeton. It is set on 105 acres and contains fine old Victorian homes. It is famous as a factory outlet town for such diverse items as designer jeans, active sportswear, shoes, lingerie, decorator fabrics, curtains, lamps, silver, bags, shoes, sneakers, and much more. There are hobby centers for toy-train enthusiasts, and doll collectors. New dishware sets from Royal Doulton, Corning glass, and Pfaltzgraff stoneware can be found at **Liberty Village,** a Colonial shopping center. Stangl pottery, Fulperware, and Flemington cut glassware was originally produced here, but is now found in antique shops, notably **Popkorn Antiques** at 4 Mine Street, (908) 782-9631, near Main. Bob and Nancy Perzel, who run Popkorn, have a huge selection of Stangl pottery as well as Fiesta ware and other popular pottery from past decades. They also carry advertising signs, cameras and toys from the 1920s, 1930s, and 1940s. Open every day except Monday from 10 A.M. to 5 P.M. The **Main Street Antique Center** at 148 Main Street has 45 dealers in a space covering 2,000 square feet. Here you can find, yes, an antique kitchen sink and everything else. They're open every day (except Tuesday) from 10 A.M. to 5 P.M. Julie Sferrazza is the manager. Her number is (908) 788-6767. The **Flemington Cut Glass Company,** 156 Main Street, has a showroom of the most beautiful pieces produced over the years and presents free glass-cutting demonstrations. The showroom is open daily from 10 A.M. to 5:30 P.M., phone (908) 782-3017.

Particularly engaging and a fun adventure-ride is the 11-mile roundtrip on the **Black River and Western Railroad** plying between the center of Flemington Township to Ringoes. You can take this farmland journey on a steam-locomotive train on Saturdays and Sundays and holidays, with trains departing every 1½

Bob Perzel of Popkorn on Mine Street (near Main) in Flemington holds up a rare 1939 New York World's Fair tapestry made in Belgium.

hours (between 10:45 A.M. and 4:45 P.M.) from mid-April to November 30. During the summer months of July and August a
Tuesday–Friday schedule includes trains leaving every hour between 12:30 to 3:30 P.M. Train trips for adults cost $5 and children
5–12 are charged $2.50, ages 3–4 $1; call (908) 782-9600. The
1870 **Union Hotel** at 76 Main Street in the downtown center of
Flemington, just across the street from the county courthouse has
a restaurant serving traditional American food, a lounge, and many
historic displays echoing the folklore of those Depression days
when Lowell Thomas, Damon Runyon, Adela Rogers St. John,
and Dorothy Kilgallen reported the sensational developments in
the famous Hauptmann case. The hotel number is (908) 792-4311.
Flemington is also the site of the New Jersey agricultural fair, a
wonderful event to attend, which runs for 10 days toward the end
of August every year. The emphasis at this fair is on domestic animals, many raised and tended by 4-H members, and numerous
Grange activities, including "best" produce and canning exhibits.
Prizes are given for the best Jersey tomatoes, relishes, and homemade preserves from local farmers and farmwives. As you walk
around the fair you will see famous country-and-western singers
belting out the classics like "It Wasn't God Who Made Honky
Tonk Angels" or "He'll Have to Go." There are aerial acts and exhibits of the latest farm equipment and spectacularly decorated,
gadget-filled home trailers.

Just a few miles east of Flemington is **Neshanic Station,** which
holds a regular weekend farm, flea, and antiques market (take
Route 567 or Pleasant Run Road at Centerville off Highway 202).
The pleasant road meanders casually for three or four miles
through a hilly farming and grazing valley along the scenic banks
of the south branch of the Raritan River, which meets the Neshanic River at Neshanic Station. It's a lovely spot for a sponta-
neous alfresco swim or fishing under the old bridge and
abandoned railroad trestle. The preserved train depot is now an
ammunition and gun supply store, featuring the latest in hunting
equipment. The market itself is always diverse, with vegetables,
baked goods, and general country flea market merchandise with
the occasional good antique dealer. This is a beautiful setting and
interesting local characters make this stopoff worth a trip. Sunday
is the best day in spring, summer, and fall; but go early as many
start packing up by 3 P.M. The homes and the farmlands in this
country area make for a nice Sunday drive.

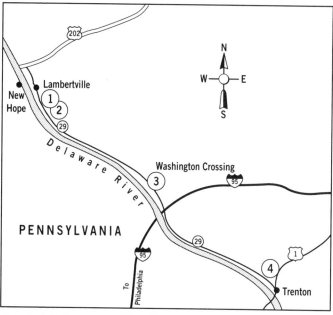

1. Lambertville House
2. Flea Market
3. Ferry House Tavern
4. The Old Barracks

To get to Lambertville: Enjoy the road and take a scenic drive in spring, summer, or fall on Highway 29 South from Frenchtown to Lambertville or drive from Trenton, the state capital, north on Route 29 to Lambertville. This highway parallels the Delaware River, and it is an enjoyable tour through many old villages along the route. This is also true along the Pennsylvania side where from Easton, Route 611 south turns into Route 32 at Kintnersville. Traveling along Route 32 you will find bridge river crossings from Uhlerstown, Pennsylvania, to Frenchtown, New Jersey, and New Hope, Pennsylvania, to Lambertville, New Jersey. Both roads are among the most beautiful drives to be found anywhere. From New Jersey there are many approaches to the Lambertville–New Hope area, including Highway 22 West out of Newark, which spurs off of Route 1-9. Route 22 leads into Route 202 West to Flemington; from there take Route 179 South into the town of Lambertville. You may also take the New Jersey Turnpike to Trenton and pick up Route 29 North into Lambertville. There is regular bus service into Lambertville and New Hope from the Port Authority Bus Terminal in Manhattan and from all points in Philadelphia.

Lambertville was settled in 1700 midway on the old road between New York and Philadelphia. It is a Victorian city located in a highly rural area, and the only official "city" in Hunterdon County. Listed on the National and State Registers of Historic Places, there are many charming inns and restaurants and a variety of unusual and inexpensive antique shops. Once in Lambertville, park the car and walk around for an architectural treat that includes Queen Anne, Gothic, and Italianate Victorian, Federal, Georgian, and 19th-century factory buildings. One of the buildings you should see is the **James Wilson Marshall House** at 60 Bridge Street. Built in 1810, this Federal-style house now incorporates a museum that shows photos and objects from Lambertville history. It is open from 1 to 5 P.M., Thursday to Saturday, April through November 15, (609) 397-0770. Another historical place to check out is the **Lambertville House,** built in 1812 at 32 Bridge Street. This was a stagecoach inn for travelers of note like General Ulysses S. Grant and General Tom Thumb, the renowned midget who stayed there with his circus troupes in 1867. Lambertville was not only on the east-west stagecoach line and the Delaware River, but was also located on a feeder-canal leading to the Trenton–New Brunswick canal system (now the Delaware and Raritan Canal State Park). It was once a bustling mill town, which produced paper, flour, lumber, hairpins, spokes, iron, sausage, bricks, linen, rubber, and crackers. In the 1920s most of the city's mills went out of business or moved south to Trenton. The factories are still there, but they now house art galleries and crafts boutiques. The city is attracting numbers of artists who are restoring the factories and interesting row houses, in addition to many antique dealers who have traditionally operated in this area. Chief among these is the **People's Store** (since 1859), Lambertville's oldest and largest antiques center. At 28 Union Street (at Church), the building was once a dry goods and furniture store. Now housing antique and collectible dealers, the fine **Left Bank Bookstore,** (609) 397-4966, and several artists studios upstairs, it is open every day from 10 A.M. to 6 P.M., (609) 397-9808. **Phoenix Books** at 49 Union Street has floor-to-ceiling shelves filled with new, old, and rare antiquarian books. You can browse for hours in a homey atmosphere; and the shop is often open until 9 P.M. and sometimes later, according to the whim of the owner; (609) 397-4960. **Fran-Jay,** at 10 Church Street, just around the corner from the People's Store, sells an array of toys and great quantities of Depression glass-

Matchbook from the Lambertville House.

Antique shop on Church Street in Lambertville.

ware (sometimes called "tank" glass) in translucent colors of green, amber, yellow, pink, and blue. Fran also has stacks of Fiesta ware in choice Mexican colors and Stangl pottery that is no longer attainable in Flemington, where it was once made. Fran has the gift of gab and will tell visitors where to go and what to do in Lambertville, as well as tell stories about the famous ghosts that haunt the area. Call (609) 397-1571. The old 5¢, 10¢ & 25¢ store at 40 North Union Street is now called the **5¢ & Dime,** (609) 397-4957—and is run by Steve Stegman who sells new and old Disneyana, 1950s and 1960s television pop-culture oddities like Flintstone lamps, Superman and Batman lunch-boxes, Soupy Sales dolls, and a complete line of new and vintage comic-character timepieces. **Seventh Heaven,** specializing in *deco-nouveau-moderne* "heavenly" artifacts, vases, mood lamps and wall sconces, is operated by Richard Golden and Robert Gajdos at 18 Church Street (weekends and by appointment, [609] 397-8419).

Lambertville has many good restaurants—and one of the largest is housed in the newly renovated **Lambertville Railroad Station.** This is an elegant Victorian-style restaurant with a dance floor and casual pub downstairs. Built in 1867, the 2½-story stone station house was the headquarters of the Belvedere Delaware Railroad, serving local passengers traveling up and down the river. The rail line, called the **Black River and Western Railroad,** has a real steam-driven locomotive and now offers a 45-minute train ride for tourists and shoppers with stops at Flemington, Ringoes, and Lambertville; call (908) 782-9600. The **Inn at Lambertville Station,** a 45-room hotel behind the station and overlooking the Delaware River, offers antique-filled decor with cozy fireplaces and whirlpool baths. Special winter weekend rates make it an attractive destination for overnight guests; call (609) 397-4400 for both the inn and the restaurant.

An excellent place to stay in Lambertville for an authentic feel of the past is the **Bridgestreet House** at 67 Bridge Street. The house was built in two sections, the back part dating from 1790 and the front addition dating from 1860. There are four guest rooms on the second floor of the house, a two-room suite with a narrow swirling staircase that leads to the old attic, now a bedroom; and other special rooms—some with baths—named after former oc-cupants of the house. The Bridgestreet House also has a very good restaurant, serving American-continental cuisine, including steamed and sautéed vegetables and fruit with cheese, sliced breast of duckling sautéed in teriyaki, ginger, and rum and broiled filet mignon. For reservations and information, call (609) 397-2503.

For a walk to New Hope, Pennsylvania, across the bridge, you should leave the car in Lambertville. New Hope is filled with in-teresting boutiques, antique shops, bars, ice cream parlors, book-stores, cheese shops, and restaurants and inns. The famous **Bucks County Playhouse,** the state theater of Pennsylvania, is also in New Hope with spring, summer, and fall productions of profes-sional Broadway musicals like *Annie, South Pacific,* and *Hello, Dolly.* Call (215) 862-2041 for tickets. New Hope is a touristy town, but it is a colorful place to explore. It is more populated than Lambertville, and is kind of like New York's Greenwich Village, with its population of swinging singles and gays all mixed up with stretch-pants-suited older couples. In fact, Lambertville and New Hope have somewhat of a kinship with Provincetown, Massachu-setts, in the sense of its oddball yet interesting population mix, in-cluding its fair share of resident artists, ex-hippies, and bike-boys. Places to eat in New Hope include **Mother's Restaurant** at 34 North Main Street, which has a bakery attached selling sinfully delicious cookies and cakes. **Backstage Restaurant and Cabaret** is next door to the Bucks County Playhouse at 50 Main Street, (215) 862-5085 for reservations, and has a commanding view of the river whether you dine indoors or on the open deck. Backstage prices are reasonable: a terrific charbroiled hamburger is $6.95. For a quick food fix there is an excellent Mexican eatery/take-out place with tables called **El Taco Loco,** 6 Stockton Avenue, next to the railroad tracks up the hill in New Hope. Under $5.00, open until 8 P.M. on weekdays, weekends until 10, (215) 862-0908. This is not like the fine organized sit-down dinners served along the river in Lambertville, but it is a great snack place as you walk and shop in the hilly little river town of New Hope.

Lambertville Antiques

Washington Crossing

New Jersey is antique country, whether north, south, east, or west, and you are sure to find what you want somewhere amongst all the flea markets, antique shops and centers, special antique shows, roadside sales, and country auctions. If you haven't found it, you haven't tried hard enough. A good place to start looking is in the **Lambertville Antiques Flea Market,** open every Saturday and Sunday all year long. This is one of the oldest antique markets in the New Hope/ Lambertville area and is considered one of the major antique centers in the country. Located about three miles south of Lambertville on Route 29, this market and the market at Lahaska (five miles southwest of New Hope) have long been favorites of New York and Philadelphia antiques dealers. Many who are in search of antiques and collectibles at the huge Lambertville market get up at the crack of dawn; but you can drop by any time up until 4 P.M. when the many dealers begin to pack away their wares. Sunday seems to attract the most dealers, and you will find among them many rural folk who are still emptying out the treasures from that proverbial grandma's attic of yore. There are inside shops and an enclosed, roofed rotunda for rainy days. The market has two pleasant refreshment stands with sit-down tables to rest the weary feet, where you can enjoy hot dogs, crullers, and other American foods with coffee or cider. The market is set just across the way from the Delaware River; and if you get tired of looking at or buying goods, you can cross the road and take a walk in the green.

The area of Lambertville and New Hope is rich with open-air markets and highly individualized antique shops, craft shops, art galleries, bookstores, and shops devoted to singular pursuits like old magazines and newspapers or fine frocks from yesteryear. You can easily spend a day or weekend here without covering the territory. Surely it will be a time well spent. A fascinating place to stay, even though it is not in New Jersey, is the **Black Bass Hotel** on Route 32 in Lumberville, Pennsylvania, seven miles north of New Hope on the Delaware River. This establishment, reminiscent of an English pub and Colonial tavern was, as a matter of record, loyal to the Crown during the Revolution and would not let George Washington in for the night. There is a veritable museum here of British royal family memorabilia, the dining rooms have wood-burning fireplaces, and the tables are made out of old-fashioned tavern planks. The food is very good; there is a good wine list and the service is excellent. There are seven rooms with

George Washington crosses the Delaware.

shared baths (about $75) and three suites ($125–$150). Call (215) 297-5770 for the restaurant; 297-5815 for rooms.

One of the best restaurants on the Delaware, and one of former New Jersey Senator Bill Bradley's favorite places, is the **Frenchtown Inn,** 7 Bridge Street, Frenchtown; (908) 996-3300. This old family-run country inn features a New Jersey tomato filled with shrimp for starters in their famous prix-fixe Saturday night dinner ($43), which might feature rack of lamb and a flageolet bean ragout with garlic sausage; the whole thing finished off with a complimentary chocolate truffle with your coffee.

Washington Crossing State Park at Washington Crossing, New Jersey is the site where in the winter of 1776 General George Washington and his 2,400 troops crossed the Delaware into New Jersey and raided the Hessian garrison at Trenton, just preceding the famous battles of Trenton and Princeton, a major turning point of the American Revolution. This historic park features the **Ferry House Tavern** where Washington conferred with the locals, a unique and beautiful outdoor open-air theater, seating 1,000 spectators, where they have summer musical and theatrical events, (609) 737-9721, plus nature trails, fishing, and camping, all situated on the banks of a broad and beautiful section of the Delaware River. Picnic tables and fireplaces for cookouts or barbecues are provided here. The park is just south of Lambertville on Route 29. At certain times of the year the historical crossing from Pennsylvania to New Jersey is reenacted in replicated outfits of the day. Washington Crossing State Park extends into the Pennsylvania side of the river, and you can cross over from Route 29 in New Jersey to Route 32 in Pennsylvania. Both towns at this point of the bridge crossing, in Pennsylvania and New Jersey, are called Washington Crossing.

Trenton

Over the Trenton-Morrisville Bridge, which crosses the Delaware River from New Jersey to Pennsylvania (and vice versa) there are the words, in giant letters: WHAT TRENTON MAKES THE WORLD TAKES. Famous for industry and manufacturing, the legend of Trenton has been enhanced by some of the very finest chinas made by Walter Scott Lenox or the Trent Tile Company, manufacturers of fancy mosaic and bathroom-kitchen tiles, or the New Jersey School Furniture Company, established by L. H. McKee & Company, or the American Steel and Wire Company, or the John A. Roebling Wire Rope Company, which produced the rope used on suspension bridges like the Brooklyn Bridge, the Niagara Bridge, and the Golden Gate Bridge.

Trenton, also famous as the New Jersey state capital, was once thought of in 1784 as the spot that might make a good permanent capital for the United States. Rich in history, Trenton is the place where George Washington attacked the Hessian troops, taking them by surprise on the snowy Christmas night of 1776. Some of the Hessians were fast asleep while others, having drunk too much from their wassail cups, were too ossified to know what was happening that historical night. Often at Christmastime, citizens of

Washington victorious at the Battle of Trenton.

Trenton, in Revolutionary attire, enact the entire battle of Trenton, from Washington's crossing of the Delaware to the siege of the garrison.

The **Trenton City Museum** in Caldwalader Park on Parkside Avenue is something you will want to see. The museum is a restored 1850 mansion designed by John Notman; and it is listed in the National Register. There are picnic grounds, concert bandstands, cherry trees surrounding a duck pond, and "swamp angel," which is a Civil War cannon. The **New Jersey State Library** is at 185 State Street. Call (609) 292-6260 for tours or special programs or write to the Bureau of Archives and History, New Jersey State Library, P.O. Box 1898, Trenton, NJ 08625. The **New Jersey State Museum** at 205 West State Street offers special exhibits in decorative and fine arts, natural science, history, government, archeology, and astronomy, weekdays from 9 A.M. to 5 P.M., weekends from 1 to 5 P.M. For more information on tours and special exhibits, call (609) 292-6464. A beautifully restored 18th-century house once owned by Isaac Watson has a parlor, dining room, kitchen, and bedroom complete with the original furnishings, lamps, and period objects. The **Watson House** is at 151 Westcott Avenue. Call (609) 888-2062 for a reservation and a free tour. The two-story Queen Ann–style brick **William Trent House** is at 15 Market Street. The handsome house with Colonial furniture and attractive gardens was built in 1719 by William Trent. Trent devised the plan for the region he named "Trent's Town"—later becoming Trenton. Call (609) 989-3027 for information. The hours here are May to September, 10 A.M. to 5 P.M. weekdays, Sundays 1 to 5 P.M. October to April they close one hour early and are closed on holidays.

The **Old Barracks** on Barrack Street, built between 1758 and 1760, housed the Hessians, who were composed of Continental and British troops. The two-story stone barracks contains firearms, Colonial furniture, and period china and silverware. These barracks are regarded as a fine example of Colonial architecture and are rich in history. Call (609) 396-1776 for information. Nearby is the War Memorial Building.

If you want to view this general region where Washington and his troops camped out and did battle, you should visit the **Trenton Battle Monument,** built to honor the Battle of Trenton. To view the capital city and its surroundings you can use an elevator to the top of the 150-foot observatory. Call (609) 292-2797 for information; daytime hours are 9 A.M. to 6 P.M. Wednesday to Friday, Saturday 10 A.M. to 6 P.M. Sunday 1 to 5 P.M.

Trenton proper, other than its grand array of impressive governmental and administrative buildings, some old, some new, has, like many capital cities, many middle-class neighborhoods, as well

New Jersey State Capitol building, Trenton.

as some that are just plain poverty-ridden slums. Chambersburg, the Little Italy of Trenton, is worth a tour for its Italian restaurants. Try **Commini's** on East Front Street or **La Gondola** on Butler Street. There is an annual Trenton state fair, held the first week of August, with livestock and farm produce brought in from the surrounding countryside. It is an enjoyable event focusing on the aspect of New Jersey as the "Garden State." Big-band dances, Budweiser fireworks spectaculars, "Bigfoot" car crush events, helicopter thrill acts, arm wrestling, and pig racing are but a few of the antic summer activities there. Further information regarding the state fair can be had by calling (609) 587-6300, or the state tourist information number at (609) 292-2470.

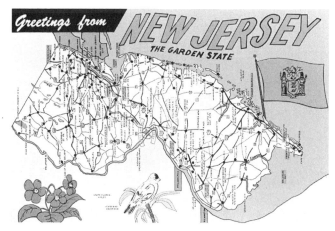

Official New Jersey state postcard, featuring state bird, flower, and flag.

Camden's Campbell's Soup

The Campbell Soup can was famous long before Andy Warhol began painting it, marketing great numbers of them over the years as subjects for his pop art paintings. Warhol, who was originally a highly paid advertising artist, ostensibly painted Nunn-Busch shoes for the ads. He once said that he hated painting the ubiquitous bowl of fruit every art student was required to copy in art school. In his memory bank he most remembered the image of a can of Campbell's tomato soup (his favorite) from his mother's pantry. When he was little Andy Warhola living in Pennsylvania during the Great Depression, this held more significance for him than the bowl of dime-store wax fruit on the family dining room table.

The Campbell Soup Company was begun when Joseph Campbell, a fruit merchant, and Abram Anderson, an icebox manufacturer, became partners to can Jersey tomatoes, vegetables, mincemeat, jellies, and condiments. Their first plant opened in Camden in 1869. Anderson left the partnership in 1876. Arthur Dorance and Joseph Campbell then formed a new company called the Joseph Campbell Preserve Company. In 1897 the concept of canned, condensed soup was originated; and in 1898 the first red-and-white label (from Cornell football colors) was introduced.

Joseph died in 1900 and the Dorance family took over. This same year Campbell's soups won a gold medallion for excellence

Three booklets from The Optimist, *which was published monthly by the Campbell Soup Company in Camden. Left to right: A Campbell's Kid in the kitchen tasting (what else?) a hearty Campbell's soup, March 1932; back cover showing the famous Campbell's tomato soup can which always used Jersey red-ripe tomatoes in its recipes, August 1926; back cover with the two Campbell's Kids saying their prayers in thanks for the bowls of piping-hot-tomato soup in front of them, March 1930.*

at the Paris Exposition, and this medallion has been featured on the soup can label ever since. In 1905 Campbell's introduced its famous pork and beans, competing with the Heinz company.

In 1905 also Grace Gebbie Drayton created the wonderful Campbell Kid trademark characters. These kids, who somewhat resembled the cherubic kewpies of Rose O'Neill, are among the first early advertising cartoon characters (others were Buster Brown and the Yellow Kid) to win wide appeal with magazine readers and consumers. Over the years many premiums and special "Campbell Kids" products such as recipe booklets, school tablets, dolls, spoons, salt-and-pepper shakers, and the like have been produced; these are highly prized as advertising collectibles in today's nostalgia marketplace. Ads with the kids usually contained some kind of poem that might link up a child going back to school in the fall while mother prepared a hot bowl of Campbell's chicken noodle soup to be served at suppertime. The idea was that children—and the rest of the American family, too—wanted a bowl of Campbell's soup all year long.

Families passed on the tradition of Campbell's soup from generation to generation; and immigrants coming to America used Campbell's products as they became associated with Americanism. An ad in *Good Housekeeping* magazine in 1905 declared: "21 kinds of Campbell's Soup—16 million cans sold in 1904." By 1911 Campbell's entered the California market and achieved national distribution. In 1915 Franco-American spaghetti with tomato sauce in a can was added to the line. In 1922 the company officially adopted the name Campbell's Soup Company; and by 1929, the year of the Crash, a second major soup plant opened in Chicago. The idea of a can of Campbell's Soup in mom's kitchen actually gained momentum in the 1930s during the Great Depression with Campbell's advertising on radio shows like "Amos 'n' Andy." In 1932, Campbell's tomato juice was introduced, and in 1934 cream of mushroom appeared. During the Depression, a can of mushroom soup with a can of tuna fish and with elbow macaroni was a favorite recipe for a cheap meal during hard times throughout America. Another Depression dinner staple was Campbell's baked beans served with frankfurters.

By 1942 sales topped the $100 million mark; and by 1947 a third plant opened in Sacramento, California. V-8 vegetable juice cocktail was added to the company product line in 1948. By 1955 Campbell's entered the frozen food market by acquiring C. A. Swanson Sons, who originated the TV dinner. Some social critics of the time regarded the TV dinner as marking the beginning of a decline in food ethics for the American family. During the 1950s and 1960s, with sales of over $500 million, Campbell's plants opened everywhere—in England, Australia, France, and Mexico. Pepperidge Farms, Inc., also became an affiliate of the company. In 1970 Campbell's introduced their line of "chunky, ready-to-serve" canned soups and also added pet foods to supermarket shelves. Also in 1970 the Campbell Museum opened in Camden, New Jersey, which is the place that will forever be known as the home of Campbell's Soup. By 1979 sales topped $2 billion, and in 1981 Campbell was chosen "food processor of the year." One can see how this company has become a symbol of the American dream.

Next time you reach for a can of Campbell's soup on the grocery store shelf, remember it all started in the Garden State and probably was inspired by the Jersey tomato, the reddest, ripest, juiciest, and most delicious of all. A famous French chef recently listed the "secret" ingredients of his special French "soupe" as:

> 1 can of Campbell's cream of mushroom condensed soup
> 1 can of Campbell's tomato soup
> 2 soup cans of light cream
> 2 tablespoons sherry
> ½ teaspoon melted butter

Heat and garnish with parsley and *Voilà!* You have *ze soupe Supreme de Paree!* On a *Nightline* television news "special report," Ted Koppel interviewed Robert Rauschenberg. The artist stated on the show that he had happily just sold his Andy Warhol soup can oil painting for a million dollars. Art, industry, commerce, television, and the Campbell soup can have become one and the same.

Though the original Campbell's Soup plant, a mammoth relic of the industrial age on the Delaware River in Camden, was blown up in 1991, Campbell Soup world headquarters, located in an L-shaped quadrangle known as Campbell Place, will continue on in downtown Camden as it has since 1876. The soups and other products manufactured by Campbell are now being processed in huge factories in Napoleon, Ohio, and Paris, Texas, and several other locations, in factories so huge that they accommodate the entrance of freight trains. The **Campbell Museum** on Campbell Place, (609) 342-6440, features an extensive collec-

The original Campbell Soup Company plant in Camden.

tion of European soup tureens in ceramic, china, and silver and exhibitions travel all over the world, wherever Campbell's soup is sold. There is also a "pop" exhibition in the lobby, featuring storefront signs, advertising merchandise, and premiums from Campbell products. Hours are Monday to Friday, 9 A.M. to 4:30 P.M.; closed holidays. The admission is free.

The **Walt Whitman House** on 330 Mickle Boulevard is the house where the poet who wrote *Leaves of Grass* lived. Three of the rooms are furnished with his belongings. There is also a library of Whitman's writings including his manuscripts and original photos. Hours are Wednesday to Friday, 9 A.M. to noon and 1 to 6 P.M., Saturday 10 to noon and 1 to 6 P.M., Sunday 1 to 6 P.M. only. The admission is free. Tour groups may call (609) 964-5383 to schedule an appointment.

Camden has a number of **White Tower** hamburger chain restaurants. These white, tiny castlelike structures serve tasty hamburgers, eggs, and coffee and, of course, you can get your choice of Campbell's soups right out of the can at any one of these establishments — served hot.

Camden, practically an adjunct to Philadelphia, somewhat akin to Queens or Staten Island to Manhattan, has a recently built aquarium and is hoping to attract crowds from the teeming metropolis just across the Delaware. The **New Jersey State Aquarium,** a lead project in Camden's revitalization, is built on an acre right on the waterfront on the site of a ferry terminal that closed more than 40 years ago. Ferry service between Penn's Landing in Philadelphia to the Aquarium was reinstituted to coincide with the opening in spring of 1992. A visit here is an ideal family expedition; there are 60 species of fish native to New Jersey, including striped bass, and the Aquarium features the second largest open ocean tank in the United States (EPCOT Center in Florida has the largest). So, pile the kids in the car and head for Camden; road signs point the way. It's open 9:30 A.M. to 5:30 P.M. March to September, 10 A.M. to 5 P.M. the rest of year, closed holidays. Admission for adults is $10.95, less for seniors, students, and younger children. Call (609) 365-3300 or toll-free (800) 616-5297.

Southwestern Farm Country

····································

*Burlington, Bordentown, Mount Holly, Timbuctoo,
Clementon, Swedesboro, Mullica Hill, Glassboro, Salem,
Bridgeton, and Vineland*

Four New Jersey counties—Burlington, Gloucester, Salem, and Cumberland—comprise the "garden spot" of the Garden State. One-third of all New Jersey's farms, which produce 70 percent of all New Jersey vegetables including sweet and processing corn, cabbage, lettuce, summer potatoes, eggplant, peppers, squash, and soybeans, 75 percent of all Jersey tomatoes (New Jersey is fourth nationally in the production of fresh market and processing tomatoes), and 95 percent of New Jersey's asparagus, are located here. South Jersey is second in the country in blueberry production, a bumper crop reaching as high as 30 million pounds; and cranberry production in this area (third-ranking producer in the United States) often exceeds 250,000 barrels annually. The whole adds up to more than $500 million a year of produce trucked

"Defy the World" brand choice Jersey tomatoes were packed into the can in Salem.

from Garden State farms, predominantly from southwestern New Jersey.

Of the tomatoes grown in the flat terrain and sandy soil of South Jersey 86 percent of them end up in processing plants run by canneries such as Campbell's, Progresso, Heinz, and Hunt. The rest, called fresh-market tomatoes, are sold to vegetable brokers at produce auctions held in Vineland and Swedesboro, in the heart of this rich farm country. The big business farmers offer a tomato plucked from the vine while still green, with thick skin and dense walls, a tomato able to withstand sorting, packing, refrigeration, repacking, shipping, and which ideally turns red by the time it reaches the supermarket shelf. Unfortunately, the flavor of these tomatoes leaves a great deal to be desired. In fact, it is missing. The reddening process of a tomato is accomplished by a natural plant hormone, which as it grows red on the vine, develops a corresponding taste in the ripe tomato. Latest developments in the automation of "rush-to-market" farming practices include a new chemical called *Ethrel* that enables farmers to spray "mature-green" tomatoes in the field, causing the entire crop to redden at once. Unfortunately again, this practice does not help the taste of a tomato.

The only thing to do, of course, is to go to one of the 500 or more roadside stands where summer tomatoes are generally grown in the immediate area. These tomatoes are allowed to mature and ripen on the vine, and are picked daily. Many roadside stand operators are members of New Jersey Certified Farm Markets, a volunteer organization that has developed guidelines for quality produce, courtesy and honest packaging and merchandising, i.e., what you see at the top of a bushel should be what you get at the bottom also. You may be lucky enough to score a few pounds of the rare and glorious low-acid yellow Jersey tomato, known far and wide by true connoisseurs of the Jersey tomato to be the most savory of them all.

Burlington, about 18 miles south of Camden on Route 130 up the Delaware, was once the busiest port in America and served for a while as the capital of West Jersey during the early Colonial days. The town is filled with historic structures including the **James Fenimore Cooper House** (at 457 High Street), where the first of America's great novelists was born (and lived for a year) in 1789 and the **Captain James Lawrence House** (right next door at 459 High Street), birthplace in 1781 of the hero of the War of 1812 who yelled, "Don't give up the ship!," a statement that later became the slogan of the United States Navy. Also on High Street is the **Pearson House,** an unusually large, for the period, beautifully proportioned frame house built in 1705 and enlarged in 1725, furnished with early 18th-century antiques. The number to call for information about touring all of these historic houses is (609) 386-4773.

Burlington contains many more Colonial structures still in use, such as **Wheatley's Drugstore** at High and Union Streets, built in 1731, in the historical district located on West Delaware, Wood, and Broad Streets. Tours are available all year long. (609) 386-3993 for information. The town is also home to many discount factory-outlet shopping centers like those in Secaucus and Flemington, for untaxed, name-brand clothing, and furniture bargain shopping.

Bordentown, 10 miles north of Burlington and just south of Trenton on Route 130, was a prosperous village settled in the late 1600s. It was, among other famous historical personages, the home of Benjamin Franklin, Clara Barton, and Joseph Bonaparte, brother of Napoleon, who had a 1,500-acre estate at Point Breeze. Along Farnsworth Avenue, Colonial, Georgian, Federal, and Victorian architectural styles offer a fantastic sweeping glance at changing American tastes in the 18th and 19th centuries. The Bordentown historic district includes the **Clara Barton School** (she moved on to other pastures to found the Red Cross after the town fathers insisted she have a male superintendent), **Bonaparte Park Garden House,** the **Friends Meeting House** (headquarters of the Bordentown Historic Society, [609] 298-1740), **Hoagland's Tavern,** the **Thomas Paine House,** and many others.

Mount Holly, on Route 541 (exit 5 from the New Jersey Turnpike—also off Routes 38, 206, and 537) is a classic example of an early American settlement with charming pre-Revolutionary houses and buildings. You can tour the houses or even the **Burlington County Prison Museum** at 128 High Street, (609) 267-2104, which is an old stone prison used between 1810 and 1965, containing memorabilia from prison life, a haunted dungeon, Indian artifacts, and a lovely prison garden. Two miles west of Mount Holly is the Greek-revival **Smithville Mansion** (1830), and **Smithville Village,** a ruined early industrial complex with workers' homes on the site of the factory where the high-wheeled Star bicycles were manufactured. This Smithville should not be confused with the Smithville on the Jersey shore. Call (609) 261-3780 for further information.

Mount Holly is a beautiful area, and **Rancocas State Park,** nearby in Mount Laurel Township (off Route 537, just north of Masonville), is an ideal place for nature study with excellent boating on Rancocas Creek. Even though it is not a designated historic town and has no notable historic structures or sites, it is recommended that you visit the small town of Timbuctoo also, just so you can tell your friends that's where you went over the weekend; it's two miles east of Mount Holly.

Clementon Amusement Park is located on the scenic Clementon Lake, 15 miles southeast of Camden near Berlin on

Route 534 in Clementon, and is open from noon to 10 P.M. from Memorial Day through Labor Day; the water park closes at 8 P.M. One of New Jersey's oldest amusement parks, it features 25 adult rides, 8 children's rides, and the biggest "log swim" in the country, called "King Neptune's Revenge," which carries riders in loglike boats over a section of the lake and down a water-filled chute, splashing them as they go. There is also a fine old carousel with hand-carved wooden horses. Call (609) 783-0263 for current admission charges. For dining in Clementon try the **Silver Lake Inn** on the White Horse Pike, (609) 783-3300, a huge restaurant with a 1950s atmosphere and special Wednesday night buffets that include lobster Newburgh and turkey mousse. They're open until midnight.

Swedesboro, a historic town south of Camden (exit 2 off the New Jersey Turnpike onto 322 West, left on Route 551) is the center of what was to have been New Sweden back in 1703. Settled by Swedish colonists around 1620, New Sweden never came to pass because the attractive Swedish girls intermarried quickly with English gentlemen. There are still many Swedish reminders here, however, and King Olaf of Sweden visited the region in 1976 during Bicentennial festivities to pay homage to his ancestors. The **Community Episcopal Trinity Church,** "Old Swedes Church," was built in 1784 and is located on King's Highway. It is open every Sunday morning or by appointment. Call (609) 467-1227. The Gloucester County Historical Society maintains the old **Moravian Church** in Swedesboro, also on King's Highway, which was built by members of the Moravian sect in 1786.

Mullica Hill (about eight miles east of Swedesboro and eight miles west of Glassboro) on Route 45 is the center of antiques country for southwestern New Jersey. Antique hunters from all over the state, Pennsylvania, Delaware, and Maryland converge on the dozens of specialty shops lining both sides of the main street on Route 45. The shops are situated in the town's historic old grist mill, an abandoned produce warehouse and other historic stone buildings, and offer 18th- and 19th-century furniture, dolls, books, glass, Victorian lace, Persian rugs, Christmas specialty antiques, arts, crafts, reproductions, and other colonial-type antiques. At one end of town there is a brick Quaker meeting house built in 1808, and at the other end the **Raccoon** (the original name of Swedesboro until 1750) **Valley General Store,** where you can buy nostalgic penny candles.

Just east of Mullica Hill is the city of Glassboro and home of **Rowan University.** The second glassworks in America was established in 1775 and most "South Jersey-style" glassmaking techniques were developed here, including log-cabin-shaped bottles made for the 1840 presidential campaign called "Booz bottles,"

named after the Philadelphia distiller who filled them. The glass-
works in Glassboro are gone now, though Owens Illinois, the Kim-
ble Glass Company, Armstrong Cork Company, Anchor
Hocking, and Gayner's continue to manufacture glass in South
Jersey, and many early bottles can be viewed at the **Rowan University Library.** The town achieved some notoriety in 1967 when
Premier Kosygin met President Lyndon Johnson there for a meeting that was determined to be halfway between Washington and
New York (where Kosygin was staying). It was widely reported that
Kosygin and his automobile-limousine entourage drove 35 miles
per hour down the New Jersey Turnpike in many places in order
to view the "beautiful industrial development." Mrs. Kosygin went
off with Lady Bird by helicopter to the Governor's House at Island
Beach State Park for tea and sandwiches. Back in Glassboro, Kosygin and Johnson had their meeting surrounded by vast tomato
fields and peach orchards where the famous South Jersey peaches
were ripening to succulent and juicy fruition.

Salem, 10 miles south of the Delaware Memorial Bridge on Route
49 (exit 1 off the New Jersey Turnpike) is a town directly related to
Wilmington, Delaware. At the turn of the century E. I. DuPont
bought vast acres of land in the area where they produced gun pow-
der and later dyes and other chemicals. In the late 1700s the land
around Salem, overcultivated by Swedish, Dutch, and English
colonist-farmers, became barren, which spurred a great migration
west where nostalgic settlers renamed towns in Ohio, Indiana,
Iowa, and finally Oregon after the original Salem in New Jersey.
Salem prospered however, after the discovery of marl (a rich fer-
tilizer) around 1820. There are 150 old pre-Revolutionary brick
and stone houses in the area, and a good place for starting a tour is
the **Salem County Historical Society** at 79, 81, and 83 Market
Street (there are 60 historic buildings on Market Street alone),
which maintains many restored houses and displays in period
rooms, historic Indian relics, rare glass, china, furniture, and farm
implements. Call (609) 935-5004 or (609) 935-2377 for information. Salem's famous landmark is the **Salem Oak** in the Friends
Burial Ground on West Broadway, a tree estimated to be 500 years
old and 30 feet in circumference. Acorns from this tree are in demand all over the world. Seven miles from Salem and five miles
from the New Jersey Turnpike on Route 49 is Finns Point, an area
on the Delaware in which the 124-acre **Fort Mott State Park** is located. It is also home to Finns Point National Cemetery, where
2,436 Confederate and 300 Union soldiers are buried. These were
prisoners who died during the Civil War at Fort Delaware. There
was never a battle at Fort Mott—in fact, its armament was re-
moved and the fort was decommissioned in 1947—when the
State of New Jersey acquired it, without ever having fired a shot in
anger. Here you can spend the day fishing, picnicking, and gazing
up and down the wide expanse of the Delaware. The **Killcohook**

National Wildlife Refuge is also located here. The historic **Hancock House,** a state historical museum south of Salem at Hancock's Bridge, was the scene of a massacre of 90 sleeping revolutionists by the vicious Tories. South of Salem is the **Second Sun Energy Information Center** on a converted ferryboat docked next to the Salem and Hope Creek nuclear generating stations. There are "hands-on" exhibits and a "century of light" theater show for adults and children, (609) 935-2660.

Route 49 takes you farther southeast (16 miles) to Bridgeton, an old glass manufacturing town and home of the **Nail House Museum** on West Commerce Street, (609) 455-4100. The museum features an excellent collection of glass, early nails, iron banks, and antique toys. The **Woodruff Indian Museum** at 150 East Commerce Street, (609) 451-2620, has over 20,000 artifacts relating to the Lenni Lenape Indians. The old **Broad Street Church,** built by the Presbyterians in 1792, is a landmark; so is **Potter's Tavern,** on Broad Street opposite the courthouse, which is an authentically restored 200 year-old tavern. Eight miles toward the Delaware, on the Cohansey River, is historic Greenwich, Cumberland County's oldest community and the site of a famous incident in 1774 wherein a group of young men, disguised as Indians, stole the tea a British merchant was trying to smuggle into the country, and burned it in a public bonfire in the center of town as a gesture against unjust taxation. The town, beautifully laid out, has many old houses carefully restored and researched by the county historical society. Call (609) 451-2310 for a Greenwich walking tour. **Ye Olde Centerton Inn,** (609) 358-3201, a Colonial stagecoach stop at the junction of Route 540 and Route 553 midway between Bridgeton and Greenwich, built in 1706, is still in operation and is a fine historic place for a traditional American "mixed entree" from seafood on up. The basic entree is $16.95 with salad and vegetable. Hours: closed Monday; Tuesday 5 P.M. to 10 P.M., Wednesday through Saturday 5 P.M. to 11 P.M., Sunday 2 P.M. to 9 P.M.

Vineland, the largest city in area in New Jersey (69 square miles, population 53,200) was created in 1861 by John K. Landis, who bought 32,000 acres of swamp and sandy pinelands. His town, in the heart of South Jersey's farmland, is a mile square, surrounded with agricultural acres. All the streets in the central area are at right angles; the principal streets 100 feet wide, the secondary streets 60 feet wide. John Landis sold land in 5- and 20-acre plots, and required that the new owners set their houses back 25 feet in the city center, and 75 feet in the country acres. He also required that property owners plant trees and grass on the streets in front of their own property. The **Vineland Historical Society** at 108 South Seventh Street has exhibits about Landis and his fascinating town, including furnished period rooms, local memorabilia, and Indian

relics. Vineland was the town were a dentist named T. B. Welch, a fierce teetotaler, developed a means whereby grapes could be made into juice without fermentation, thereby establishing the famous Welch Grape Juice empire. Another man from Vineland, John L. Mason, invented the famous mason jar. Vineland is the poultry center of the East and is known as "the egg basket of the nation," with the largest egg cooperative in the world. Just west of Vineland is **Seabrook Farms,** which is one of the largest agricultural farms in the world, with over 60,000 acres.

◆

"Take Me Back To My Boots and Saddle" at Cowtown, New Jersey

Cowtown Rodeo is a professional "ride 'em cowboy" authentic rodeo in the true tradition of the Old West. You don't have to travel as far as Oklahoma, Montana, or Colorado to see exciting bareback bronc riding, calf roping, saddle bronc riding, steer wrestling, Brahma bull riding, team roping, or enjoy the thrill of seeing hearty cowgirls barrel riding against the clock in the breathless barrel race. It is all happening here in beautiful Salem County at

Riding the buckers at Cowtown is part of the fun of a rodeo; these two buckaroos from a cardboard cut-out doll book, Whitman Publishing Company, 1950.

Woodstown—about 15 miles west of Vineland in the southwestern area of New Jersey called "the cow capital of the first frontier," referred to by regulars simply as "Cowtown." This arena features the best performing cowboys and cowgirls from across the country each Saturday night at 7:30 P.M. from Memorial Day to Labor Day. Tickets to the show are $10 for adults, $5 for children, kids under two free. There are special group rates for parties over 25. There is room for 4,000 in the stadium. This rodeo has been run by the Harris family since 1929, only interrupting its rodeo activities during the World War II period. The current owner-producer is Grant Harris, who himself is a champion rodeo cowboy performer with national prizes in the saddle bronc category. Cowtown raises its bucking horses and most of its bulls as well. At Cowtown on Tuesday and Saturdays from 8 A.M. to 4 P.M. there is a farmer-flea market with over 500 merchants selling everything from prize Jersey tomatoes to sweet white "silver queen" Jersey corn. On Tuesdays a livestock market is included. The word at Cowtown is "you name it, we sell it." Put on your cowboy boots, jeans, snapbutton western shirt, and ten-gallon hat; join in the fun. Bring along the whole family or a gang of friends. Parking is free, and there are refreshment stands. Call (609) 769-3200 for information. Cowtown is affiliated with the Professional Rodeo Cowboys Association and the Cowgirls Rodeo Association. Write: Cowtown Rodeo, Route 2, Box 23A, Woodstown, NJ 08098, to receive a rodeo brochure with pictures of real cowboys in action—in color.

Directions for Cowtown— Cowtown Rodeo is actually in Woodstown; to get there take the New Jersey Turnpike to exit 2 to Swedesboro. The rodeo is located on Route 40, eight miles east of the Delaware Memorial Bridge and two miles west of the township of Woodstown itself. Take Route 40 West if you are coming from Vineland. If traveling south on Route 295 take exit 4 (the Woodstown exit) and follow the road signs pointing to Woodstown. The rodeo is about six miles down the road on the right side of the highway. If traveling from Delaware, cross the Delaware Bridge and follow signs for Route 40 East to Atlantic City. From this point the Cowtown Rodeo is eight miles down the road on Route 40 on the right side.

Delaware Water Gap Day Trip

1. Clinton Historical Museum
2. Auto Graveyard
3. Hot Dog Johnny's
4. Delaware Water Gap National Park

The **Delaware Water Gap National Recreation Area** is a 70,000-acre region located on both sides of the Delaware River in northwest New Jersey and Pennsylvania. It is connected on the Jersey side to Worthington State Forest and Stokes State Forest by a section of the **Appalachian Trail.** The famous trail runs through Worthington and Stokes to High Point at the very top of the state and traverses over to Wawayanda State Park. There are designated areas permitted on this trail for overnight stops, but it is not recommended as a hike for the uninitiated. A day trip to the region to investigate might be a good idea; and having someone pick you up, if you *do* come back one day to make the hike, is another good idea. Then you won't wear out your hiking shoes and you won't have to retrace your steps. There is much to see and do in northwestern New Jersey. One way to get there, directly on Interstate 78, would be to start with a visit to the historic town of Clinton. The entire town has been designated a bird and wildlife sanctuary owing to its location on the migratory route of many rare bird species. At the center of town is a 200-foot wide waterfall at the junction of the Spruce Run and Raritan Rivers, flanked on either side by two historic mills. On the west bank is an old red-frame mill, housing the **Clinton Historical Museum,** its four floors exhibiting a variety of rural daily life artifacts from the 18th, 19th, and 20th centuries. Additional buildings connected to the museum include a blacksmith shop, general store, post office, an 1860 schoolhouse, and a log cabin. On the east bank stands a carefully restored stone grist mill dating back to Colonial times. This mill, on the National Register of Historic Places and now operating as an art gallery, is a fine space to see, with its beautifully restored wood floors, original ceiling beams and interior supports, and white plastered walls. The art gallery is open all year round; the museum is open from April through October from 1 to 5 P.M. and Saturday and Sunday from noon to 6 P.M. Clinton Historical Museum, at 56 Main Street. The phone number is (908) 735-4101. Special events and concerts are regular occurrences and the Clinton antique show, usually held on the weekend before Memorial Day, features the early American country look in antiques. The town of Clinton is charmingly Colonial and well worth a visit for its preserved architecture. Try the **Old Clinton House** for fine country dining (908) 730-9300. Two state parks are nearby, **Spruce Run State Park** and **Round Valley State Park,** located in the crater of Cushetunk Mountain with 4,000 acres of woods and water, encompassing the second largest lake in the state.

For an overnight stay in Clinton, try the **Holiday Inn** ($87 to $93 double occupancy, [908] 735-5111). The **Stewart Inn** is a fine bed-and-breakfast easily accessible from Clinton (take Route 78 West to exit 4, about 12 miles). The Stewart Inn has modern conveniences, private baths, cable television, all set in a bucolic country landscape. Rates are reasonable, around $75 to $85 per night with breakfast. Stewart Inn, R.D. 1, Box 571, South Main Street, Stewartsville, NJ. Call (908) 479-6060 for reservations. The inn is equally convenient for visitors to the Delaware River, Flemington and Lambertville.

The city of Phillipsburg, just minutes west of Stewartsville is like a miniature Pittsburgh, an industrial town set on a series of hills that steeply drop down to the Delaware. This is a city with a rich history, attested to by the neighborhood on the hill above the river filled with Victorian mansions built to order for the business executives who ran the iron mills at the turn of the century. The view west from Phillipsburg is of the larger, more prosperous city of Easton, Pennsylvania, just across the river. After a tour of Phillipsburg you may want to investigate the **Washington Auto Graveyard** in Washington—take 57 East out of Phillipsburg to Washington; turn right at the light with the **Dunkin' Donuts** on the corner, and drive eight miles to Montana Road across from the old *inn* sign. Follow the road over a small mountain and turn right at the bend. Whether you need a part for your 1950s Hudson Hornet dream car or not, this place is a must. You will find an autophantasmagoric scene here the likes of which you have never seen before. The swampy, low-lying meadows yield row upon row of different makes, models, and vintages of America's late, great automobiles. You will uncover, amid the bugs and quacking ducks, 1920s, 1930s, and 1940s Packards, 1950s Buicks and Cadillacs and everything in between, from Grahams to Studebakers to aerodynamic streamlined Nash bed cars. The older cars, long rusted out, stand side by side in rows often overgrown with thorny berry bushes. Some are stacked one upon the other. This is a junk-art happening to be experienced. Bring tools to dislodge that rare door handle you've been looking for; pay the proprietor as you leave.

Back in Washington, take Route 31 North to the intersection of Route 46 at Buttzville. Here is where you'll find the unique **Buttzville Hot Dog Johnny's,** famous throughout New Jersey and Pennsylvania. This highway spot is run by original founder John Kovalsky's daughter Pat, who has been working there since she was eight years old. Established in 1935 and still going strong, Buttzville Hot Dog Johnny's specializes in farmfresh buttermilk supplied by a local farmer, birch beer served in frosted mugs, and hot dogs. These hot dogs are really *hot,* not in the sense of a burning taste, but the sense of warmth; roll and dog are served to you steaming and wrapped in old-fashioned wax paper. These are truly mouth watering and afterward you may never want to eat a Nathan's Coney Island dog again. According to John and Pat, Hot Dog Johnny's was originally located at the stoplight in Buttzville, and business was booming when the Atlantic Gas Station across the highway provided the funds for a complete move down Route 46 to Buttzville center. It seems they were interfering with Atlantic Gas's own food concessions and causing congestion in the busy traffic flow in this little crossroads hamlet, which traditionally attracted the far-flung citizens from the Scranton coal region area. The customers always demand and get the best at Hot Dog Johnny's, and there is no trouble parking the car. There are picnic-style tables here and in nearby **Island Park** on the **Pequest River,** a spot shaded by tall trees and long favored by trout fishermen. The hours at Hot Dog Johnny's are loose, but usually open from 9 A.M. until quite late. Call (908) 453-2882.

After fueling up at Buttzville, drive west on 46 to the Delaware River, to Manunkachunk, to the Kittatinny Mountains and the **Worthington State Forest.** Explore!

Northern Mountains and Lakes
Bergen, Passaic, and Sussex Counties

The northern hill and lake country of New Jersey was thought of by the Germans who settled there at the turn of the century as reminiscent of old Bavaria and the green mountainous areas of the Old Country. Some of these early immigrants fondly referred to New Jersey as "New Germany." Today a variety of ethnic groups live in this verdant region; much of it continues to remain intact and unspoiled, only miles away from modern civilization. Travelers in the region should explore some of the exciting back roads like scenic Route 515, which has many steep curves and turns that take the driver up and around and into the forest valley that possesses great majestic beauty. We have all traveled over hill and dale in search of this and that, but here you will discover the same serenity of mountainous and mysterious woodlands so often associated with the Berkshires, Bear Mountain, Vermont, or New Hampshire. A fairy-tale Hansel and Gretel forest is all to be found here, in what is called the "Highlands" of New Jersey.

To get there: Take Interstate 78, a beautiful east-west highway, which connects Phillipsburg to Newark and New York, Route 80 (also east-west) connects the Delaware River at the Delaware Water Gap to the Hudson River at the George Washington Bridge. Route 206 is a viable north-south route off I-78 or I-80, and Routes 15 or 23 are good alternate roads for traveling into the regions of New Jersey north of Interstate 80. Forty-three percent of New Jersey is still forest, and the Division of Parks and Forestry maintains a great deal of it in state forests and parks, natural areas, and historic sites. Fish and wildlife management areas administered by the Division of Fish, Game and Wildlife comprise 154,000 acres, which are open for hiking, but without official swimming or camping facilities.

There are many parks, state forests, and specialty "good time" spots to hike, canoe, swim, ski and play in New Jersey's "skylands." One particular vantage point with a wondrous view of the surrounding area is **High Point State Park** that is in the extreme northwest corner on the crest of Kittatinny Mountains. The park, which has a camping area called **Sawmill Lake,** is connected at its southern tip to the 15,319-acre **Stokes State Forest,** which extends 12 miles southwest. Elevations here range from 420 to 1,653 feet (Sunrise Mountain). Highway 206 crosses the forest at Culvers Gap. There is daily bathing at the **Stony Lake** bathing area and camping is permitted here also.

Jenny Jump Forest has 1,118 acres with beautiful panoramas of the surrounding country and the Delaware Water Gap (between Interstate 80 and Route 46 off Route 519 near Hope). **Swartswood State Park,** located on the shores of both **Big** and **Little Swartswood Lakes** near the village of Swartswood in Sussex County (off Route 206), offers bathing in a sheltered cove with lifeguard protection and bathhouses. Picnicking and camping are allowed and in the winter cross-country skiing is the main outdoor activity.

Hopatcong State Park contains 107 acres including a section of the old Morris Canal. The clear water of Lake Hopatcong may be enjoyed by bathers at a safe sand-filled beach under lifeguard protection. A well-graded lawn, sloping toward the lake, encourages sunbathing. This park may be reached from I-80 (exit 28) by way of Landing or from Route 206 at Netcong. Amusement park aficionados like to remember and associate Lake Hopatcong with Bertrand Island Amusement Park, which, alas, was torn down. **Waterloo Village,** near Stanhope (off I-80 at exit 25 to Route 206 to Route 604—Waterloo Road) in the undeveloped **Allamuchy State Park,** is a beautifully preserved and restored 18th-century town. The **Waterloo Festival for the Arts** (May through October) offers a complete program of chamber music, a Saturday orchestra series, and afternoon concerts of jazz, folk, classical, and pop music on Sundays. There are 23 authentically restored homes and buildings with period furniture, rare antiques, and objects of art on display. Crafts can be bought at the well-stocked general store, including such novelties as period pottery, hand-dipped candles, brooms, wrought iron pieces, pine incense, and hand-loomed scarfs. Waterloo Village is a National Historic Site situated on the winding towpaths of the old Morris Canal and there are dense forests, dark lakes, and rushing rivers to explore in the region.

Wild West City, located in Netcong near Stanhope (exit 25 off I-80 to Route 206 north) is the place where the old wild west comes back to life in northwestern New Jersey. You can watch the reenactment of the fight at the O.K. Corral, ride a stagecoach, ponies or an old iron horse railcar. Stop off at the **Golden Nugget Saloon** and enjoy food and a real Western stage show.

The Land of Make Believe (on Route 611 in Hope, 2 miles off exit 12 off I-80) is a real treat for children under 12. Here they can watch a Punch and Judy show, investigate Old McDonald's Farm, talk to a scarecrow that talks back, ride on the Indian River ride or a Civil War train. They can visit the Haunted House and receive a gift from Santa Claus at the North Pole. There are plenty of amusement rides here for kids from 3 to 12 and a large picnic grove.

Space Farms (Route 519 in Beemerville, open from May to November) is also fun for kids who enjoy the petting and feeding zoo and the large collection of wild animals and birds. For parents there are classic automobiles, farm tool displays, carriages, Indian artifacts and a display of antique dolls to ogle. Call (973) 875-5800 for information.

Vernon Valley Action Park Route 23 to Route 94) is the largest "self-participation" theme park in the world, with rides that include the Avalanche Water Ride, Alpine slides, Lola formula race cars, speedboats, four water slides, super go-carts, the Kamikaze Rapids Ride, and the Tidal Wave Pool. A bathing suit is a must here. For smaller kids there's Water World and play park. Call (973) 827-2000 for information.

The Quarry (in Hamburg on Route 517 off Route 23) near the Gingerbread Castle (see High Point day trip) offers swimming and scuba diving during the summer in its spring-fed crystal-clear water. During the winter you can cross-country ski on its 70 acres and afterward relax in the lodge's cocktail lounge or buy your new ski equipment in the pro shop. Call (973) 827-7630.

Vernon Valley/Great Gorge Ski Area (Route 23 to Route 94 or I-80 to Route 15 to Route 94) is an ideal spot for a winter vacation. With over 50 trails and slopes, 14 chairlifts and 3 rope tows, everyone from expert to novice can join in the winter wonderland fun. Great Gorge also has ski rentals, lessons, and the world's largest snowmaking facility (in case Mother Nature doesn't provide!). There is also night skiing for the truly adventurous. For further information about resort hotels and dining in this area call (973) 827-2000.

Hidden Valley (Breakneck Road, Vernon, on Route 94 off Route 23) has ski slopes that range from beginner to expert. Hidden Valley Ski Lodge, in the pines at the base of the mountain, has a limited lift-ticket policy that ensures short lines and uncrowded slopes. During the summer, visitors can hike, boat, play tennis, and platform tennis. Banquet and party facilities are also available. Call (973) 764-6161.

An Alpine racer at the Great Gorge Resort in McAfee. (Photo courtesy of the Great Gorge Resort)

The Craigmeur Ski area (off Route 23) is ideal for beginner skiers with smaller slopes specially designed to make skiing fun and easy. Quality instruction is available, and during the summer people find the grounds excellent for picnics while enjoying a ride on the wet and wild bumper boats and mountain coaster slide. Reservations only; (973) 697-4501.

The Franklin Museum (on Evans Street in Franklin off Routes 23 and 517) has beautiful displays of minerals from the zinc mines of New Jersey including the unique franklinite. There are fluorescent rock shows here, and family rock hunts between April 15 and November 15. Wednesday to Saturday, 10 A.M. to 4 P.M. Sunday 12:30 to 4:30 P.M.; call (973) 827-3481 for information.

Wawayanda and **Greenwood Lake State Parks** and the undeveloped **A. S. Hewitt State Forest** form a vast green belt at the New York–New Jersey border. There is swimming, boating, and hiking a-plenty here—the **Appalachian Trail** runs through Wawayanda. Northern Passaic and Bergen Counties are dotted with lakes including **Pompton Lakes** (off Route 23) in the Ramapo Mountains and **Franklin Lakes.**

The Lorrimer Nature Center (790 Ewing Avenue, Franklin Lakes) is a charming area maintained by the New Jersey Audubon Society offering self-guiding trails, outdoor classrooms, natural history programs, and courses for children and adults. Take Route 208 and follow the green-and-white Audubon Nature Center signs.

The Mahwah Railroad Museum (Route 17 North to Mahwah–Pompton lakes exit to Island road, right turn to East Ramapo Avenue) is open from May to October, Sundays from 3 to 5 P.M. (other times by reservation) and includes old-time historic passenger cars and diesel engines, railroad memorabilia, models, historical documents, maps, and photos.

The Ramapo Valley County Reservation provides excellent hiking and camping facilities beside the Ramapo River on Route 202, Mahwah. There is a lake for canoeing and rafting, a fishing pond, and a waterfall. Write the ranger for sketch maps of the trails (610 Ramapo Valley Road, Mahwah, NJ 07430).

Darlington County Park in Mahwah has three lakes, two for swimming, one for fishing. There are snack bars, comfort stations, and playgrounds provided for summer residents and visitors. Call (201) 327-3500 for a schedule.

Ringwood State Park (from Route 23 to 511) is located on the New Jersey–New York state line and offers fishing and boating in Shepherd Lake with facilities for bathing in the summer and ice skating and skimobiling in the winter. There are hiking trails and picnic areas, a small pond, a blacksmith shop, formal gardens, and the beautiful **Ringwood Manor House.** Built during the Victorian period, it is a beautiful 51-room mansion, and is now a museum with American furniture, firearms, implements, and artifacts. Also located here is a 44-room Jacobean mansion with a 300-acre botanical garden called **Skylands.** There is a lodge with a cafeteria, snack bar, and boat and canoe renting facilities. Call (973) 962-7031 for further information regarding the many special activities held year-round at this lovely spot. At the park's south end is the **Ramapo Mountain Forest,** an undeveloped but beautiful area encompassing another 3,500 acres with many hiking trails and good fishing.

A particularly charming spot is **Lake Girard,** a small intimate place with hillside picnic areas with tables and fireplaces and swimming and canoeing, located at Hardyston on Route 23, halfway between Stockholm and Hamburg, situated next to the **Hamburg Mountain Wildlife Management Area.** Also near Hardyston on Route 23 is a legendary country restaurant, in business for over 40 years. **Jorgensen's Inn** serves American fare in an old-fashioned style. Open year-round, Fridays from 5 P.M. to 9:30 P.M., Saturdays until 10:30 P.M. Sundays from noon to 7, and holidays from 11:30 A.M. to 8:00 P.M. Call (973) 697-7355. For an exceptional drive before dinner at Jorgensen's, take Route 515 off Route 23 at Stockholm. This is a *scenic* road you will surely enjoy.

Another scenic region, in a different sense, is Boonton, which was the largest iron center in the country in the 1800s. It's an industrial town from the past, built into a ledge overlooking Rockaway Gorge. Route 202 goes through the center of town (take 202 from Route 46 or I-80, five miles away) and you won't believe the precipitous mine-stripped view of the Gorge and the train embankments beyond offered from the pavilion next to the bank. The antique shops on the steeply twisting streets of the old city offer rewards to collectors of hard-to-find records and early recording machines. Pop-culture enthusiasts will find shops carrying early industrial antiques including porcelain enamel advertising signs. Automobilia is also a craze in Boonton—stop in at the **Kanter Auto Products** showroom at 76 Monroe Street and prepare to ogle the Packards—Fred Kanter supplies mechanical, trim and restoration parts for collector cars, with a full line of engines, suspension, brakes, and water and fuel pumps as well as convertible tops, carpets, car covers, leather and seat covers. He ships worldwide, and sells and repairs all kinds of vintage cars, and his specialty is America's best—"Ask the man who owns one." Call (973) 334-9575.

High Point Day Trip

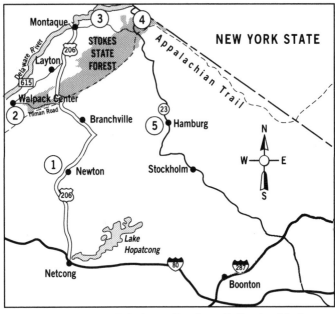

1. Newton Fire Museum	3. Deckertown Turnpike	5. Gingerbread Castle
2. Walpack Inn	4. High Point	

This is a day trip to the highest point in New Jersey, located in the northwest corner at **High Point State Park.** The quickest way to get into the region of Sussex County is to take Interstate 80 to exit 25 to North 26. **Lake Musconetcong** and **Lake Hopatcong State Parks** are on your right, the undeveloped **Allamuchy State Park** on your left as you drive northwest to Newton, the Sussex County seat. Newton is a 19th-century town filled with historic brick buildings set on a public green. The most impressive building is the 1847 County Courthouse, a Greek Revival structure on a steep hillside. The **Town Hall** at 39 Trinity Street distributes free pamphlets for sightseeing highlights and the **Newton Fire Museum** (150 Spring Street), built 150 years ago, has a museum with antique firefighting equipment and memorabilia, open Tuesday through Saturday, 10 A.M. to 2 P.M. Call (201) 383-0396. The **Sussex County Historical Society** headquarters and **Museum** is located in the Hill Memorial Building at Church and Main, (201) 383-6010. The museum has local handmade furniture, old household utensils and clothing, photographs and postcards; but the really exciting thing here is the mastodon found outside town in the 1960s, which is on display also. If you're hungry, try the **County**

Seat restaurant on Route 206 and Clinton Street on the north side of town. **Swartswood State Park** for swimming and boating and **Whittingham Wildlife Management Area** (with 1,500 acres apiece) are to the west and south of Newton on Route 619.

From Newton continue north on 206 to Branchville. Diverge off 206 to 630 and drive to the middle of town to Branchville's **Gourmet Wine and Cheese Shop.** Marty, the proprietor, will stock you up with goodies for your trip into the wilderness ahead. If it's staple food at a classic diner you're after, stop at the **Five Star Diner,** Route 206 North, Branchville. The very last place you might want to stop at is the **Yellow Cottage,** between Branchville and Culver Lake. The Yellow Cottage, on the lefthand side of he road, has been there for decades. They make sandwiches, sell their own pies and breads, and feature out-of-this-world brown Bettys. Get them with coffee and fill the thermos. Drive past Culver lake through **Culver Gap** and you'll find yourself in **Stokes State Forest,** deep in the Kittatinny Mountains. Pass the entrance to Stokes Forest, watch carefully (there should be a state 4-H camp signpost here) and take your next left onto Strubble Road. Drive down scenic Strubble, which turns into Dimon Road to **Tillman Ravine.** This is a designated natural area, undisturbed by man, a virtual laboratory where natural forests, rocks and soil as affected by climatic conditions and natural processes may be observed. It is spectacularly beautiful, canopied over with tall, graceful hemlocks and other kinds of old growth trees. There are masses of native rhododendron on the steep banks of Tillman Brook, which slides down long waterworn channels over huge boulders in fine cascades. There are parking areas here; but no picnic tables, camping or other recreational facilities exist to mar the natural beauty. After hiking the forest paths and crossing the quaint wooden bridges, drive on down the mountain on Brink Road to Main in **Walpack Center.** This is a preserved ghost town (complete with ancient cemetery) maintained as part of the **Delaware Water Gap National Recreation Area.** If you thought the forest was something, the great natural beauty and the vistas across the beautifully maintained fields in Walpack Valley will take your breath away. Take a swim, if you like, in Flat Brook and drive up north on Route 615 (Walpack–Flatbrook Road) to the **Walpack Inn.** This is a no reservation place with a lovely outdoor eating terrace where you can eat while watching the deer eat. Specialties run from steak and fresh fish served with salad bar and baked potato or rice with prices ranging from $15 to $34. They are open on Friday and Saturday from 5 P.M. to 9:30 P.M., Sunday 11 A.M. to 2:30 P.M. brunch, and 4 P.M. to 8 P.M. dinner. There is a wonderful piano player named Jim Woolsey who will play anything you want on his grand piano. Call (973) 948-9849 for more information. To get back onto Route 206, drive north on 615, take a left on 521 to 206. The Walpack Inn is about seven miles south of Route 206.

Left to right: Humpty Dumpty statue at the Gingerbread Castle in Hamburg; the Gingerbread Castle itself.

The summer months are the most beautiful to catch the sunset from High Point. To get there after dinner or after a picnic in Stokes State Forest take Route 206 North to Route 653 (Clove Road) to Route 650 (Deckertown Turnpike). Turn right and drive east on Deckertown Road into Stokes Forest to Sawmill Road. Take a left on Sawmill Road and drive north along the crest of the Kittatinny Mountains. You can't miss **High Point Monument,** (201) 875-4800. Dominating the summit of the mountain and astride the greatest elevation in New Jersey (1,803 feet), this 220-foot-high granite-faced landmark, built in 1930, has views westward across the valley of the Delaware to the ridges of the Pocono Mountains in Pennsylvania. Nestled in the valley 1,300 feet below lies Port Jervis, New York, with Tri-State Rock marking the common boundary of three states at the juncture of the Neversink and the Delaware Rivers. The Port Jervis line (Metro North commuter railroad operated in conjunction with NJ Transit) out of Hoboken travels up in New York through Orange County and terminates in the bustling railroad town of Port Jervis. Northeast in the distance one can see the Catskill Mountains. To the southeast lies the valley of the Wallkill River, checkerboarded with the farms and woodlands of Sussex County. Sunrise Mountain in Stokes State Forest may be seen in the middle distance. This 13,398-acre park was a gift of the late Colonel and Mrs. Anthony R. Kuser of Bernardsville, to the people of New Jersey, in 1922. Mrs. Kuser's money came from the Prudential Insurance Company.

Route 23 is the best way to get back to civilization from High Point. Take it east about 18 miles all the way to Hamburg in the Pochuck Mountains where you will have to screech on the brakes when you see the **Gingerbread Castle.** This unbelievable place was built in 1930 by Florenz Ziegfeld's famed stage designer Joseph Urban, at the behest of a successful businessman named F. H. Bennet, who loved the immortal stories of "Hansel and Gretel," "Snow White and the Seven Dwarfs," "Little Red Riding Hood," "The Three Little Pigs," "Little Miss Muffet," and "The Old Lady Who Lived in a Shoe." This is the place to recapture the spirit of childhood; conducted tours of the castle and its adjacent grounds are led by expertly trained local school children dressed quaintly in period costumes. The boys are transformed into "Hansel" and the girls become "Gretel," all of them reciting in awed tones the fairy tales connected with each display in the castle. They point out Humpty Dumpty perched atop his famous wall and Prince Charming astride his prancing charger. Then they will show you the spitting black cat that stands guard over the castle up in a turret, and the wise old owl who watches every move through unblinking yellow eyes. Children are warned not to touch the walls of the castle lest they turn into stones. There is a dungeon, a witch's trophy room, and in the main hall your Hansel and Gretel guides will point out the gingerbread cookies and peppermint sticks studding the walls. Later they will show you the evil witch astride her broom ready to flee from reproachful eyes, and the witch's evil kitchen where a big black cauldron contains the bones of the hapless children trapped in her lair and cooked alive. The tour over, you will be led through a narrow door onto a landing high up in the battlements and down a brick stairway past animal-cracker balustrades formed by elephants. This unique Humperdinck German-style castle was closed for 10 years but was brought back to life by Joseph Difiglia and Brian Hamilton, who have added a petting zoo with baby animals, a snack bar for gingerbread cookies, and a gift shop for souvenirs. There are picnic tables nearby beside the Wallkill River. The Gingberbread Castle is open every day from 10:30 A.M. to 5:30 P.M. during the summer. Call (973) 827-1617 for more information. Route 23 will take you to Route 46 or I-80 near Paterson, where you can connect up with the Garden State Parkway.

"Hello from the Jersey Shore"

Notes on Road, Ferry, and Train Travel

The old route to fun and sunny good times at the Jersey shore out of Manhattan Island from the Lincoln or Holland Tunnels is New Jersey State Highway I-9. Route I-9 becomes simply 9 at Woodbridge (US Route 1 goes straight on down to Trenton). Some drivers at this point followed 9 through the Cheesequake State Park area, Freehold, Lakewood, Toms River, and farther on down all the way to Cape May. US Route 9 originally was an old Lenape Indian trail, and later became Kings Highway before being designated an official state highway. Other drivers preferred to swing into South 34 at Cheesequake, which is actually closer to the shoreline, taking the road through the beautiful farm regions of Holmdel and Colts Neck. During the summer months fresh white-and-yellow Jersey sweet corn and every variety of Jersey tomato is sold at farm roadstands on Route 34. Highway 35 will also take you to the shore through the antique-center town of Red Bank, which has many historic buildings, Shrewsbury, Eatontown, and eventually into Asbury Park and Spring Lake all the way south to Seaside Heights. Much of Route 35 is now mostly commercial with immense shopping malls.

The route to the North Jersey shore, Keyport, Keansburg, Atlantic Highlands, Sea Bright, Monmouth Beach, and Long Branch is the old Route 36 (north coastal highway). Route 36 is a beautiful drive along the Atlantic Highlands with many views of Sandy Hook Bay, the Navesink and Shrewsbury Rivers, and the Atlantic Ocean. Often you drive almost alongside the crashing waves. At Long Branch "the shore drive" changes into Route 71 through Deal, with its splendid ocean-front mansions and into Asbury Park, Ocean Grove, Bradley Beach, Avon-by-the-Sea, Belmar, Spring Lake, Sea Girt, and Manasquan. Most New Yorkers prefer the relatively fast-lane travel along the New Jersey Turnpike to the Garden State Parkway at Woodbridge. North Jerseyites will simply get onto the Parkway at an earlier point from the Meadowlands Arena, the Oranges, Union, or other points north. Philadelphians can travel to the southern Jersey shore on any number of interesting old highways like Route 70 to Lakehurst and to Point Pleasant Beach, or from 70 onto Route 72 to Barnegat or Ship Bottom on Long Beach Island. The old Route 30 to Pleasantville and into Egg Harbor City, Absecon, and finally Atlantic City is a wonderful and rewarding ride in and of itself. Routes 40 and 49 are also well-traveled South Jersey highways that connect the shore region with the Delaware Memorial Bridge. Of course, speedsters in a hurry to gamble must take the Atlantic City Expressway; but the old roads

Seashore resorts booklet (back cover) showing New Jersey coastal towns from the Pennsylvania Railroad system, 1923, printed by Edward Stern & Company.

out of Philadelphia and Camden are a great deal of fun if you can enjoy just the sense of motor touring as people did in the old days, when there was no cause to be in such a big hurry. It was one of these old roads that Thronton Wilder refers to in his play *The Long and Happy Road to Camden.* No one today thinks of the turnpike as a "happy" road, though the southern part of the Garden State Parkway is quite beautiful, particularly through the Pine Barrens. Even so, old Route 9, which almost exactly parallels the Parkway, is far more leisurely, beautiful, and interesting. The added benefit is that you may stop at roadside points of interest, farm stands, antique shops, old taverns, and eateries along the way. Old-style motels, cabins, and trailer parks can be found on these routes for a night's rest that can be more fun and intimate than one of the bigger chains. However, there are Holiday Inns, Howard Johnson motor lodges, and many other fine chains offering clean and reasonable lodging and dining. Recommended, therefore, is a sane and happier return to a slower, more enjoyable pace on a back road or an old highway.

✧　　✧　　✧

To get to the shore area via water from New York, take the ferry to Pete's Pier and the Conyers Hotel in Atlantic Highlands—call T.N.T. at (732) 872-2628 for ferry schedules leaving Pier 11 on Wall Street. Express Navigation, Inc., at (800) BOAT-RIDE, has high-speed ferries between Atlantic Highlands and Manhattan as well. By car begin your coastal adventure just South of the Edison Bridge in Sayreville with a visit to the **Peterpank Diner,** run by the original owner's son Alex Panko Jr. The Peterpank is at 967 Route 9 North, so if you are heading south, which

Lighthouse tile on bathing pavilion in Spring Lake.

you will be if you're going down to the Jersey shore, you'll have to go under the butterfly at the gigantic shopping mall in Sayreville, just down the road, and come back up. Open 24 hours a day, it's easier to get that last hot cup of Jersey java on the way home as well. Chow down on good diner food and home-baked goodies at this popular spot for truckers and shore trekkers from New York and New Jersey. Chief waitress Marilyn offers local gossip along with hash and scrambled eggs.

You can also get to the New Jersey shore by train from New York's Penn Station or Newark's Penn Station (NJ Transit's North Jersey coast line). The train stops at 10 seaside towns from Long Branch to Bay Head (the end of the line) and most beaches are only a 5- to 15-minute walk from the station. During the summer NJ Transit runs a Shore Express with bargain excursion and round-trip ticket offerings (from New Jersey call [800] 772-2222; from out of state call [973] 762-5100). Buses, of course, travel to all points. In May 1989 Amtrak began direct-rail service to Atlantic City from points along the northeast rail corridor. Round-trip fares from Philadelphia to Atlantic City are low and encourage train trippers with special deals to specified casinos. Call Amtrak for rail connections from New York, Newark, and other points at (800) USA-RAIL. A Cape May ferry to Lewes, Delaware, makes the southern Jersey shore points and the Delaware Bay (New Jersey side) easily accessible to Delaware and Maryland. The Chesapeake Bay Bridge Tunnel from Maryland to Norfolk make points from Cape May a distance from Virginia not much further than from New York City. The Cape May–Lewes Ferry has been in operation since 1964. They are 5 immaculate vessels 320 feet long, 68 feet wide, and 17 feet deep. Each ferry holds 800 passengers and 100 cars. Call 1 (800) 64-FERRY for information.

Sandy Hook Day Trip

∙∙∙

Via Keyport and Keansburg

Sandy Hook, part of the **Gateway National Recreation Area,** is a narrow barrier beach that curves out off the mainland at Atlantic Highlands. Sand beaches along the oceanfront are on one side of this seven-mile-long peninsula, once an island, at the tip of New Jersey's north shore. On the other side are the shifting marshland ecosystems of the Sandy Hook Bay. The road leads down the middle to the visitor's center, a ranger station, and the dunes and ocean. **Seagull's Nest** is a popular spot noted for its two-story cement concession stand, and entertainment is scheduled throughout the summer. **Spermaceti Cove** (named after a whale), **Horseshoe Cove,** and historic **Fort Hancock** are on the bayside. At the tip is the **Sandy Hook Lighthouse,** the oldest in the United States (1764), a US Coast Guard station and weather station. A trip to Sandy Hook may be made at any time of year; spring and fall are preferable to the strong bitter winds of winter, though some fishermen, birdwatchers, a few lone hikers, and other appropriately dressed hearty souls enjoy the bracing elements off-season. Year-round the area is home to hawks, peregrine falcons, seagulls, ducks, osprey, great horned owls, whippoorwill, and 270 more types of birds, 50 of which are considered rare. Pack a lunch, bring the family, don't forget plenty of liquids and coffee, and get there early. Sunrises and sunsets at Sandy Hook are remarkable.

Two waterfront towns, less than 40 minutes from the Holland Tunnel, between the Raritan River crossing at the Edison Bridge and Atlantic Highlands on the coast, are good beginnings or ends for a day trip to the shore. Just over the Edison Bridge or the Garden State Parkway bridges turn onto Route 36 to Keyport. The Matawan Creek enters Raritan Bay here and the estuary makes for a beautifully green and natural spot with a sweeping water-level view of Staten Island, New York City, and Long Island. Keyport is a quiet, turn-of-the-century town and at 149 West Front Street, right on the water is a landmark 1920s lunch and dinner restaurant called **Ye Cottage Inn,** (732) 264-1263, serving seafood specials and steak platters at comfortable tables and affordable prices. There is ample parking and you can stroll along the waterfront dock out to the municipal pier to catch a sea breeze and a closer view. Just across the road from Ye Cottage Inn is the **Keyport Fisheries** at 150 West Front Street, (732) 264-9723, which sells fresh seafood and probably the best deep-fried seafood sandwiches and platters to go anywhere. Try a shrimp or flounder sandwich and go sit on a bench on the dock and enjoy a little bit of gourmet heaven out in the open air. Prices here are just over $10. They're closed

on Monday and Tuesday, open the rest of the week from noon to
7 P.M. Ye Cottage Inn is open from noon to 10 P.M., Fridays and
Saturdays until 11 P.M., closed Monday. Don't forget to take a
walk into the town of Keyport, which is close to the dock; it has the
small-town charm of long ago.

Just as unique a town, but in a different and funky way, is Keansburg, a few miles east of Keyport, also on Route 36, situated on the
banks of the lower Raritan Bay. Signs along the road will direct
you into Keansburg. In the old days a steamship took passengers
from Manhattan to Keansburg for a night of fun. The 1930s movie
actress Ruby Keeler, who was married to Al Jolson, vividly recalls
her days as a chorine in Texas Guinan's club in the 1920s. "We all
piled into a boat after the New York speakeasies closed—and
sailed across moonlit waters to party away the rest of the night in
Keansburg." Sometime after World War II Keansburg became a
wild shanty town filled with raucous bars like **Nickerson's** or the
Club Miami, which are still there. Barflies, factory workers, and
ex-cons who wear rose tattoos, accompanied by their Sadie
Thompson–type broads, all intertwine here in search of a crazy
wild night or honky-tonk fun on the boardwalk. Motorcyclists and
their leather gals eat what may be the best french fries on the East
Coast. They have been dousing them with white vinegar and salt
for years from the same boardwalk vendor. The **Old Heidelburg
Inn** has been on the midway for almost 90 years; it serves an authentic red hot (a hot dog with hot red relish) with a mug of beer
or root beer, both on tap. At another concession try a cinnamon
cruller with a cup of Maxwell House coffee. There are amusement park rides, games of chance with numbered spinning
wheels, penny arcades, and an old-time merry-go-round. Keansburg has a beach on the bay for those who like a dip, and there is
a large outdoor pool for those who prefer chlorine.

Continuing on Route 36 five miles you reach the Highlands;
watch for signs that point to a road that says "scenic drive" (near
Stewart's Root Beer Drive-in). Drive up for a scenic overlook
from the highest point on the East Coast, **Mount Mitchell** on
Ocean Boulevard. This will give you a very good view of Sandy
Hook; and (on a clear day) Coney Island, New York's answer to
Keansburg.

Following this viewpoint, head back down the road to Sandy Hook
for a day of sun and fun. Sandy Hook, site of the strategic **Fort
Hancock,** was a gift from the United States Army to the public in
1962.

North Shore

Atlantic Highlands to Deal

Just opposite Sandy Hook's entranceway at the top of Jersey's north shore are the historic **Navesink Twin Lights,** which once signaled the entrance to ocean ships as they sailed into New York Bay and harbor. The view out to sea, across the harbor and down the Jersey coast, is breathtaking from this high point where the bay converges with the ocean. Visit the Twin Lights museum and climb the steps of the north tower for an even higher view. The north tower has a small blinking beacon, though it's nothing like it used to be when sailors could see its glow 70 miles out to sea. Decommissioned as a light station in 1949, Twin Lights is now maintained as a state park.

Restaurants notable for seafood right in Atlantic Highlands (just next to Sandy Hook) include **Bahrs** at 2 Bay Avenue, (732) 872-1245, and the **Clam Hut** at the foot of Atlantic Street, (732) 872-0909. Both places serve moderately priced seafood dinners and lunches, and have lobster specials. Gourmet seafood preparations at a higher price are superb at **Doris and Ed's** at 36 Shore Drive, (732) 872-1565. If you are looking for something other than seafood try the **Hofbrauhaus** at 301 Ocean Boulevard, (732) 291-0224, for German food. Ocean Boulevard is also called "scenic drive" and just across the road from this restaurant is a spectacular view of the ocean, bay, and surrounding areas. Specials here are the best of German meats and sausages, including *kloster Weiss-beir,* jaeger schnitzel, Wiener schnitzel, Kassler rippchen (smoked pork chops), sauerbraten with potato dumpling, and German pot roast with potato pancakes. A Hofbrau special including pork chop, knockwurst, bratwurst, sauerkraut, and German potato salad is also offered. On Friday and Saturday nights and Sunday afternoons during Oktoberfest (the end of September running into the middle of November every year) there are authentic German bands and Bavarian dancers. Highway 36 continues south from the Highlands right alongside the Atlantic Ocean. As you drive along you can hear the pounding of waves against the man-made rock seawall. There are points at which you may want to stop and climb up the wooden stairways to the top of the rocks to look at the ocean and breathe the fresh salt air. The town of Sea Bright has a small public beach, restaurants, and shops.

Turn inland at this point for a side trip (take the Sea Bright–Rumson Bridge, Route 520) through swanky Rumson to Red Bank, a town long frequented by antique dealers and enthusiasts. Red Bank is easily accessible on Route 35 (exit 109 off the Parkway). The town was established in 1870 and is set on the Navesink

River, bordered by the towns of Shrewsbury and Little Silver. There are lovely parks, like Marine Park at the foot of Wharf Avenue on the Navesink River, old Victorian homes, and a first-rate hotel-restaurant, the **Molly Pitcher Inn,** (732) 747-2500, which is right on the river. You can also dine on the Navesink at the **Olde Union House** (since 1791), which serves American fare at reasonable prices; it was rated three stars by the *New York Times*. The number is (732) 842-7575. You can find anything in antiques at the **Red Bank Antiques Centers** at 195 and 226 West Front Street. There are four buildings housing over 200 permanent dealers in indoor booths. Call (800) 479-4621 for further antique center information. Back at the shore, Monmouth Beach, just below Sea Bright, with its big rock formations and yellow sand is a good "stop point" for a refreshing dip in the ocean. You should have your swimsuits on underneath your casual summer attire however, as facilities for changing are not provided.

Long Branch is the point on the North Jersey shore that opens up to the vast expanse of the sea (exit 105 on the Garden State Parkway or continue to follow Route 36 south). The seaside town of Long Branch, once famous for its fishing pier and amusement area, which collapsed in a fire a few years ago, is still known far and wide for great Italian food. One of the best spots for pizza in New Jersey is **Freddie's Pizza** at 563 Broadway, (732) 222-0931, featuring a small personal pizza for $3.18 up to $8.11 for the 16-inch plain. This is an attractive restaurant with a beautiful Pizzaman neon sign in the front. Johnny Scialla is the host. Another charming small restaurant for ziti and ravioli, served piping hot and freshly made, is **Nunzio's** at 230 Westwood Avenue, (732) 222-9798, located in a glass brick-and-neonized building near the railroad station. The pizza pies here are also first rate. The prices at Nunzio's are not the only attraction; the food is very tasty and is prepared by the Nunzio family with care and in an authentic old-world style. Don't let the plain decor fool you, this is no-nonsense Italian food at its best. Right next door to Nunzio's is **Tuzzio's,** a fancier restaurant with a full bar at 224 Westwood Avenue (732) 222-9614. Prices here are more than reasonable, and well worth the price. Meat entrees (all served with salad and pasta) are the specialty and they have veal and peppers, calamari, and shrimp marinara served hot and sweet. Since everything is cooked to order you must allow about one half hour over a drink. All the Long Branch restaurants are family owned and operated. The food is served with love and care; and a trip to Long Branch at anytime — even just for dinner — is highly recommended.

A site to see in West Long Branch is the **Monmouth College** campus clustered around the graceful old French-style 130-room mansions, which was the setting for the movie *Annie*. It originally contained a theater, a chapel, and gold-plated fixtures. The man-

California Mission-style mansion on Ocean Drive in Deal, which has some of the most beautiful homes to be found in New Jersey.

sion is now named **Woodrow Wilson Hall** to commemorate the period in which it served as a summer White House. The **Guggenheim Memorial Library** at Westwood and Norwood Avenues was the Guggenheims' 35-room mansion. This manse, with its high ornate iron fences and luxurious gardens, was later given as a gift to the college.

The five-mile Ocean Avenue drive along the shore from Long Branch through Deal and Allenhurst is a wonderfully scenic car tour of the old Georgian and Mission-style mansions of these two classy resort towns. There is minimum access to the beach in this area since most of the homes are right on the ocean.

Monmouth County Side Trips

Other things to see and do in the Monmouth County area include the **Monmouth Battleground State Park** at Route 33 and Wemrock Road in Manalapan Township. This is where Molly Pitcher struck a blow for freedom and ultimately for the cause of women's liberation in a pivotal 1778 Revolutionary battle. The 1500-acre park has walking trails, two picnic areas, and a playground. Hours are 8 A.M. to 8 P.M. **Owl Haven** at Route 522 in Manalapan Township is a park maintained by the New Jersey Audubon Society, where you can hold a live owl on your arm. Other than these big-eyed birds that eat live mice and other rodents, there are snakes, turtles, and other special wildlife-related exhibits to be seen. Open Tuesday through Sunday from 1:30 to 4:30 P.M. **Longstreet Farm** in Holmdel Park is a working New Jersey farm near the shore area that still uses farm equipment of the 1800s. It is maintained by the Monmouth County Park System. The farm's hours are 9 A.M. to 3:30 P.M. daily. The **Garden State Arts Center** at Holmdel, located right on the Garden State Parkway (exit 116) just one hour away from New York and one hour away from Philadelphia, is a futuristically designed 9,000-seat outdoor amphitheater in which you can buy a ticket to see classical or pop concerts, musicals, operas, dance events, and ethnic folk festivals. The likes of Bob Dylan, Bon Jovi, and Liza Minnelli attract record crowds. The **Monmouth Park Racetrack** is at Oceanport Avenue in Oceanport just off Route 36 (Parkway exit 16). For more information call (732) 222-5100.

A favorite outdoor antique flea market in Monmouth County in the Tinton Falls area on Route 34 and Route 33 (exit 100A, Parkway) and just beyond the US Naval Weapons Station Earle (often itself the scene of weapons protestors) is the **Collingwood Auction** (732) 938-7941. Here you will find old and new mixed together at outdoor stalls. A large indoor market features bargains galore in clothing, homemade pickles, homemade Polish bologna, bread counters, a spice shop, a pet store (with puppies and kittens for sale), hardware shops, a bookshop, a vintage magazine and comic book dealer, canned goods, vacuum cleaner attachments, a vinyl upholsterer, plaster statuettes, *junque*, endless whatnot stalls, and several small restaurants specializing in good home cooking. One outdoor area is devoted to local farm produce. Jersey tomatoes, red or yellow, and Jersey sweet corn, white or yellow, are the order of the day in the summer months. Peaches, apples, and the Jersey eggs sold here are the freshest and best. The indoor market is open Friday from noon until 10 P.M. and all day Saturday, 10 A.M. to 10 P.M. and Sunday from 10 A.M. to 7 P.M.

The **Delicious Apple Orchards** store on Route 34 in Colts Neck sells its own sweet apple cider by the cup, half gallon, and gallon. The homegrown apples are also used in fresh doughnuts, home-style pies, and cakes. Delicious Orchards sells farm produce (New Jersey summer produce, autumn squash, and select winter shipments), fancy cheeses, hickory-smoked bacon, home-baked breads, specially packaged homemade cookies (buttercrunch, chocolate chip, and oatmeal raisin), Vermont maple syrup, sugar candy, and other fine culinary items. It is certainly worth a stop along the road; and picnic tables are provided for your doughnut-and-cider repast or to eat the lunch you packed at home. If not, you can pick up whatever you need at Delicious Orchards, and you can be sure it is better quality than what you will buy at a highway supermarket.

The granddaddy flea market of them all is **Englishtown Auction Market** on Route 527 (Old Bridge Road) five miles south of Route 18, a tradition since 1929. Englishtown is one of the first flea markets that originated out of the country farm market in the early 1950s. There are buildings housing produce, dealers in canned and dry goods and butchers, bakers, and candlestick makers. You can buy fresh fish, cheese and dairy products, and goats and live chickens, turkeys, and rabbits. In recent years the merchandise at the outdoor market has tended toward the new, and it is harder than ever to find a treasure there now, prompting most people to bring out their flashlights and get there before dawn. It is an important market, attracting up to 10,000 people at the height of the season, and worth the long trudge from the parking lot to the dealer sections, which themselves spread out over vast acres of land.

Freehold is horse country and the **Freehold Raceway** offer this best in harness racing—trotters and pacers. There is dining in the track's clubhouse, located at Route 9 and Route 33 in Freehold; (732) 462-3800.

Open April through Thanksgiving is the renowned **Wall Township "Demo Derby"** on Route 34 (Garden State Parkway exit 98, or exit 35B off I-95) that also hosts sporting events and concerts. Call (732) 681-6400. Also in this area is the **Allaire State Park,** boasting a restored Revolutionary bog iron community, the Pine Creek Railroad (for a short steam ride), picnicking, campsites, riding trails, walking, bicycling, a nature center, and playgrounds. Allaire also hosts many fine antique and crafts markets throughout the spring, summer, and fall. Route 547 at Farmingdale; (732) 938-2371. Call for special events and a seasonal schedule.

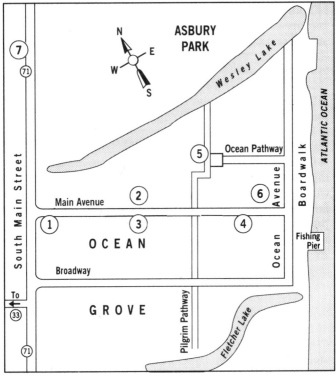

1. Main Entrance
2. Gifts by Tina
3. The Kitch and Kaboodle
4. Sampler Inn
5. The Great Auditorium
6. The Amherst Hotel
7. Ocean Grove/Asbury Park Railroad Station

B y the Belle of The Amherst, Madeline Hoffer, Ocean Grove poet:

Telling the Ocean Slant

A sandpiper pipes her scales of loss,
The crab persists, clutches a piece of her mate
Returns to the sea.

But the sun still rises—
A peach parrot with teal tail
Weightless against the gravity of the sky.

Remind me—a beach tilted sideways
Will always be a waterfall.

Ocean Grove is a very easy day trip to take in spring, summer, and fall, and up through the Christmas season when there are special events and pageants. It is no more than an hour from Manhattan by car and NJ Transit's north shore line leaves Penn Station at reasonable intervals; there are late-night train returns as well. Exit 100A off the Garden State Parkway onto Route 33 East through Neptune and onto Route 71 leads you to the majestic town gates of Ocean Grove, and the moment you enter Main Avenue, the main thoroughfare, you are transported to yesteryear.

This is a truly old-fashioned magical place that almost feels out of another century. Founded by the Methodists as a camp meeting resort in 1869, Ocean Grove is an architectural treasure of Victorian and American Picturesque-style seaside hotels, homes, cottages, gazebos, open bandstands, and other turn-of-the-century buildings, which are still standing intact as a testimony to the function and beauty of things past that continue to serve us well in the present. The boardwalk and ocean are at the end of all east-west streets, and the bathing beaches are immaculate. The huge **Great Auditorium** is used for various religious services and meetings, and also attracts special pulpit speakers such as Dale Evans. Summer entertainment appearing at the auditorium might include gospel singing groups, the Lettermen, the Ferko String Band, Pat Boone, Lou Christie, Lesley Gore, and Little Anthony. In previous years the Fred Waring Orchestra and Glee Club were a popular attraction.

The grove was thought of as a tonic for those in need of both physical and spiritual recovery, and even today attracts many who retire there to live out their last years near the ocean, breathing in the salt air. Of late many more cosmopolitan people have come to Ocean Grove in search of a relaxing time. The Great Auditorium is a Victorian wooden structure that was 100 years old in 1994. It has an 18-foot neon cross on the outside, a huge electric-light bulb American flag inside, 7,000 seats, plus one of the largest pipe organs on the eastern seaboard. Surrounding this auditorium are 114 summer tent houses. This is not a typical tent community,

Ocean Grove tent houses.

Vintage cars abound on the streets of Victorian Ocean Grove.

with outside latrines, kerosene lamps, and outdoor campfires. Instead, the tents fit onto permanent wooden structures that give the occupants 336 square feet with open porches and flower gardens filled with zinnia, black-eyed Susan, and petunia. When lit by electric light at night these big-sized canvas house tents with striped tops are a restful sight to behold. Tent houses have been in existence in Ocean Grove for over 115 years. The many Victorian hotels on Pilgrim's Pathway and Lake Avenue, with their gingerbread finials, fretwork, cupola, transoms, turrets, and tracery have spring and autumn rooms for rent at off-season rates. The town center on Main Avenue is filled with quaint Victorian-style shops. At **Kitch & Kaboodle,** 76 Main Avenue, (732) 869-0950, chenille bedspreads, floral and geographic-print tablecloths, linens and doilies, kitchen chatchkas, dinnerware from the forties and fifties, and other homey oddball usables abound in this fun-filled kitschy store run by Beth Miller. Across from "The Kitch" stop at **Gifts by Tina,** 73 Main Avenue, (732) 774-0457 owned by Tina Skokos, who specializes in jewelry. Art Deco lovers should walk over the bridge to 718 Cookman Avenue in Asbury Park to **Of Rare Vintage,** whose proprietors, Bill Meisch and Michael Rispoli, always carry a full range of furniture, accessories, radios, decorative items, and collectibles. As their prices are reasonable, several big-city Art Deco stores stock up here. Call (732) 988-9459. Don't forget to look at the Victorian skyline of Ocean Grove as you return from your Asbury walk. Many of the hotels have large airy open-to-the-public restaurants that serve full course American home-cooked meals for a nominal amount. The **Sampler Inn** (established in 1917) is such a self-serve cafeteria in the **Sampler Hotel** at 28 Main Avenue, serving home-style cooking that attracts residents, not just from Ocean Grove, but the surrounding area.

※　　※　　※

Called "God's square mile of health and happiness," Ocean Grove's hotels and white-sand ocean beaches welcome anyone of any denomination to its healthful, old-fashioned, and serene environment. Ocean Grove was designated landmark status by the New Jersey Register of Historic Places, and is also a National Historic Monument. It is in Neptune Township, and it can be seen as the setting for Woody Allen's film *Stardust Memories*. In fact, Woody Allen repaired the neon cross on the auditorium, which had not been working, as a gift to the town.

If you want to spend a weekend or longer in Ocean Grove, the following is a list of recommended hotels to call for reservations. The Ocean Grove Chamber of Commerce, (732) 774-1391, will send you a list of others with brochures.

The Cordova 26 Webb Avenue (732) 774-3084 or (212) 751-9577

Park View Hotel 23 Seaview, (732) 775-1645

Ocean Plaza 18 Ocean Pathway, (732) 774-6552

The Pine Tree Inn 10 Main Avenue, (732) 775-3264

The Amherst 14 Pittman Avenue, (732) 988-5297

The House By The Sea 14 Ocean Avenue, (732) 775-2847

North Shore

··

Asbury Park to Bay Head

The famous resort town of Asbury Park, just north of Ocean Grove across Wesley Lake, is now in the process of development and revitalization. Though many things are changing, the beautiful parks that gave the town its name are still there. The restored **Convention Hall** and **Paramount Theater** on the boardwalk are active. The **Stone Pony** (on Ocean Avenue and 2nd Street) is featuring rock groups that promote the Asbury Sound, like Bruce Springsteen, a Jersey boy who began his illustrious career here. Bruce's album *Greetings from Asbury Park* and his follow-up albums were inspired by the tough, gritty, leather-jacket lifestyle that has been so much a part of this honky-tonk seaside town. Springsteen drops in (with Bobby Bandiera of Southside Johnny) to sing and play guitar at the Stone Pony and at **Rum**

Antique saltwater taffy box from the Criterion Tea Shoppe and Restaurant. Criterion Candies are gone, but the spectacular 1950s Howard Johnson still serves up good grub on the boardwalk in Asbury Park.

Greetings from Asbury Park, New Jersey, picture postcard.

Palace funhouse in Asbury Park.

Runners in Sea Bright. National label bands play at the Stone Pony and Rum Runners at the **Brighton Bar** in Long Branch. Live rock and new alternative music and dance music—including some punk—(like the Nerds)—is heard all over New Jersey. Two other places in Asbury: **T-Birds Cafe,** 707 Main Street, which has an acoustic unplugged venue, and **Fast Lane II** at 4th and Kingsley, a rock concert bar. The place to stay in Asbury Park is the attractive and recently renovated Art Deco **Berkeley Carteret Hotel,** a landmark built in 1925, at 1401 Ocean Avenue, (732) 776-6700. Danny DeVito likes to eat at the **Adriatic,** and Nat Lane's **Fishermen's Pier** draws seafood lovers in. Nightlife in Asbury can often be raucus and rip-roaring—the place to be on Friday and Saturday nights is **Down The Street** on Cookman, with its four bars, disco dance floor, outdoor terraces, clubhouse, and volleyball beach. Compared to Ocean Grove, which is a dry town, Asbury Park is filled with bars. If you take one of the old pedestrian bridges across the Wesley Lake from Ocean Grove, it's as if you entered into some kind of pleasure island. If you are looking for char-

Though Bruce Springsteen sang in other Asbury Park clubs, it is the Stone Pony where the great New Jersey rock-and-roll singer first gained recognition and a following of fans that remain faithful to "the Boss" to this day.

A fantasy seahorse detail from Convention Hall on the boardwalk in Asbury Park (top). The bottom photo shows the old carousel building in Asbury Park.

acters, you will see them in Asbury Park, which was once seen as a smaller version of Atlantic City in its more elegant days.

The following restaurants are a short drive from Ocean Grove and Asbury Park, and are good places to eat after a day of sun and fun. **Mom's Kitchen** is the place for dinner in Neptune, 1129 5th Avenue, (732) 775-4823 and is one of local son Jack Nicholson's favorite hangouts. There are pictures of the actor, who grew up in Neptune, with John and Anjelica Huston on the wall. Mom's pasta dishes are out of this world, the saltimbocca and calamari are delicious, the pizzas excellent, and the atmosphere friendly and upbeat. Booths and tables are in a spacious pine-walled dining room and there is a comfortable bar. They're open every day except Tuesday from noon to 10 P.M., 11 P.M. on weekends. **Pete and Elda's Tavern and Carmen's Pizzeria** is another *must* in this area. Operating together as one establishment, it is located on Highway 35 in Neptune City; (732) 774-6010. The hours are 11:30 A.M. until 2 A.M. for drinks; with dinner served until 1:15 A.M. Here the pizza is cracker-thin and melts in your mouth. Pasta dishes are very good, and it is not unusual to have dinner for two at this friendly tavern (since 1954) for under $20. Also on Route 35, farther south in Wall Township, is **The Circus,** a roadside drive-in restaurant that is built to resemble a circus tent. The carnival at-

Born in New Jersey, USA, in Freehold, Bruce Springsteen found fame singing in Asbury Park. Many of the songs he sings are ballads about the ordinary life of workers and bikers in Bruce's home state.

mosphere here is as much fun as a barrelful of monkeys, and it's a great place for families and children. There are specials for kids under 12, like a hamburger, an ice cream cone, and a soda for $2.99. Other than tasty hamburgers and charcoal hot dogs there are shrimp dishes, soft-shell crabs, and barbecue meats, some with names like "wild animal special" (½ pound of ground beef on a hard roll) or "the juggler" (a grilled cheese and tomato sandwich), and "the fire-eater" (hot chili). There are sundaes, malteds, and combos of all kinds for kids and adults. This sideshow of a drive-in is a perfect place for a birthday party or special celebration—call (732) 449-2650—or just drive in. The Circus has been here since the mid-1950s.

Due West out of Asbury Park on the "Circle" at Routes 33 and 34 in Wall Township is the **Roadside Diner,** which will transport you to yet another twilight zone. The '50s jukebox plays only 1950s 45s of Buddy Holly, Elvis, or the Big Bopper. The waitresses wear 1950s "new look" outfits with poodles and rhinestones appliquéd onto their skirts, and wear their hair in ponytails. The bright clean walls are covered with nostalgic icons of that decade, including Coke signs and photos of vintage cars and James Dean. You don't need a reservation here and the food runs from deluxe sandwiches to blue plate specials such as meat loaf and mashed potatoes. The "in" colors to wear on a date are pink-and-black—and if you drive a pink convertible (circa 1955) park it right in front. If you want to stick close to shore, head on over to **Klein's Waterside Cafe,** 708 River Road in Belmar, (732) 681-1177, for grilled fish, steamed lobsters, clambakes, and fried shrimp outdoors on the shore of the

Shark River, between two highway bridges. For affordable outfits for diner visits stop at Pat Tecza's **Nostalgic Nonsense,** 903 Main Street, (732) 681-8810 in Belmar. Pat, Rosalita, or Ken will help you look like Sandra Dee, Connie Francis, Fabian, or Elvis with dressy and casual dresses, separates, "unisex" men's jackets, and a full line of accessories.

As you drive south on Highway 71 from Ocean Grove to Bradley Beach to Avon-by-the-Sea to Belmar, you will note that each town is separated by lakes, rivers, and parklands. A major inlet to the ocean is at Belmar on the Shark River. A good geographic point for boat watching, it attracts fishermen year-round. Driving along the oceanfront south from the youthquake Fort Lauderdale–style playground beach town of Belmar you pass through a gateway structure just over Lake Como that serves as the entranceway to the resort town of luxurious and very upper-crust Irish Spring Lake. The **Boardwalk Pavilion** and **Municipal Pool,** decorated with 1920s art deco tiles depicting fish and wading birds, is one of the architectural high points here, as well as the lovely two miles of beaches, with their white sand and black rocks, and the gracious boardwalk that proudly contains no amusements or rides in favor of spatial elegance.

Spring Lake has a beautiful lake next to its small but charming old-style downtown shopping center. The park and the lake are surrounded by tall, beautiful shade trees, shrubbery, pine groves, winding gravel paths, rustic wooden bridges, and contain indoor tennis courts. By the lake you can feed the many ducks and swans. Spring Lake is a wonderful blend of country, town, and shore, which make it a truly special place in which the traveler can es-

1920s advertising fan for early real estate development of Shark River Hills near Belmar on the Shark River Inlet.

cape the hurly-burly of congested city living. In fact, in the film *The Subject Was Roses* (1968), starring Jack Albertson, Martin Sheen, and Patricia Neal, it is Spring Lake that Patricia Neal goes to by bus to escape her dingy New York flat, her loudmouth drinking, unfaithful husband, and her unfeeling son, who has just returned from World War II. In Spring Lake, the sad and tragic woman finds a sense of peace and serenity, if only for a few hours, walking along the beach and dining in an elegant hotel restaurant. Outstanding here is the **Warren Hotel** (circa 1890), a

The grand Essex and Sussex, once one of New Jersey's finest seashore hotels, in Spring Lake.

huge Victorian building at 901 Ocean Avenue, (732) 449-8800. It has 200 rooms, a private ocean beach, a pool, tennis courts, as well as a putting green. Breakfasting is open to the public from 8 to 9:30 A.M. and dinner in the Audubon Room from 6:30 to 8:30 P.M., with jacket required for gentlemen. There are many fine places to stay in and around Spring Lake, from the grand to the humble. A good time can be had at Annette Bergins bed-and-breakfast **Down the Shore** at 201 Seventh Avenue in Belmar, (732) 681-9023. Write for a list to: The Greater Spring Lake Chamber of Commerce, 1315 Third Avenue, Spring Lake, NJ 07762, or call (732) 449-0577. There are also summer rentals of individual houses in the area. Try contacting the MacGowan Agency (732) 449-9400—a local realtor—in March or April to see what kind of listings they have. You could start in December at the **Spring Lake Christmas Bed and Breakfast Tour.** This is an annual event featuring a tour of gaily decorated and beautifully appointed Victorian inns, usually followed by a festive holiday tea. Call the Chamber of Commerce for the exact date.

One restaurant on the beachfront in Spring Lake just in front of the Warren Hotel is the **Beach House**, (732) 449-9646, a Victorian-style house with screened-in porches that serves excellent dinners in a relaxed and pleasant atmosphere. There is a buzz of friendly activity at the Beach House that will make you feel right in the center of things and right at home at the same time. You can order cocktails at a bar while waiting for your seats, and the bar has a view of the ocean. The lunch menu includes sandwiches, quiche with soup or salad, a shrimp salad platter, five-ounce charbroiled burgers and franks, gazpacho, and clam chowder. Dinners of chicken marsala, shrimp Capri, broiled filet of sole, twelve-ounce charbroiled sirloin steak, Beach House shrimp, fettuccine Alfredo, seafood Newburgh; all entrees include vegetable du jour, salad and potato or rice. Dessert is available and chocolate mousse Grand Marnier is recommended.

The Beach House Restaurant and the Tudor-style Warren Hotel on Ocean Avenue in Spring Lake.

From Spring Lake driving south you will pass through the small seashore communities of Sea Girt, Manasquan, and Brielle, which is known as a commercial fisherman's town. Brielle is at the mouth of the Manasquan Inlet, and you can buy bluefish, striped bass, tuna, fluke, kingfish, big bull stripers, snappers, and other fish at well below market cost directly from the fishermen at the Brielle landing just off Route 34 (under the bridge). At 503 Route 71 in Brielle be sure to stop at **Escargot Books,** run by Richard Weiner, a lawyer who has extended his interest in books into this pleasant store stocked with antiquarian and novelty collectible readables like early paperbacks, first editions, comic books, post-cards, and early sheet music and magazines. Call (732) 528-5955.

In Manasquan try the **Carriage House Antique Center** at 140 Main street, (732) 528-6772. Residents of Manasquan and the sur-rounding towns all know about the gourmet food at **Squan Tav-ern,** 15 Broad Street, (732) 223-3324; it is served up every night but Monday. Dominic and Marguerite Bossone started the restau-rant in 1964, and with the help of Dom III, Joe, Ro, Trish, and Mike, all members of the family, have turned the place into a leg-end. The pizza is good, salads and antipastos are carefully pre-pared, pastas and entrees are superb, and the wine list includes everything from a glass of Chablis for $2 to a $65 Brunello di Montalcino Riserva from Italy. The pinewood paneling on the walls and the neon lighting create an intimate setting for dining and bar drinking here.

Crossing the Manasquan River over a drawbridge south of Brielle you will enter Point Pleasant Beach and the township of Point Pleasant. This is where Agnes Boulton and playwright Eugene O'Neill had a house together; and the place where Sean O'Neill and Oona O'Neill Chaplin played as children. Agnes Boulton continued to reside year-round in the old house in old Point

Pleasant until her death. Point Pleasant is an inviting summer resort lying along the coast on the peninsula between Manasquan
Inlet and the Metedeconk River at the head of Barnegat Bay. The
road along the inlet toward the beach (first turn over the bridge
onto Broadway) is lined with motels and eateries.

Recommended for seafood is **Spike's Fish Market and Restaurant** at 415 Broadway, (732) 295-9400; and **Peter Skoko's Drive-In**
at the end of Broadway, (732) 892-3420, for delicious chargrilled
hot dogs, hamburgers, and clam chowder. The **Broadway Bar**,
across the road, is good for a quick beer and a submarine before
boarding a fisherman's boat at **Ken's Landing** for a day of sea fishing or a night of moonlight cruising. In season call (732) 528-6620
or 892-3377 to reserve a spot on the *River Belle*, a 140-passenger
replica of a Mississippi River paddleboat, which cruises the Manasquan River and Barnegat Bay on a variety of daylight and
evening cruises. There is a two-hour Sunday brunch cruise with
an all-you-can-eat brunch as well as hour-and-a-half and two-hour-
and-a-half cruises with lunch, Monday through Friday. The *River
Belle* is moored at the inlet on Broadway in Point Pleasant Beach
where you can book yourself for ocean voyages as well. The boardwalk amusements in Point Pleasant mainly consist of the kiddie
type; Jenkinson's maintains a fun train ride on the sand from the
Inlet to **Jenkinson's South Amusement Park** (732) 892-3274.

Point Pleasant has a number of very good, unpretentious Italian
restaurants—one of the best is **Tesauro's** at 401 Broadway. John
and Audrey Tesauro offer pizza appetizers—their specialty the
classic Trenton "tomato pie" for $3.95 for two. Famous seafood
specialties include "flounder formaggio," which is a fresh filet
baked in a Dijon cheese sauce with mozzarella, $12.95, and
"Tesauro's 'famous' scampi," $15.95. Their telephone number is
(732) 892-2090.

Point Pleasant Beach is the point that separates the northern shore
from the beginnings of the southern shore. The ocean seems to
change here, the water is clearer and it is also more turbulent. In
fact, New Jersey historian John Cunningham writes about what is
called among experienced men of the sea "the treacherous shoals
of Barnegat," which pounded ships to pieces, flinging their cargos

*The Ocean Bay Diner on Route 35 and Route 88 on the circle in Point Pleasant as
it used to be.*

Point Pleasant Beach souvenir postcard folder.

and the dead and dying sailors and passengers onto the sands. He described how ships destroyed by the moody ocean littered the beaches in the old days. The coast he referred to stretched from Point Pleasant to Little Egg Harbor, an ocean area that merited the reputation as the most dreaded and feared shoals north of Hatteras.

The small downtown area of Point Pleasant is now noted for its many interesting antique shops. The **Point Pleasant Antique Emporium,** which is housed in what used to be a furniture showroom, has three floors and 100 dealers under its roof. Many fine antiques from yesteryear are to be discovered here from among the individual little shops that create an antique "department-store" ambience. Open seven days a week, the emporium is at Bay and Trenton Avenues, and the hours are 11 A.M. to 5 P.M. Call (732) 892-2222. Check out shops like **Pomegranate** for antiques, jewelry, flowers, and cards at 707 Arnold Avenue, Point Pleasant Beach's old-fashioned "main street."

After you pass through Point Pleasant, keep to the shoreline on Highway 35. The road narrows down to two lanes when you hit Bay Head, the end of the line of the NJ Transit North Shore Railroad. The beach is only a few blocks from the tiny railroad depot. Bay Head is the beginning point of Barnegat Bay and the first seashore town on the peninsula that eventually ends at Island Beach State park. From Bay Head on the Metedeconk River all the way south to Beach Haven where Little Egg Harbor joins the Great Bay and opens onto the Atlantic, the expansive stretch of water that comprises Barnegat Bay, filled with blue crabs, turtles, mollusk-horseshoe crabs, clams and fish, varies in width from 3 to 6 miles and extends itself alongside almost 50 miles of barrier beach with the ocean on one side and the swampy, marshy borders of the mainland on the other. Extending for almost one third of the entire Jersey coast, it resembles in many ways the protected bays along the eastern coast of Florida. The big Barnegat Bay offers many unexcelled facilities for motor-boating, sailing, rowing, swimming, fishing, and crabbing. Many varieties of wildfowl and bay birds are to be found in the salt marshes along the fresh streams of the mainland. It is at Bay Head that vacationers may begin to enjoy the advantage of the attractions of the Atlantic Ocean and the delights of the wide waters, tides, and bay breezes.

The beach at Bay Head is one of the best on the coast with black-rock jetties creating interesting deep-water pockets for swimming. The beautiful old oceanfront homes are right on the beach. Initially the 1.25-mile stretch of beach was open only to residents and their guests and those visitors who stayed at the old hotels or rooming houses. Now nonresidents can buy day beach privileges although you must already be dressed for the beach since there is no bathhouse in which to change clothes. Bay Head was a resort as early as the 16th century, when it was used as such by the Lenape Indians, who were later referred to as the Delawares by early white settlers. Seashore land and improvement companies began here in 1879; and Bay Head truly opened up to visitors in 1882 when the railroad arrived. The town of Bay Head is architecturally pure New England–Cape Cod with a bit of Victorian Rococo thrown in for good measure. Bridge Avenue at Bay Avenue is the main shopping area that contains the Victorian-style **Dorca's Ice Cream Parlor and Restaurant,** a cheese shop, an antique emporium set on a wharf, a German bakery, a bookshop, a liquor store, a delicatessen, and a few smart clothing shops.

Lodgings in Bay Head include: The **Bay Head Sands** bed-and-breakfast, open from April through November at Main Avenue and Twilight Road, (732) 899-7016; **Conover's Bay Head Inn** bed-and-breakfast at 646 Maine Avenue, (732) 892-4664; and the lovely old **Hotel Grenville,** 345 Main Avenue, which offers a complimentary continental breakfast, (732) 892-9883.

Seaside Heights Day Trip

••

How to get there: Take the pleasant drive down the peninsula between Barnegat Bay and the Atlantic Ocean to Seaside Heights. Starting at Bay Head, Highway 35 is a two-lane road until it widens south of Mantoloking, the latter sometimes called "millionaire's row" because of the huge summer mansions along the beachfront and bayside. Katharine Hepburn, Mary Roebling (Roebling Steel), and Richard Nixon have all summered here. Continue driving south from Mantoloking, passing through many small beach communities like Normandy Beach, Lavalette, and Ocean Beach until you hit Seaside Heights. If you use the Garden State Parkway, exit at 82 onto Route 37, which takes you directly into Seaside. If you are coming from Philadelphia or western New Jersey, hook up with Highway 70 East that will lead you into Route 37 West at the US Naval Air Station at Lakehurst.

For a great day trip, a day at the beach, good food, and an exciting time, bring your date or the whole family to Seaside Heights, definitely Funtown USA, New Jersey-style. Its expansive mile-long boardwalk and a lengthy pier that stretches out over the ocean are jam-packed with the latest fantastic rides like the Himalaya, Bobsled, the Wild Mouse, or the Zipper. There is a beautiful Dentzel/Looff carousel at the north end of the boardwalk of the classic variety, and it is the best to be seen and ridden anywhere. Dr. Floyd Moreland, a classics professor and dean at City University in New York, was instrumental in saving the carousel from destruction, and now devotes much of his time operating and

Seaside Heights Greetings, published by Parlin Photo Service.

The Casino merry-go-round with its beautifully carved horses at Seaside Heights.

restoring it. The music is provided by the only continuously operating Wurlitzer Military Band Organ, built in 1923. It plays with a
pneumatic system generated by leather bellows, and the notes are
activated by perforated music rolls, like a player piano. The horses
and other animals, many dating from the 1880s, and the snare and
bass drums, the cymbals, the handmade wooden organ pipes and
the 16 bell bars on the glockenspiel combine to transport you to
another less-stressful century. Dr. Moreland operates a gift shop
featuring carousel miniatures and music boxes; the carousel operates daily during the summer from 10 A.M. to midnight. Weekends
and holidays it's open all year-round from noon to early evening.
Games of chance with their spinning wheels continue to be a
main attraction on this wooden walkway right next to the Atlantic.
Here you can win stuffed panda bears, tigers, even sharks and
snakes; and you could go home with a basket filled with canned
groceries and boxed products, a turkey, a television set, or a carton
of factory-fresh cigarettes. From sweaters to the latest in T-shirts to
Popeye the Sailor and Mickey Mouse, you will find it all on the
Seaside Heights boardwalk. It's a veritable feast of Italian sausage
or meatball sandwiches, corn on the cob, clams on the half-shell,
and pizza. In fact, the pizza pies (or tomato pies as some of these
establishments still like to call them) are in themselves a reason for
stopping by this glittering amusement area. Actually, the very best
pizza to be found in New Jersey or anywhere for that matter is
right here at **Maruca's Pizza.** Maruca's on the boardwalk will not
reveal the treasured secret of their family recipe, but it is guaran-
teed to literally melt in your mouth and delight your taste buds.
Connoisseurs of good pizza—take heed—you will not want to
miss one of these hot-out-of-the-oven pies served up by the
Maruca twins, Joseph P. and Domenic A., or their sister Maria.

The Maruca twins, Dom (left) and Joe (right), showing off the best pizza pies on the Jersey coast, at Maruca's Pizza on the Seaside Heights boardwalk.

Maruca's emanated out of Trenton in 1947 where the family had a pizza parlor restaurant for many years, but since 1950 they only operate on the boardwalk. There are sit-down stools and booths with very friendly waitresses to accommodate larger groups and families. Pennsylvania Dutch root beer, coffee, or other drinks accompany your mouth-watering slice or whole pie (with or without extras). The Maruca clan satisfies hungry travelers at **Maruca's Tomato Pies West,** at 751 Route 37 West, (732) 473-9190, and **Maruca's Tomato Pies East** at 2206 Route 37 East, (732) 288-0033, with special Italian dinners with fresh salads and garlic bread, pastas, the famed Maruca pizza, and everything else to eat in and to go.

One old-time bar that is a really good-time hangout (and has been for years) is **Klee's Bar** on Dupont Avenue and the Boulevard. A mix of singles, regulars, and local characters, it is worth the trip to come there whether in summer or winter for the entertainment, which is a hodgepodge of country-western and true-blue American. The atmosphere is old-fashioned and the knotty pine walls and neon beer signs give this place a special warm glow. The thin-crusted pizza is very good and the tap beer is ice cold. Mussels, deli sandwiches, and basket foods (chicken, fried mushrooms, etc.) are served until 1:30 A.M., when the kitchen closes. The bar stays open late and you will have a helluva lot of fun. Tropical drinks are a specialty, but Rolling Rock beer seems the most popular brew. Ireland-brand coffee is served up on the fishing pier (same as the amusement pier) in a little shack perched right on the edge and looking out over the breaking waves of the ocean. Accompanied by a bag of Oreo cookies or caramel popcorn from

Klee's Bar beer coaster (left).
Klee's Bar on Boulevard and Dupont serves excellent pizza and New Jersey's favorite Rolling Rock beer.

Johnson's on the boardwalk, the coffee often hits the spot after playing the pinball games at the **Central Arcade** on the boardwalk at Hamilton Avenue. This arcade, one of several in Seaside, is run by a handsome, enterprising man named Gary Phillips, who bears a striking resemblance to the movie actor George Montgomery when he played a carney barker who tames a honky-tonk singer played by Betty Grable in the 20th Century–Fox 1940s techni-color film *Coney Island*. Gary loves the amusement parlor busi-ness, and will eagerly tell you about another one he owns in Beach Haven at the tip of Long Beach Island. He calls this new complex **Fantasy Island Amusement Park.** Gary also collects antique amusement park games, fortune machines, pinball machines, and early Wurlitzer jukeboxes that he lovingly restores. Some of these are on display for all to see and enjoy, and you can still drop a coin

Gary Phillips, the handsome George Montgomery look-alike, with his prize 1930s bakelite, wood-and-chromium jukebox, and 1932 baseball game at his Central Arcade on the boardwalk of Seaside Heights.

Early animated Madame Zita machine will pick out your fortune for a dime at Gary Phillip's Central Arcade.

and play a few of the oldies like a baseball game with miniature players (such as Jimmy Foxx and Hank Greenberg) in painted lead from the early 20th century.

The **Berkeley Sweet and Taffy Shop** is a place from times gone by that continues to exist on the great boardwalk. At the Berkeley, located at the enclosed merry-go-round to the south, you can send anyone a box of saltwater taffy, eat a caramel or candied apple, or a particularly good chocolate, strawberry, or vanilla-coconut candy patty. Other homemade candies are available in bags or in colorful boxes. A second Berkeley Taffy branch is several blocks down the way on the boardwalk, in case you passed it up the first time. **Johnson's Popcorn** has served its own particular brand of delicious caramel popcorn or salted buttered popcorn in simple cardboard boxes on the boardwalk for decades. A primitive hand-painted mural at Johnson's shows Goofy and his pal Mickey Mouse downing the sweet gooey caramel concoction. **Kohr's** soft custard stands (there are at least three on this boardwalk) serve blueberry ripple, fresh banana and peach, orange-and-raspberry sherbet, and chocolate peanut-butter custard creme as well as their trademark fresh-squeezed refreshingly iced orange drink. The design concept of the Kohr's stands is pop art in a combination of blue, orange, and white colors. The sanitary and efficient manner of Kohr's and the clean and immaculate porcelain interiors make these stands a nice place to patronize.

Seaside Heights seems to really sparkle at nighttime when the boardwalk lights glitter and the bars and discos, like the **Bamboo Club, Yakety Yak Club,** or the **Chatterbox,** and funky juke joints are in full swing. The lights from the amusement rides on the pier as they reflect into the ocean and the night sky are a sight to behold. After a day in the sun, a walk on the boardwalk at night seems just right, seeing the sights and the people, some in outlandish offbeat attire, and feeling those cool evening breezes from the sea. The beach at Seaside Heights has soft white sand and the

ocean waves here are often powerful, attracting large numbers of surfers. You can swim on the beach at Seaside Heights for $2 weekdays, $3 weekends, and in-season there are some bathhouses along the boardwalk for changing your clothes.

Tiny Tim continued to perform before his passing in 1996 at clubs like the old Parrot Club and the VIP Lounge in Seaside Heights. Here he looks like one of the live screaming characters who frighten visitors to the haunted castle on the Seaside Heights boardwalk amusement pier.

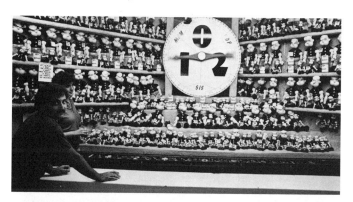

A game of chance in which you can take home a prized Popeye the Sailor doll, boardwalk, Seaside Heights (top). A spectacular pop culture sign display at Kohr's famous custard and orangeade stand on the boardwalk at Seaside Heights, one of several such outstanding concessions up and down this boardwalk (and in other locations on the Jersey shore) (bottom).

Island Beach to Island Heights

Island Beach is a state park divided into a botanical zone, wildlife sanctuary, and recreation area for beachgoing and swimming. This is the best place to swim on your Seaside Heights day trip. It is a 10-mile long natural barrier beach going to the tip of the peninsula. One side of this land is Barnegat Bay while the other is the Atlantic Ocean in its wildest and purest state. This is a truly wondrous environmental showcase for the state of New Jersey. To visit Island Beach with its snow white sand, its natural grassy dunes, its thick shrubbery, its holly trees, and its swamp grass and many varieties of wild plant life, is to confront the elements at the shore as they have been since the very beginnings. Wild rabbits, red fox, and other creatures inhabit the thick brush, and there are many varieties of birds that make this spot a bird-watcher's delight. Recently the hawklike ospreys returned to their nests of twigs and branches perched on top of telephone poles. There are two public beach areas located halfway down the park with modern bathhouses with showers, refreshment stands, as well as beach lifeguards. The "aeolium" has a display of plant and wild animal and bird life. There is a pathway here into the dunes with signs naming the various outdoor pine bushes, plants and trees, including cacti and beach plum shrubs. There is an oceanfront Cape Cod–style summer mansion on Island Beach, used by the incumbent governor of New Jersey, and the estate has a smaller house on the bay for visiting dignitaries and guests. South of the public beach area there are numbered parking lots for fishermen who consider Island Beach a paradise, winter or summer. For 30 years the State of New Jersey pondered whether to buy this strip, which was privately owned; they finally decided to go ahead when real estate developers were beginning to make propositions. In 1952 the state acquired it for $2.75 million and the park was opened in 1959. Eight miles south of the entrance the two-lane road ends at parking area A-23. Here is a good opportunity to park the car and take a hike down the beach at the water's edge. A mile and a half down you will reach the tip of Island Beach, the Atlantic Ocean surging into Barnegat Bay through Barnegat Inlet. Barnegat Lighthouse—"Old Barney"—is across the inlet at the northern tip of Long Beach Island, and to your right, on the bay side of Island Beach, are the dunes and marshes of a protected bird nesting area. Bathe your feet and linger in the changing pools of the inlet before returning to your car. Note: When the parking lots at Island Beach are filled (mostly on hot weekends during the summer) traffic into the park is halted at the entrance, and you must either wait for a certain number of exiting cars or bathe elsewhere.

Bordering Seaside Heights to the south is Seaside park, which claims a small portion of the Heights boardwalk but in the main is a quiet, sedate beach resort town that stands in sharp contrast to the Heights's frenetic activity, in the same way that Ocean Grove separates itself from the crazy nightclub activity in Asbury Park. Seaside Park's boardwalk is built over the wide, powdery-white sand beaches and has no amusements; it does have a number of summer house gazebolike structures with green rooftops that are more like open porches, jutting over the sand. These have benches for a respite from the sun or a sudden lightning storm or summer shower. Seaside Park has many large barnlike houses that are almost like summer mansions as well as a few rental houses, and two or three places of the rooming house variety; but for the most part it is very private. There are day beaches and bathhouses in the northern part of Seaside Park. You can dine on "the best of land and sea" seven days and seven nights a week year-round at the **Top O' the Mast Restaurant,** (732) 793-1110 at 23rd Avenue at the ocean in Seaside Park, abutting Island Beach State Park. With its 65-foot surf bar, two happy hours (3:00 to 6:00 and 10:00 to 1:00 A.M.), and its excellent food the "new" Top O' the Mast (under new ownership—the 400-plus seat restaurant was completely re-modeled and renovated in 1997) is attracting nature lovers and travelers all year round. Right alongside the restaurant stretching west from the ocean, is a two-story, double-sided motel called **Island Beach Motor Lodge,** (732) 793-5400. Call them to reserve one of their 76 units from single-bed motel rooms to a swanky penthouse facing the ocean, as well as efficiencies (kitchen, separate bedroom, Castro convertible couch in the living room) that can accommodate 4 to 5 people. During the season these go for $170 per night (July and August); single units are $85 per night during the week and $87 on weekends. Doubles with two beds are $105 during the week and $110 on weekends. Special rates apply in September, October, May, and June, as well as November through April, when single units re $25 per night during the week and $30 on weekends. This is definitely the place to go during the cooler months, or anytime, so be sure to call and make a reservation for rates in all seasons. Joe Leon, your gracious host at Island Beach Motor Lodge has recently opened the **Atlantic Bar & Grill** for wild and cozy beach rendezvous. **Ebby's Deli** in South Seaside Park (open 7 days from 7 A.M. to midnight) features famous giant submarine sandwiches and excellent homemade crumbcakes, cannollis, fresh breads, fine meats, and other take-out goodies. **Ebby's Cafe Alfresco** serves sit-down dinners from 4 to 11 P.M., featuring premier Italian dishes like pasta frasioli, spiedini, mozzarella in carozza, and chicken Rossini. Call (732) 830-4775 for specials and delivery. Ebby's also has a place in Chadwick Beach on the "strip."

✻   ✻   ✻

Bum Rogers, on Central Avenue at 23rd Avenue (just outside the entrance to Island Beach State Park) in South Seaside Park is a bar and restaurant that stays open late (until midnight) and cooks up the very best hardshell crabs, softshell crabs, blackened fish (Creole style), lobster, and good seafood combo platters. There is the sense that this is an "in" restaurant. The lively casual ambience makes it a fun place to go, and prices are moderate. If you need to take a walk after eating you are just a block from the ocean and two blocks to the great Barnegat Bay.

The **Pier House** on Central and 22nd Avenue, (732) 830-2250, serves breakfast from 7 A.M., lunch and dinners of steak, seafood, whole stuffed lobster with imperial crabmeat stuffing with linguine or potato and bouillabaisse. The **Berkeley Fish Market,** (732) 739-0400, **and Restaurant** is at 24th Avenue and Central. On the upper floor of this family restaurant you can view the expanse of Island Beach. Here you can enjoy fresh seafood specials and fish combinations deep fried or broiled at very reasonable prices. The homemade clam chowder is excellent; and at the fish market you can take a container home with you as well as prepared fried seafood. Breakfast (7:30 to 11:30 A.M.) here includes two eggs, toast, home fries, and coffee. Lunch (noon to 4 P.M.) of a hamburger or fish sandwich with french fries, coleslaw and chowder is a bargain and economical family dinners are served from noon to 10 P.M. The restaurant and fish market are open Mother's Day to the week after Labor Day. The family opened a new restaurant at 1747 Hooper Avenue (inland to Toms River on Route 37) in Silverton (in the Anchorage Square Plaza) that is open year-round. At Central Avenue and First (still in Seaside Park) the **Windjammer Motor Inn** has an amiable cocktail lounge, good to visit to listen to the live organ music and eat the complimentary hot and cold hors d'oeuvres served at poolside. The **Aztec Motel Bar,** in Seaside Heights, offers a raunchy good time. This place, with a pool, a restaurant, and a fast-food emporium, is located right on the boardwalk north of the amusement pier, in the loudest and most crowded section of the Heights. It is fun, and there are live bands. Call (732) 793-3000. Both of these last places are open year-round. If happy hour is not your thing, rent an outboard motorboat or a rowboat at the **Wheel House Marina** (24th Avenue and Barnegat Avenue in South Seaside Park) on the bay. Gary J. Grob and Don Matthews, who run this place right at the northern tip of Island Beach (a kind of end-of-the-line location), also have a no-nonsense coffee shop with home-cooked breakfasts and American-style sandwiches on the premises, open from 6 A.M. to 8 P.M.

The weekend after Labor Day Seaside Heights has its annual Mardi Gras. (In Seaside Mardi Gras comes after Labor Day, not before Lent—a mercantile maneuver cooked up by local bars to cash in on the lingering summer mood.) It features incredible low,

The original Barney (standing) sold homemade clam chowder for 10¢ and served his root beer out of a barrel.

low price sidewalk sales, parades, floats, and merrymaking of every kind. Outlandish costumes, men in full drag as prom queens or street hustlers are everywhere, camping it up at Klee's and the other hot spots for two whole days and nights. For some it is all innocent fun, laughs, and a happy time. For others it is a bargain hunt. Still others are on the proverbial "lost weekend," raising hell well before All Hallows' Eve when things are very quiet indeed in these parts. However, it should be mentioned that the Seaside Heights boardwalk concessions are open for business, chiefly on weekends, with many places open until Christmas and again, certainly, well before Easter (as soon as it warms up even a bit). The skilo and bingo parlors never close and keep the locals fascinated and away from their homes and the television set for many hours. Usually these are the places grandma can win a butterball turkey for the holidays. And the historic carousel on the boardwalk is open weekends all year round. In Lavallette (north of Seaside on Route 35) at 601 Grand Central is the **Crab's Claw Inn,** (732) 793-4447, in the town center. It's noted for its fresh seafood dinners and its choice steaks. The Crab's Claw also has a 100-bottle wine list and serves up 135 different brands of domestic and imported beers. There is nightly entertainment with happy hour (half-price drinks) serving exotic and regular cocktails from 4 to 6 P.M. Lunch on the porch is a pleasant experience here. Lavallette has a charming, old-fashioned boardwalk laid right out on the sand. From here you can see the glittering lights of the Seaside Heights boardwalk just south.

West over the bridge from Seaside Heights and a few miles inland on Route 37 there is a turnoff before you reach Toms River. This

A Victorian summer house in Seaside Park.

is the beautiful, secluded community of Island Heights, which began as a Methodist camp meeting ground in 1878. Situated on
Toms River proper, where it enters Barnegat Bay, this Victorian
town, with its tall trees and spacious front lawns and gardens, its
small yellow sand beaches, its quaint wooden boardwalk along the
bayfront, is a varied area of hills, valleys, and lowlands, and a fine
place to take in the bay breezes commingling with the sweet smell
of the river, the pines, and the ocean. The **Ocean County Artists
Guild** is located in a fine old home at 22 Chestnut Avenue, and
often has art shows and related events. There is an art school, a
dance school, several churches, and a few small shops, adding to
the rustic flavor of this town. There is little that is gaudy or commercial and everything is pastoral, spacious, and green. The great
Victorian homes by the bay, and the wide-paved streets, dimly lit
at night to retain the old-time flavor of the past, make this geographic spot on the inland-waterway an ideal place to take a
moonlight walk if you are staying out on the strip in Seaside
Heights, and want to experience something very different and very
pleasant. Highway 37 is filled with motel after motel for overnight
accommodations and there are fish markets, farmers' produce
markets, gas stations, automobile dealerships, a junk hubcap shop,
plant and garden supplies, shopping malls, movie houses, diners,
and fast-food spots galore. when you make the turnoff to Island
Heights the changeover is remarkable and that is what is fun about
New Jersey—its many "round the bend" surprises.

The Legend of the Jersey Devil

The great area known as the Pine Barrens and other sections of southern New Jersey are said to be menaced by the Jersey Devil, a demon reported to have a horselike face, red eyes, bat wings, cloven hoofs, and a forked tail. This demon beast, as legend has it, likes to play mischievous tricks on innocent tourists and children, sometimes half-scaring them to death from fright. The "Pineys," the local folk who live in the Pine Barrens, are said to be dominated by this devil and will themselves "give a scare" to outsiders for no apparent reason. Many Pineys are descendants of Hessian troops (German soldiers hired by the British) who hid out in the barrens after the American Revolution to avoid being captured. The Pineys call the Jersey Devil the "Leeds Devil," referring to the original legend that it was originally born to a Mrs. Leeds in 1735 at what is now known as Leeds Point near Smithville. One of the myths has it that the Devil's first meal was several sleeping children and another handed-down tale has him devouring the entire Leeds family. The monster so menaced this area that a clergyman in 1740 was called in to perform an exorcism that was said would last for 100 years. Unfortunately, the Jersey Devil did not com-

Two postcards, left: The most famous New Jersey folklore character, known as the "Jersey Devil" or the "Leeds Devil," was said to be a monster born of a woman named Leeds in the early 1700s. The 1975 postcard is by Ed Sheetz. Right: "Atlantic City by Moonlight," a 1908 postcard with what appears to be a Jersey Devil creature emerging out of the sea to confront one vacationer who has had one too many highballs.

Jersey Devil by Earl Tyler, 1970.

pletely disappear during this time; he came back in 1840 with a vengeance and has not left since. Sometimes, throughout the 1,700 square miles of the Pine Barren wilderness region, blood-curdling screams and agonizing moans are heard at night that are attributed to this weird beast. The Jersey Devil is said to hide out in swamps and near dark ponds and lakes, and has been spotted often in the Atlantic City meadows as well as in the depths of the forests around Batsto.

In the Pine Barrens near Weekstown, not far from the winding Mullica River, there is a tiny coffee shop-restaurant called **Pat's Stand** with a screened-in porch, a whirring overhead fan, and rusty old 1940s Coca-Cola signs. One of the proprietors, a woman named Gladys A. Wilson, talks about the Jersey Devil. She tells the tale told to her by her grandfather, who knew of a family that lived deep in the woods. Traveling by horse-and-buggy these folk had to ride through a large cedar swamp and cross a rail bridge. One night on one of these journeys they had to fight their way across the bridge when a big hairy monster came out of the swamp and menaced them. The man grabbed a rail off the bridge and hit the beast, knocking it into the water. Then he jumped in his buggy and took off faster than lightning. Gladys's great-uncle William Bozarth used to be the caretaker at Batsto Village. At midnight he would go with his lantern to the barn to check the livestock. Walking down the path to the barn late one night he suddenly saw a strange-looking animal with a horse face, walking on two feet just in front of him. "Uncle Willy," she recounted, "was sure it was the Jersey Devil on his way into the barn to make a killin' for a midnight snack." Gladys also tells tales about recent occurrences of dogs, cats, geese, chickens, and ducks disappearing without a trace. When a group went into the woods with shotguns, the posse discovered deer bones, hides, dog bones, feathers, and the like all in one single spot. All suspected the Devil's work was at hand.

There were other stories of children being whacked so hard on the back of their necks by some kind of creature in the pinelands that their collar bones were broken. Gladys looks thoughtfully out at the horizon and says, "Things have been quiet of late. It's about time for that rascal to come galloping out of the swamps. I do hope he comes out and scares the hell out of the developers for messing in our Pinelands. They'll be sorry they destroyed the forest if their paths cross that of the Jersey Devil. Oh, by the way," Piney Gladys Wilson pauses, "the Jersey Devil is most certainly in Atlantic City!" Other Pineys now joke about the notion that the Jersey Devil took over the body of the person who originally sold out Atlantic City to gambling interests. Could she be referring to Reese Palley? In any case we know the Devil is alive and well in A.C.!

Lakewood to Lake Rova to Forked River

Devotees of the American road always have loved old Route 9, a two-lane highway that parallels the Garden State Parkway on the eastern shore of New Jersey. When the pace was slower, Route 9 was the main roadway to Atlantic City and other southern Jersey seashore resorts. Jersey jaunters, in search of something simple and different, still can appreciate the many roadside diners and funky motels like the '50s-style **Moon Motel,** just north of Lakewood, with its fanciful neon sign of animated rockets heading for the moon. If you enjoy waterbeds, overhead mirrors, mirror-ball lighting, and special video installations, stay at the Moon or at one of the dozens of other motels—most of them clean and respectable—that dot the old road.

Lakewood on Route 9 became famous on the East Coast as the place where you could breath in the fresh pine air. In the late 19th century it was the fashionable spot to vacation in the winter. Right up to the 1950s you would see women sitting in the noonday sun with their dyed hair and full-face makeup, wearing furs, diamonds, and pointed rhinestoned sunglasses on the front porches of the old Lakewood resort hotels, on Highway 9. Of course, many come in the summer to be among the pines, and to swim and hike along the many pine-needle trails in and around Lakewood. Great estates and mansions were built here when this health resort was at its peak, including those of John D. Rockefeller and George Jay Gould. You can still see **Georgian Court,** built along Lake Carasaljo's northern shore as the home of George Jay Gould in 1898–1900, with its Georgian and Renaissance architecture and elaborate gardens and fountains. The site is now a Catholic college for women. The former estate of John D. Rockefeller Sr., was acquired by Ocean County in 1940, and though the mansion has been torn down, the remaining trees from around the world and planted by Rockefeller himself form a public park with picnic grounds and a lake for swimming. To experience the great pines of Lakewood and to swim in its mineral-rich lakes you should turn right on Route 88 off Route 9 to **Ocean County Park** where you can picnic at tables with fireplaces and swim in the lake. Here are over 300 acres of white pine and hemlock trees towering high.

On the Manasquan River, boaters ply east and west but their favorite tie-up place is **Peterson's Riviera Inn,** 1600 Highway 20, Brick Township, (732) 840-1110, replete with docking facilities. Dock and dine on the à la carte menu and daily specials in the $14.95 to $20.95 price range. Hours are 11:30 P.M. to 10 P.M. Sunday through Thursday. Friday and Saturday they're open with a late-nite menu until 11 P.M. but are closed Mondays in the winter. Also on the premises at Peterson's on the Manasaquan River there is an extravagant Liquor Centre with everything imaginable available.

Out of Lakewood there are many chicken farms where you can purchase candlelit eggs, eggs from free-running hens, organic eggs, or just plain Jersey eggs, which are delicious any way you like them. Some places also will sell fresh-killed chickens. Farm produce stands in this area always sell the best of the summer harvest from New Jersey farms. In the summer, silver queen white corn, every variety of Jersey tomato, including yellow acid-free tomatoes, eggplant, squash, peaches, and beach plums flood old Route 9.

◆

Six Flags Great Adventure

Heading west on 526 from Lakewood off Highway 9 toward Jackson and Trenton is **Six Flags Great Adventure** on Route 537 (about six minutes from Exit 91 off the Garden State Parkway). In the theme park is a 3-lane, 4.5-mile drive-through safari (about 350 acres) with 1,500 wild animals from all over the world, some of which will jump on your car; so convertibles or vinyl-top hardtops are not permitted in this area of the park unless you want a hairy orangutan or mandrill on your lap. This family-type planned environment has a kiddie kingdom with merry-go-rounds and other rides. There are over 100 rides, shows, and attractions here. You will find restaurants and five hours of specialty shows daily, concerts, dolphin acts, aquatic acts, and more.

The 2,200-acre park has a daily season that runs from May 18 to September 4 and a weekend-only season (Saturday and Sunday) during March 24 to May 14 and September 9 through November 10, including a special Columbus Day celebration and hayrides, a Halloween party, and costume events on October 31. At the end of October there are also Oktoberfest Bavarian festivals with German entertainment, food, and strolling oompah-pah brass bands. One of the main attractions for this family-oriented park is a 15-acre water ride called Adventure Rivers, a collection of water slides, tubes, and streams that will leave you wringing wet—so dress accordingly—bring a change of clothing or wear a rubber suit. There is also a hair-raising roller coaster called "The Great American Scream Machine" that is a-thrill-a-minute with loops, dives, and curves that create a rush of terror, fear, and excitement for those young and brave souls who enjoy a good scare and a good scream.

If twists and turns don't excite you, you might want to try the parachute jump. Bring plenty of extra dollars for souvenirs, food, and parking. The safari trip, in which car windows must remain closed, can be stifling in summer if your auto does not have air-conditioning. The drive-through takes an hour with giraffes and wild elk sometimes standing in front of the car looking for a treat to eat.

Great Adventure is very much a shlock pop-culture experience, but it can be an entertainment and distraction for a family looking for a good time. Some return again and again; and it is the closest you can get to the controlled environment of a Disney park in the northeast. It is just one hour either from Manhattan or Philadelphia. In summer put on insect repellent as you will find yourself at the top of the Pine Barrens region and mosquitoes are legendary. Theme Park and Safari ticket prices can be purchased separately or as a package; there are special discount prices for seniors and kids under 54 inches—infants three and under free. From Garden State Parkway take Exit 91, from the N.J. Turnpike use Exit 72. Call (732) 928-1821 for further information.

There are lakes farther west on Route 526 for swimming and picnic grounds to enjoy as well. Route 528 West out of Lakewood is a lovely drive to Cassville, where you will turn right at the sign to Rova Farms, an old White Russian resort. At one point Routes 528 and 527 are joined, but at the Van Hiseville Juncture stay west on 528. On the 527-528 neck of the journey **Butterfly Pond Fish and Wildlife Management Area** (which features a quail farm) is an interesting stop.

At **Rova Farms** in the Pines is **Lake Rova.** The **Rova Farm Bar and Restaurant** serves excellent Russian peasant-style dishes, sauerkraut and homemade kielbasa, pelmini in butter and sour cream, roast duck with kasha, and delicious Russian borscht. The old White Russians—and their offspring—sing Russian songs and drink Russian vodka without ice. The large simple restaurant room has pictures of Anton Chekhov and other Russian greats on the wall. Throughout the year there are many festivities such as folk festivals, Russian picnics and concerts, and all are always welcome here. A great open porch winds around the restaurant, and a little store sells folk items imported from Russia. There is an enclosed dance pavilion on the lake where these folk will dance wildly into the night. The grounds, including the formal **Pushkin Gardens,** dominated by an imposing statue of the famous Russian writer Pushkin, has the feeling of old Russia: the pine trees, the shrubbery, the holly trees, the thick grass and wildflowers, and the broad gravelled walks evoking the novels of Turgenev and Tolstoy. Even the dark Lake Rova seems more like a great pond than a lake. **St. Vladimir's Church** at Rova Farms is a copy of a 16th-century Russian chapel with a great ornate gold dome, and with many broad stairs climbing up the hill to its prominent site. It is painted cream-white and has colorful tile mosaics of the saints. There is also a gazebo and a small graveyard where many of Tolstoy's kin—including his daughter—are buried. The Russian priest wears long white robes and has long red hair and a red beard. Russian Christmas and Russian Easter are celebrated here, and the restaurant is open all year long with very reasonable prices. This is a wonderful Sunday drive and you should call (732) 928-0928 for the restaurant hours, a calendar of the special festivities, and to ask about overnight accommodations. This is a restful vacation spot that seems to be not only from another time, but another country. The area is surrounded by small farms where you can buy honey, corn, tomatoes, summer squash, and other products.

"Old Peg-Leg John" drained a swamp near Cassville in 1845 to grow cultivated cranberries in the pines. He was so successful in selling them in Philadelphia that soon a cranberry industry flourished throughout the Pine Barrens. There are still cranberry bogs in the Pines as well as blueberry farms, but not to the degree that there were in earlier years. (See "Southwestern Farm Country" for cranberry and blueberry statistics.) Sailing vessels used to take supplies of cranberry on board for a long voyage, believing these tart red berries prevented scurvy. The Lake Rova–Cassville area is also approached out of Toms River on Route 571 that crosses Route 528 at Cassville. Check your map.

Take Highway 547 one mile out of the Borough of Lakehurst to the Lakehurst Naval Historical Society (732) 323-2620 for a self-guided tour past Blimp Hangar #1, which contains a memorial at the site where the famous *Hindenburg* burst into flames on May 6, 1937 after its third transatlantic crossing, 36 passengers perishing in the flames. The folk of the Pines, the "Pineys," are not lovers of progress—in fact, during Prohibition the men who made "white lightnin'" in the pineland stills thought the airships were "revenoors" and were always shooting them up with holes as they glided over the woods. The *Hindenburg* disaster, broadcast to the world from an on-the-site observer, spelled the end of airship travel in the 1930s, though in recent times, with safer methods, there has been talk of reinstituting such travel. Nearby **McGuire Air Force Base** has tours by appointment, (609) 724-2154, for those interested in what the Department of the Air Force has to offer. Call Ocean County Parks and Recreation (609) 971-3085 for special group tours of the area.

The **Ocean County Historical Society,** 26 Hadley Avenue, in Toms River, (732) 341-1880, is a must-not-miss museum visit. The ladies of the society have helped to create a house in which history lives. The schoolroom on the second floor, with all the original articles of its reading and writing work in place, the charming playroom, the roughhewn bedrooms of its former occupants as well as the kitchen and family rooms downstairs, create a startling effect. The ladies will point out such curiosities as the pot at the foot of the bed. "A spittoon?" you will ask. "No, it's for holding turpentine to kill the bedbugs." The Victorian mansion, which seems to be waiting for that family to return a century later, is connected to another exhibition area that features historical aspects of Ocean County, including impressive dirigible memorabilia and a research center.

The **Cowboy Steakhouse and Saloon,** built to resemble an Old West cowtown, is below Toms River, in Bayville, on Route 9. It is owned and operated by Louis "Tex"

Gigantic two-gun painted-metal road sign, 45 feet high and vividly red neon at night, beckons travelers to the Cowboy Steakhouse and Saloon on old Route 9 in Bayville.

Gotsis, a fan of cowboy culture. Gotsis has combined a vast dining room with an extensive menu, a roomy, circular barroom, and a sweeping dance floor that features live country dance till 3 A.M. every night. Special concerts in the past have featured the likes of Willie Nelson and Mickey Gilley. You can't miss the Cowboy Steakhouse's 40-foot-high animated red neon cowboy waving customers in off the road. Call (732) 269-5545 to find out what's going on, pardner.

Farther south on Route 9 there is a state game farm at Forked River where you can see thousands of penned-in peacock, golden pheasant, quail, and other wild game, including deer, all in a beautiful setting, just drive in off Highway 9.

Long Beach Island and "Old Barney"

Four miles out to sea, 19 miles from its northern tip at the **Old Barnegat Lighthouse** to its southern tip at Beach Haven Inlet on Little Egg Harbor, Long Beach Island has long been a favorite vacation resort for New Jerseyans, New Yorkers, and Philadelphians. "Old Barney," the main attraction on the island, is over 100 years old, but ceased being used as a lighthouse in 1927. It was saved from destruction by concerned citizens in the 1920s who rallied to save the lighthouse beacon that once guided ships into the narrow and fast-moving Barnegat Inlet, and helped to rescue those that were in distress or sinking. It is still an experience to see this red-and-white tower, designed by George Gordon Meade, from a distant approach or at close range. A gift shop, a museum, a restaurant, and a bait and tackle shop now surround Old Barney, which was built of thick strong brick and is a great symbol and monument to the sea and of times past; if it could speak like some of the old fishermen who like to spin tall tales of the ocean, it would have many adventurous sea stories to tell.

◆

Sinbad, the Legendary Four-Legged Sailor

A legend has developed around a 24-pound brown, black-and-white mongrel named Sinbad who came aboard the Coast Guard cutter *Campbell* in 1937 and served as a "sailor-mascot" aboard this vessel throughout World War II. Sinbad was buried in 1951 at the ripe old age of 14, at Barnegat lifeboat station. Many stories about the heroic dog have been chronicled in *Life* magazine and in newspapers. A book about his life, *Sinbad of the Coast Guard* was published, and there was a film called *Dog of the Seven Seas* that was released by Universal Pictures in 1947. The "salty sea dog" ate and slept with the crew, and was also known as a "bar hound" who, when on shore leave, frequented the bars with his buddies, jumping up and sitting on a barstool, lapping up his boil-ermakers just like any sailor. First he would lap up a mug of beer, followed by a shot glass of bourbon, which he favored over Canadian whiskey blends. His pals always paid for these drinking jaunts. Staggering back to the boat with the others he would be given aspirin the next morning to help bring him back to a "ship-shape" condition. Sometimes Sinbad would remain on board but would always be sitting on deck when the ship was in port to help escort a drunken sailor to his bunk. Sinbad was regarded by his crew not just as a mere mascot but as a good-luck charm, having seen the gobs through many World War II battles, such as the one

Sinbad the Sailor, United States Coast Guard dog.

when the *Campbell* had a 12-hour duel with a wolfpack of German submarines. When the ship rammed a German sub, sinking it into the icy waters of the North Atlantic, the Coast Guard vessel itself was badly damaged, and the crew, including Sinbad, had to be transferred onto a convoy escort. The many fighting battles that Sinbad was an active part of brought him a good deal of attention in state-side newspapers; following the war this sailor-dog went on a publicity tour all over America for the benefit of the US Coast Guard. It is fitting that this outstanding and unusual canine, who served honorably for 14 years in the Guard, should come to a final resting place near his beloved beacon of light—Old Barney—New Jersey's world-famous lighthouse.

At Beach Haven you can visit **Lucy Evelyn,** the site of a three-masted schooner that was destroyed by fire in 1972, and the wharf has several shops as well as **Schooner's Wharf** at the corner of Bay Street and 9th. Since 1985 Beach Haven has **Fantasy Island Amusement Park,** owned and operated by Gary Phillips of Seaside Heights. This family fun park includes a casino arcade, a beautiful miniature Victorian golf course, rides, games, food concessions and a Victorian ice cream parlor. Before leaving Long Beach Island have a sit-down dinner at the **New Horizon Restaurant.**

Many people came to Long Beach Island to seek relief from pollen and hay fever in the old days. Surf City established itself as a resort in 1873, and Barnegat City, at the north end where the lighthouse stands, began in 1881. North Beach Haven developed in 1887, and Ship Bottom in 1898. The ride from Highway 72 (off Route 9) from Manahawkin becomes a series of high bridges that give one the scope of the bay and the marshes that surround it. New Yorkers like to think the island itself resembles Long Island and its many beaches. Long Beach Island is very accessible from Philadelphia and Camden on Route 70, which switches into Route 72 at Lebanon State Forest. From New York, of course, it is the Garden State Parkway (exit 63) or old Highway 9 to Manahawkin.

Old Route 9 Day Trip

From Barnegat to Oyster Creek

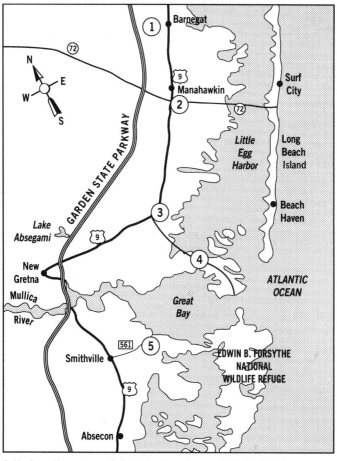

1. Hurricane House
2. Bay Avenue Diner
3. Tuckerton Emporium
4. Great Bay Boulevard
5. Oyster Creek Inn

The old New Jersey road south to Atlantic City and Cape May, for those who lived and toiled in the industrial northern towns like Newark, Perth Amboy, Rahway, Elizabeth, Paterson, or Passaic and the suburbs that surround them, was always-wonderful two-lane Highway 9. In times past when life seemed easier and the pace was slower with no superthroughways, turnpikes, and parkways, you could enjoy the towns and places Route 9 passed through. Often your destination might not be the ocean resorts

Abandoned fishing shack on an island in Barnegat Bay in Barnegat.

but one of the towns on Route 9 that were on Barnegat Bay, Manahawkin Bay, or the series of smaller bays and inlets down the eastern seaboard to the very tip of the state. Cabins and overnight lodgings were always to be found along this highway and still are. This is quite a surprise when you consider that most of these places from the twenties, thirties, and forties were replaced in the 1950s with the newer, cleaner, more efficient motel equivalent. The giant Holiday Inns of later decades were unimaginable back then and are still scarce in this laidback southern region. As you drive south into the Pine Barrens, you will notice that tall shrub pines, open meadows, yellow sandy soil, and great pine groves predominate, giving the feeling of being in Georgia rather than Jersey. Barnegat is a quaint bay town with a boat dock and small boardwalk on the bay, practically inside **Barnegat National Wildlife Refuge.** Barnegat has several antique shops in the town center, some interesting Victorian architecture, and an old ice cream parlor called the **Hurricane House,** which serves Arctic Ice Cream and sandwiches in a pleasant atmosphere with whirring overhead fans and an old screen door.

Old Highway 9 is still noted for its many antique shops, and things do mysteriously turn up in this Jersey Devil country out of the attics and into some of the stores and flea markets. Usually, prices are very fair along this highway now, because most vacationers are speeding along the Garden State Parkway, which parallels Highway 9 all the way down to Cape May—but the old route is for the adventurous and back roads are always where the good times are.

The next point south on Route 9 following Barnegat is Manahawkin, which is an old Lenape Indian expression meaning "good corn land." Right at the crossroads of 9 and 72 there is a small cranberry bog lake, and a pine grove for picnics or just to park and relax (no charge). Just off 9 in Manahawkin there are a few eateries, notably the **Bay Avenue Diner,** at 32 Bay Avenue, (609)597-9804, which serves breakfast eggs with scrapple, charges 25¢ for tea or coffee, and is open around the clock.

In Tuckerton, situated on **Lake Pohatcong** (another good spot for a picnic) there is a very nice drive-in: **Stewart's Root Beer,** situated on the highway just opposite the lake, and the town proper has a diner as well as small shops. One of the most interesting spots is the **Tuckerton Emporium,** with a dozen different shops at 2 East Main Street (Highway 9), (609) 296-6278, open from 10:30 A.M. until 6 P.M. every day, offering new stained glass, custom framing, pine furniture, local art, imported fashion sweaters, Victoriana, and flower arrangements, as well as a shop that sells unique things like handmade black dolls, and "exquisite curiosities" in addition to exotic Chinese kites and garlic jellies. Out back of this boutique-antique-craft cooperative department store at 1 Shourds Lane is a specialty Jerseyana bookshop called **Clam Town Books** (609) 296-6278.

Just beyond Tuckerton and off Route 9 the road signs will direct you to Little Egg Harbor and Mystic Island, which leads you into the **Great Bay Fish and Wildlife Area** on Beach Haven Inlet, Little Egg Inlet, and the Great Bay. This is a particularly beautiful southern New Jersey wildlife area. The drive along the Great Bay Boulevard, a sandy dirt road, is breathtakingly beautiful. Following Route 9 again south you will pass through the **Bass River State Forest** (9,400 acres), and **Lake Absegami.**

The next town, New Gretna, has some good seafood restaurants; and one of the best is **Allen's Clam Bar,** a plain affair run by Win Allen, who is a New Jersey state oyster shucking champ. The oysters and scallops here come from the Great Bay, just a few miles away, and for $4 you can truly enjoy a platter full of clam fritters with french fried potatoes, coleslaw, and Jersey tomatoes, or deviled crabs, clams, flounder, or lobster (from $4 to $14). The clam chowder is filled with vegetables, potatoes, onions and tomatoes, and the oyster stews (when in season) are rich and creamy. Be warned: the horseradish will clear out your city pollution sinus condition. During the summer Allen's is open from 11 A.M. until 9 P.M., winter from 11 A.M. to 8 P.M., closed on Monday.

Just beyond New Gretna, Highway 9 merges with the Garden State Parkway to cross the vast marshes at the mouth of the broad Mullica River, which enters the Great Bay here at **Brigantine National Wildlife Refuge.** This is a 20,000-acre area of bays, marshes, and tidal inlets that serves as a vital system in the ecology of the entire Pine Barrens region, home to such rare birds as the Canada geese, snow geese, brant, blue-winged teal, black ducks, gadwall, shorebirds, egrets, herons, ibises, and warblers. After crossing the river take the very first exit (48) over the bridge and get back onto Highway 9.

This will bring you right into **Smithville**, which was a stagecoach stop in the late 1700s on Kings Highway (eventually called New York Road, now US Highway 9). Today Smithville is a restored town, which also has many quaint shops in rebuilt and restructured small buildings, each with its own history: a general store, a tobacco store, a bakery, a bookshop, a Jersey Devil souvenir shop with the infamous devil imprinted on T-shirts, postcards, posters, and other Pine Barren souvenirs, a cheese shop, a Christmas shop, a toy shop, and a candy shop, as well as several antique shops and an indoor antique center.

Smithville might have remained just a forgotten little hamlet had it not been for Fred and Ethel Noyes, who were antique dealers from down the road in Absecon. The Noyeses bought a deteriorating inn for $3,500 and restored it into a 42-seat restaurant in 1952. The inn, built in 1787 by James Baremore, originally served travelers on a stagecoach route between Leeds Point and Camden. The Noyeses had a vision of surrounding their restaurant with restored 18th- and 19th-century buildings, which typified those found in this area of southern New Jersey. Old houses and stores were literally "collected" and brought onto the land in the 1950s. In 1975 Fred and Ethel severed their association with Smithville when they sold the entire village to a subsidiary of the American Broadcasting Company. When the tourist spot did not

Bonny Wyckoff, in early American garb, at the Smithville Antiques Center on Route 9.

live up to ABC's expectations of profitability, it was sold again to the Cadillac-Fairview Corporation, which then included two subsidiaries called Inns and Shoppes Inc., and Historic Smithville Development Company. Smithville is thriving now with infused business from the people who live in nearby developments, built to house the Atlantic City casino workers. The Noyeses, meanwhile, opened the **Noyes Museum** farther down the road in Oceanville (Lily Lake Road), which features selected works from Fred Noyes's collection of American art plus "working" decoy ducks, sculptures, and summer string quartets; call (609) 652-8848.

The **Smithville Inn**, (609) 652-7777, is a focal point here for tourist dining, serving South Jersey American fare for lunch, including chicken shortcake, chicken apple crepes, and eggs Benedict. The "Pony Express" lunch in the tavern section offers sandwiches, quiche, and chef salads at reasonable prices. A buffet of over 50 hot and cold specialties draws a large daily crowd (mostly in busses from Atlantic City.)

Waterwheel mill is now an antique shop at Smithville historic village.

You will find a few other fancy "Ye Olde Tavern" type eateries in Smithville, but if you turn left on Route 9 near the old graveyard—at a sign that says LEEDS POINT, you can take a three-mile drive along Old Moss Mill Road (Alt. 561) through woods and marshes—to the very tip of Leeds Point on the Great Bay and smack in the middle of the Brigantine Wildlife Refuge. At Oyster Creek you will come upon the **Oyster Creek Inn** where boats dock up at the pier, some sailing and motoring in just for dinner. Rustic sea shanties and fishermen's shacks surround this old restaurant that serves excellent seafood dinners in a plain atmosphere—and you can come dressed as you like. An "old salt" serves cocktails at a friendly bar (in the shape of a boat) and the open-view picture windows look out onto the bay. On a clear night you can spot the glittering lights of not too distant Atlantic City to the south and Beach Haven on Long Beach Island to the northwest. Big fish are mounted on the knotty pine walls, and the lights are cheery and bright so that you get to see exactly what you are eating. The fisherman's combination platter is a real taste treat and the crab cakes, soft-shell crabs, bluefish, shrimp, and oyster fries are all excellent. A clam stew is nicely creamy without being too thick, and the clam chowder is just right. Dinners include the typical choice of french fries or baked potato, coleslaw, with coffee or soda. The seafood combination at the Oyster Creek Inn includes flounder, scallops, a crab cake, a deviled clam, and shrimps—either fried or broiled. The Oyster Creek Inn at Oyster Creek is open Tuesday to Saturday from 4 to 9 P.M. and Sunday from 1 to 9 P.M. Call (609) 652-9871 for reservations or just drive out. The inn is set practically on the spot where the Jersey Devil is said to have been born, so watch out for queer happenings in these parts. An after-dinner walk down the old dirt road among the tall marsh grass and along the bay is a very pleasant experience here.

Pine Barrens Day Trip
and the Carranza Memorial

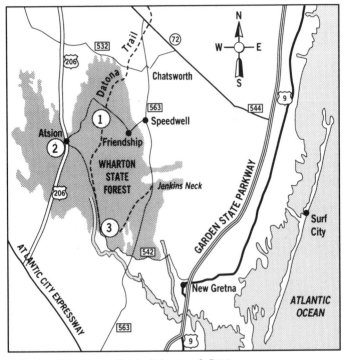

1. Carranza Memorial   2. Lake Atsion   3. Batsto

Wedged in between the New Jersey Turnpike on the west side of the state and the Garden State Parkway and Route 9 on the eastern estuaries forming the Barnegat Bay, Little Egg Harbor, and the Great Bay, are the 337,000 acres of New Jersey's famed Pine Barrens. US Route 206, state Routes 70 and 72, and secondary highways like 532, 534, 541, 542, and 563 cut through the Barrens, but it's still a vast wilderness that includes over 50,000 acres of pine forest, a rare dwarf pine tree (sometimes called stunted pygmy pine) forest and 17 trillion gallons of pure glacial-ice-quality water (beneath the Pines' deep sand beds). The great wild beauty of this vast area, with its more than 400 varieties of wildflowers, its blueberry, gooseberry and huckleberry bushes, its cranberry bogs and varieties of pine trees, its wild orchids, waterlilies, and curly leaf ferns, is breathtaking and awe inspiring. Congress created the Pineland National Reserve in 1978 and it was later designated as a coastal plain reserve by UNESCO, the United Nations agency.

Chatsworth, at the junction of Route 523 and Route 563 in Woodland Township, is the central town in the Pine Barrens, with about 100 homes, a post office, a church, a firehouse, and a schoolhouse. Like a town of days gone by, the Pineys, the folk of the region, many of whom work in the cranberry bogs, gather in the general store to drink coffee and tell tales of the forest and the Loch Nessian creature known to them as the "Leeds Devil."

Naturalists, canoeing enthusiasts, bird and wildlife watchers, poets, writers, and artists seek peace and solitude in this natural wilderness area, filled with deer, rabbit, opossum and other creatures of the wild who are protected against the encroachment of suburbanization. The Pine Barrens are primarily in Burlington County, which is New Jersey's largest, but they also extend into Ocean, Atlantic, and Camden Counties.

To experience it firsthand drive the back roads, walk, or if you like, paddle a canoe. Hikers can walk for hours in the Pines without seeing another soul—other than forest folk (the gremlins, Devils and demons of the mind), some deer, a hawk, and an occasional screech owl.

For an exciting day trip into the Pine Barrens turn right off Highway 9 at New Gretna onto Route 542 to **Batsto Village** and **Batsto Lake.** Batsto is located in the southern realm of the **Wharton State Forest,** which contains almost 108,000 acres and is the largest tract of land administered by the state park service in New Jersey. The word *baatstoo,* or *steambath,* was introduced by the Scandinavians and Dutch. The Indians borrowed the word, referring to it as *Batstow,* or *bathing place.* Here you will see an early industrial village where a glass factory and a lumber business in the 19th century replaced the 18th-century bog iron settlement, which flourished during the Revolutionary War. Complete with the gentleman's mansion on the hill, workers' homes, an iron furnace, a grist mill, a sawmill, glassworks, and a brickyard, this now "deserted village" once was a community of 1,000 people and was an important part of the industrial development of the United States. Batsto has a pig slaughterhouse, a general store, a blacksmith shop, a typical worker's home, a craft and pottery house, and other interesting buildings from days gone by. You can almost "feel" and "see" the retrogressive photographic images (the ghost presence) of those that had been here before as if you were in the twilight zone in another century. You also have the dark eerie feeling here of the Jersey Devil, but then—this is Jersey Devil country. Batsto is open Memorial Day to Labor Day from 10 A.M. to 6 P.M. and Labor Day to Memorial Day from 11 A.M. to 6 P.M., (609) 561-3262. Guided tours are conducted through the Victorian **Batsto Mansion,** former home of Joseph Wharton, the Philadelphia industrialist who over a period of 30 years bought the many parcels of land that comprise the Wharton Forest. He planned on damming the streams to create reservoirs so he could sell water to the city of Philadelphia, but his scheme was stopped by the legislature of the state of New Jersey, which prohibited the exporting of water. The state acquired the land in 1954 and 1955 and has left large areas undeveloped in order to preserve the natural habitat.

Primitive campsites are found throughout the forest and there are two family camping areas with numbered sites, and seven group campsites, including the **Batona campsite** (150 people), the **Mullica River wilderness campsite** (100 people—no cars or vehicles of any kind allowed), and **Goshen Pond** (200 people). There are nine cabins situated along the north shore of **Atsion Lake**. They can accommodate from four to eight people and have indoor toilets and showers and hot and cold running water. Reservation information may be obtained from the Atsion ranger station or the Batsto visitors center. Atsion Lake also has a protected bathing lake.

Located deep in the heart of the forest is the famous **Carranza Memorial**, notating the spot where Emilio Carranza, a 23-year-old Mexican pilot, challenging Lindbergh's solo flying record across the Atlantic, tried to fly solo from Mexico City to New York. Tragically he crashed in the first hours of his return flight to Mexico City, on July 13, 1928, and died deep in south Jersey's Pine Barrens. To get to the Carranza Memorial (a trek undertaken by not a few) take Route 563 south out of Chatsworth to Speedwell. Turn right and drive to the **Batona Trail.** Here, after walking through a long stretch of scrub pine, you will find the stone and cement memorial to that brave pioneer of flight, Señor Carranza.

Though rich in history and well stocked in ghosts, the Pine Barrens are sparsely populated, though most small settlements and villages have grocery stores and places to eat and there are many cut-out-of-the-woods-by-the-side-of-the-road taverns which serve up hearty fare and good drink. When you're ready for "fancy dining," head to the shore regions. Remember that this is a vast area and not to be explored in a day.

Atlantic City Day Trip

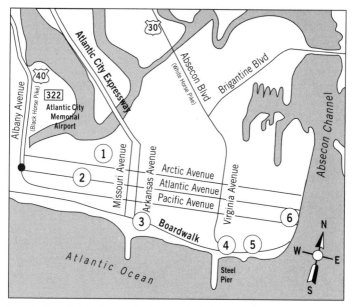

1. White House Sub Station
2. Tony's Baltimore Grill
3. Caesars Atlantic City
4. The Taj Mahal
5. Garden Pier
6. Absecon Light House

It has been said in aggressive Jersey travel-tourist advertisements that "all roads lead to Atlantic City," and in a sense this is true. Atlantic City has been and still is at the center of things in New Jersey; and the geographic point in which it is located has always been ideal for sea breezes and a swim in the ocean.

Route 9 leads directly onto Absecon Highway (Route 30) into Atlantic City. This old causeway has a number of 1930s cabins and 1950s motels and interesting pop-culture architectural oddities, notably the **Santa Maria House,** built by J. Vaughan Mathis in 1926 as a landmark for his real estate development north of Atlantic City. The building, a two-story replica of Christopher Columbus's ship, has been a restaurant and is now an antique shop.

Route 322 out of Pleasantville (also off Route 9) is the southern road into Atlantic City and is known as the Black Horse Pike. Two pop oddities are the old **Studebaker Showroom** in the 1920s mission-architectural style (now an antique-boutique complex) and the **Sand Castle,** a charming fairy-tale building in the Spanish-adobe architectural style, facing an unbroken expanse of bay and

sky. This building, now unoc-
cupied, used to be one of Barbara Hutton's—the poor little
rich girl Woolworth heiress—
summer getaways.

The Atlantic City Expressway, a
toll road, will get you there in a
big hurry from Philadelphia;
and, of course, for Philadelphians and others who connect at
Philadelphia and Cherry Hill
from all points, there is the Amtrak train into Atlantic City. Naturally people are now loaded onto
daily and hourly express buses
from local candy and cigar stores,

Sheet-music cover for the song "At-
lantic City" from the Novelty Music
Company.

and from points all over the
Northeast for a big day of gambling at the casinos. But in the
spirit of old times, it is still rec-
ommended that you take the old routes by car into the excitement
of Atlantic City. Maps of Atlantic City are plentiful in the casinos.

One spot that still has the quality and Boardwalk "flavor" of old-
time Atlantic City, and is surely the best place to start a visit (or
end one) is the **White House Sub Station** at 2301 Arctic Avenue,
right near the Atlantic City bus station. The White House, which
claims to have originated the submarine sandwich, has been in
business since the early 1940s, and still makes its own bread and
uses U.S. grade #1 bolognas, salami, steak, hot sausage, and other
meats with its own special green hot relish. The original hot or
cold submarine sandwiches are meticulously made with the inside dough pulled out and the meat piled on thick. There is no
stinting here; good Ireland-brand perked coffee and Pennsylvania
potato chips (made with pure lard) are served, all at very reasonable prices. The gleaming white interior is set off with blue-and-
orange neon advertising signs, bright lighting, comfortable sit-down
booths, and friendly waitresses who serve with a smile. Some of

The Black Cat (outlined in green neon) Tavern in Absecon is just outside Atlantic
City.

the celebrities who loved their delicious White House subs include the Beatles, Frank Sinatra, Eydie Gorme, Jerry Lewis, Liberace, and countless others. The walls are adorned with photographs of smiling, satisfied movie stars, radio and television personalities, sports figures, and nightclub entertainers, all holding their giant subs. The White House is open until midnight and some nights until 1 A.M., and should not be missed by food buffs who never have tasted a real sub sandwich. No soft, skimpy blimpies here; phone (609) 345-1564.

New Jersey resorts booklet showing a bathing beauty and a lady in a rolling wicker chair on the Boardwalk in Atlantic City during its golden era; from the Pennsylvania Railroad system, 1923.

Tony's Baltimore Grill at 2800 Atlantic Avenue is one of the great mainstay establishments in Atlantic City. As you enter the restaurant, lit by red neon light, there is a horseshoe-shaped bar on one side and comfortable booths on the other. Another large room is filled with booths and tables throughout. The kitchen is in full view, and patrons can watch, for all practical purposes, their meals being cooked or the pizza dough thrown. There is a buzz in the place, and an atmosphere of warmth and good cheer. The food served here is good Italian-style seafood, spaghetti concoctions, and first-rate pizza (whole pies only). The prices fit the tourists' pocketbook, and the servings are ample. Try antipasto, fried shrimp, or crab cakes for starters. The Baltimore Grill seafood special, including fried shrimp, scallops, and crab cakes, or spaghetti with meatballs, sausage, clams, or anchovies are both good choices for entrees. Cheese pizza is served with sausage or other ingredients—the special is a cheese, mushroom, and sausage pizza. The Baltimore Grill pizza is mouth-wateringly delicious, and is big

Two Fralinger's Saltwater Taffy containers. Left: an original from the 1930s. Right: a 1990s tin-litho reproduction.

Atlantic City Boardwalk at night.

enough for a meal for two. The prices are low, but the service and food are just fine. Atlantic City regulars rave about this place and the proprietor—in the manner of Atlantic City—says he keeps the joint open around the clock; phone (609) 345-5766 or 345-9461.

In its biggest boom since gambling started in 1978, Atlantic City expanded its airport and built a new **Convention Center** (1997). The original **Convention Hall** is now used as a special events arena.

For more information on Atlantic City tourism, contact the Atlantic City Convention and Visitors Authority, 2314 Pacific Avenue, Atlantic City, NJ 08401, or call (609) 449-7154. To go from the future back to the past, visit the preserved and restored Garden Pier on the Boardwalk at New Jersey Avenue, where you can visit the Atlantic City Art Center and the Atlantic City Historical Museum.

Fun and Games in Atlantic City

Charles Darrow, a Philadelphian who vacationed in Atlantic City, sat down in his living room one day in 1930 and created a game based on Atlantic City real estate called *Monopoly*. Like a good many others, Darrow needed money in the Great Depression to support a wife and child. This play-money property game contains a pertinent fantasy element that holds players' interest beyond the normal 45-minute attention span of most board games. However, initially Parker Brothers were skeptical of the game's sales potential on the marketplace, and turned the proposed game down in 1934. They changed their thinking, however, when Darrow proceeded to have a few thousand sets made up that sold like hotcakes at Philadelphia department stores. Needless to say, Darrow made his own Atlantic City fortune out of this Monopoly game. Oddly enough, the success of the game in the Depression arrived on the scene at a time that the Big Bad Wolf nearly did in the biggest resort on the eastern seaboard. After the Wall Street stock market crash and bank closings, many Atlantic City hotels were empty and nightclubs and restaurants were forced to shut down. By 1933, the worst year of the Depression decade, the city could not meet its own payroll, and issued the equivalent of "play" money in scrip certificates, which were to be

Mickey Mouse pushes Minnie, who is sitting in a rolling chair, on the Boardwalk. The famous cartoon mice are shown on an Atlantic City tin sandpail, which originally was filled with saltwater taffy. Pail is marked Walter E. Disney Enterprises, circa 1934, and was purchased recently at the Atlantic City Antique Show for $1,200.

redeemed when the American economy returned to normalcy. Today it is not play or scrip money, but the clinking of coins in paper cups and the clatter of rolling dice on the crap tables, the high rollers and the low rollers, all out to win big in the new fun and games stakes of Atlantic City.

The casinos provide the excitement of gambling, fancy dining, and nightclubs with top performers, which have included Joan Rivers, Diana Ross, Dean Martin, Al Martino, and Frank Sinatra. Comfortable hotel rooms are not the least of Atlantic City's attractions. The casinos are: **Merv Griffin's Resorts International Casino Hotel,** (609) 344-6000, the first to open, May 26, 1978, located on the Boardwalk between North Carolina Avenue and Pennsylvania Avenue. Resorts features a 1,700-seat superstar theater where it presents top-name entertainment and championship boxing. The actual casino area of Resorts is almost the size of two football fields, with more than 1,700 slot machines and 120 gaming tables. There are over 700 guests rooms in the renovated Chalfonte-Haddon Hall and more than half-a-dozen restaurants from gourmet to moderate to economical.

Caesars Atlantic City extends from Pacific Avenue to the Boardwalk between Arkansas and Missouri Avenues. A prime attraction is the 18-foot-tall exact replica of Michelangelo's **David,** weighing nine tons and handcrafted in Italy from Carara marble. Caesars was the second casino to open in Atlantic City, on June 26, 1979. Entertainment at the **Circus Maximus;** lounges include the **Cleopatra,** and the **Forum,** restaurants include **Ambrosia, La Posh, Primavera, Hyakumi, Imperial Steakhouse, Cafe Roma, Oriental Palace, Pompeii, Boardwalk Cafe, Italian Festival,** and **Venice Bar.** Caesars' telephone number is (609) 348-4411.

Caesar Augustus of Prima Porta, an 18-foot replica of the original, dominates the corner of the Boardwalk and Arkansas Avenue. (Photo courtesy of Caesars Atlantic City)

Bally's Park Place, A Hilton Casino Resort, (609) 340-2000, opened in December 1979 on the Boardwalk between Park Place and Michigan Avenue, on the site of the destroyed Marlborough-Blenheim Hotel. It also incorporates the completely gutted and

The most obvious feature of Bally's Park Place Casino is its size— 60,000 square feet, accented by neon lighting and diagonal ceiling mirrors. (Photo courtesy Bally's Grand Casino Hotel)

refurbished Dennis Hotel, and a 37-story tower. There is a cabaret, lounges and restaurants.

Sands Hotel and Casino, (609) 441-4000, opened in August 1980 between Indiana Avenue and Illinois Avenue just off the Boardwalk at Brighton Park, and advertises itself as "the most precious jewel in the tiara of East Coast gaming!" The Sands has an aggressive entertainment program and has gained the reputation of being the boxing center of the East Coast. There are three restaurants.

Harrah's Casino Hotel, (609) 441-5000, was the first casino to open away from the Boardwalk in November of 1980 on a 14-acre site located adjacent to the Brigantine Bridge. This 15-story, brightly lit glass hotel casino can be seen for miles around. Special features here include the marina for nautically minded gamblers, and an 850-seat Broadway-by-the-Bay Theater, lounges galore, and restaurants.

Bally's Grand (originally the Golden Nugget), (609) 340-7111, on the Boardwalk between Boston and Providence, opened in December 1980 and features a Victorian decorating theme, including a 120-foot-wide by 10-foot-high mural depicting the 1890 Atlantic City Easter parade, and a 35-foot

brass birdcage complete with five audio-automated birds, which perform a musical review every fifteen minutes. Balley's Grand featuring more than 100,000 linear feet of brass railings and grills, has an opera house, and several restaurants from gourmet to economical.

The **Trump World's Fair,** (609) 441-2888, at Florida Avenue on the Boardwalk, was originally the Playboy Hotel and Casino. The complex, currently comprising two buildings with two glass skywalks, has a theater and three floors of casino gambling. There is a lounge, the Travel Pavilion (open 24 hours), and a moderate priced restaurant, O'Flynn's Irish Pub.

Joyous craps players at Bally's Grand Casino, which also offers Big Six, Bacarat, Blackjack, Mini-Baccarat, Roulette, Red Dog, and Sic Bo. (Photo courtesy Bally's Park Place Casino)

Claridge Casino Hotel at the boardwalk between Indiana Avenue and Park Place, (609) 340-3400, is in the refurbished Claridge Hotel, which was built in 1930 and modeled after the Empire State Building. The original Claridge closed in 1973 after playing host to world celebrities like Princess Grace of Monaco, Bob Hope, and Alfred G. Vanderbilt. The present hotel casino, originally done all in English style, has been revamped into a sporting all-American decor in keeping with the fast-paced style of Atlantic City; it includes a theater, a cabaret, and four restaurants.

Tropicana Casino and Resort, (609) 340-4000, (formerly the Tropicana Hotel and Casino) opened in November 1981 at the Boardwalk between Iowa Avenue and Brighton Place, on the site of the former Ambassador Hotel. The Tropicana resembles a geometric work of art with its multilevel cubical design and 17-story tower with bands of black and white. The motto here is "where every second sizzles" and an interesting feature is the glass elevator ride to the **Top of the Trop,** a lounge with an observation corridor providing panoramic views of the entire Atlantic City area, there is a showroom, lounges, seven restaurants, and **Tivoli Pier,** an indoor amusement park.

Trump Plaza Hotel and Casino, (609) 441-6000, opened at Mississippi Avenue and the boardwalk in May, 1984. It features a 37-story gleaming white-and-black obelisk, called Atlantic City's "centerpiece." Panoramic views can be had here also, and why not try **Ivanka's,** named after Donald and Ivana's daughter, a gourmet restaurant featuring such a lavish display of food that it is worth the price of admission to *see* it once.

Trump Castle, (609) 441-2000, which opened in May 1985 (at the Farley Marina area) is on Brigantine Boulevard and is popular with boaters; Donald Trump's yacht was docked here for use by the high rollers in the first few months of the gala opening. It has theaters, lounges, and six restaurants.

Showboat, (609) 343-4000, at Delaware Avenue and the boardwalk, has two showrooms, the **Bourbon Street Lounge,** and the **Hall of Fame Lounge;** Missis-

sippi Steak and Seafood, Casa di Napoli, Deli on the Square, Snack Bar & Pizzeria, Basin Street Cafe, 11th Frame Snack Bar, Sun Deck, Captain's Buffet Restaurant, and the Showboat Bowling Center, open from 10 A.M. to midnight for more active sportsmen and women.

The Taj Mahal, (609) 449-1000, at Boardwalk and Virginia Avenue, is the most recent and, of course, the largest casino in the world. Its casino, the size of four football fields, is glittering with hundreds of crystal chandeliers, and its miles of public corridors are studded by rare works of sculpture and art. Here is the **Etess Arena** (for shows), the **Casbah** and **Oasis** lounges, the **Scheherazade Restaurant** and **Safari Steak House,** both gourmet, the **Bombay Cafe, Sultan's Feast** (moderate), and **Rock and Rolls** (an economical eatery in the 1950s style, with neon and life-sized figures of Elvis on the walls). At the top of the escalator, hung with

The Smothers Brothers have performed at Donald Trump's resort, the Taj Mahal, which can feed 13,000 people at one sitting. (Photo courtesy Trump Taj Mahal Casino and Resort)

The late, great crooner Dean Martin and his sidekick, comic Jerry Lewis, got their big show biz break as a duo playing at the 500 Club in Atlantic City, where Frank Sinatra and Jimmy Roselli often appeared. Jerry Lewis still likes to make return trips to the Chancellor Avenue neighborhood in Irvington where he was born and raised.

three of the world's largest crystal chandeliers, is a granite-faced branch of Tiffany's, the great New York jewelry store.

For a breath of air try a walk at the northern end of Atlantic City at the **Abesecon Light House.** Take a drive north across Absecon Bay to Brigantine Island with its "haunted castle," other attractions, and funtime bars. The **Lagoon** at 3700 Brigantine Boulevard, has the area's "hottest" deejay for disco dancing Thursday, Friday, and Saturday nights in the **Boat Bar;** they also serve good seafood, steaks, and veal dishes. Call (609) 266-7057.

Atlantic City itself features more restaurants in just the casinos alone than exist in the entire state of Rhode Island. Three good ones, outside the casinos, include the architecturally fascinating **Knife & Fork Inn** at Atlantic and Pacific Avenues, (609) 344-1133, presided over by the brothers Latz since 1927, serving fine seafood, of course, fresh vegetables, and an extensive wine list; **Dock's Oyster House** at 2405 Atlantic Avenue, (609) 345-0092, serving seafood since 1897, and specializing in poached salmon and live lobsters in the tank; and **Angelo's Fairmount Tavern** at Mississippi and Fairmount Avenues, (609) 344-2439, established in 1935 and featuring the best in Italian pasta.

Remember, this is an all-night town for bars, casino, and some eateries. Something is always happening in A.C.!

Old Atlantic City

I n the 20th Century–Fox technicolor musical film *Three Little Girls in Blue* (1946), Vivian Blaine, June Haver, and Vera-Ellen, three beautiful blonde farmgirl sisters, go to one of the old Atlantic City hotels in 1905 in search of millionaires. The film, which also starred George Montgomery, Frank Latimore, and Celeste Holm (now a New Jersey resident herself and also an active conservationist), contains the well-known standard "On the Boardwalk in Atlantic City" written by Josef Myron, Harry Warren, and Mack Gordon, which extols the virtues of boardwalk rolling chairs, summer love, and saltwater air in a magical place. The popular rendition of this happy seashore tune was recorded by Dick Haymes in the 1940s. After renting a fabulous suite for $9.25 a day (quite a sum in 1905) one practical-minded sister complains about expenses while another more romantic one says breathlessly, "Atlantic City! Oh . . . come on . . . what's money? At last we're free!"

Such has always been, it seems, the reckless spirit of a city known as America's answer to the Riviera, built on sandy Absecon Island on the Atlantic Ocean. The first tavern inn to operate in Atlantic City was licensed to Aunt Millie Leed in 1839. Could this have been a relation of the same Leed family at nearby Leeds Point who let loose a Jersey Devil into the world? By 1854, with the advent of

Three Little Girls in Blue, a 1940s technicolor 20th Century–Fox musical set in Atlantic City at the turn of the century, introduced the song "On the Boardwalk in Atlantic City." 1946 lobby card.

The beautiful Marlborough-Blenheim Hotel depicted on a 1908 postcard printed in Germany. Though this grand and sturdy structure had been declared an official landmark by the State, it was nevertheless demolished to make way for casino gambling.

a steam-powered railroad line from Camden, more than half-a-dozen rooming houses appeared, and by 1860, 4,000 people could rent a room with breakfast and dinner at places such as the Surf House, Congress Hall, the Mansion, and Odd Fellows. People flocked here initially believing that salt air and the ocean could cure illness, particularly sinus, bronchitis, walking pneumonia, consumption, and other 19th-century ailments. Even the mentally infirm who suffered from various "nervous disorders" or "attacks" were brought to Atlantic City for a cure.

Atlantic City historian Vicki Gold Levi, who wrote the book *Atlantic City — 125 Years of Ocean Madness* with Lee Eisenberg, remembers an Atlantic City filled with deep blue, pink-and-purple hydrangea bushes. They surrounded the old hotels and were particularly lush at the Marlborough-Blenheim. Vicki herself was the "Hydrangea Queen" of Atlantic City, and her father was Al Gold, Atlantic City's chief photographer from 1939 to 1964. Vicki wanted to be the girl on the high-diving horse on the Steel Pier, but her dad discouraged that occupation when he showed her some of the dangers involved in such a feat. There was a lot going on in Atlantic City that Al Gold told his wide-eyed daughter; one story involved a high-level mobster convention held there on May 14, 1929, attended by Al Capone, Louis "Lepke" Buchalter, Meyer Lansky, Dutch Schultz, Frank Costello, and Lucky Luciano. Much of the changeover from old world Atlantic City charm to the Las Vegas–style stretch pants pomp of casino Atlantic City can be seen in the brilliant film *Atlantic City* directed by Louis Malle, written by John Guare, and starring Susan Sarandon and Burt Lancaster.

✣   ✣   ✣

In 1994, the **Atlantic City Art Center,** (609) 347-5837, and the **Atlantic City Historical Museum,** (609) 347-5389, celebrated the Gala Opening of their permanent homes, both located on the Garden Pier on the Boardwalk at New Jersey Avenue. Vicki made the initial gift to the museum, seven cartons of memorabilia she had collected over the years, including period postcards, change purses made from seashells, porcelain mermaids, china bathing dolls manufactured in West Germany, and plates and saucers made in Japan—all with an Atlantic City overprint—mother-of-pearl pins, salt-and-pepper shakers resembling lobster tails, kewpie dolls, snowflake glass balls with Miss America inside—and hundreds of photos she assembled from her own collection of her father's photos of Atlantic City, now designated as the Al Gold Memorial Collection. Vicki , who was the founder of the museum with Florence Miller and Tony Kutschera, was also the principal consultant for the Walt Disney World "Atlantic City Boardwalk" Resort, which opened in Florida in 1995.

Bess Meyerson, after having been crowned Miss America, is ecstatic while Atlantic City's own Vicki Gold Levi (author of Atlantic City, 125 Years of Ocean Madness*) carries the velvet train.*

The first saltwater taffy sold in Atlantic City was produced at a James saltwater taffy stand in 1883 (six pieces for a nickel) with Joseph Fralinger following with his taffy shops in 1885. In 1985 **Fralinger's,** the most famous candy-taffy-maker in Atlantic City, celebrated its 100th anniversary. These gooey chewy concoctions in pastel colors and a variety of flavors (originally just chocolate, vanilla, and molasses), were just the thing to offer a beautiful lady in her rolling chair on the Boardwalk.

Official program and souvenir album of the famous Miss America beauty pageant. Diving girl, Convention Hall, and the sunburst pattern make a striking cover for this 1933 event.

The great Boardwalk, as we have come to know it, is 40 feet wide and 4 miles long (some 1920s brochures described it as 7 to 8 miles long and 60 feet wide), and was completed in 1896 following in the footsteps of 5 smaller previous boardwalks. The Boardwalk flourished at the turn of the century and in the teens, with many commercial establishments, restaurants, and piers such at the Heinz (57 varieties) Pier, known as the Crystal Palace by the Sea, which offered real pickles, pickle pins, and other free samples until 1944, when the pier was swept away by a hurricane. The Steel Pier opened in 1898 and was known as the "showplace of the nation" and the Steeplechase "funny place" Pier opened in 1904. The Million Dollar Pier opened in 1906, offering entertainment through the years with Harry Houdini featured, as well as being the site of the crowning of the earliest Miss Americas.

Two great "sandcastle" style hotels that once stood on the Board-walk were the Marlborough-Blenheim and the Hotel Traymore. The Blenheim was one of the first hotels to be made of reinforced concrete. Thomas Edison, who developed this method of construction, was on hand to supervise the raising of the building, which was completed in 1906. The ornamentation of imaginary sea creatures and devils, sea horses, bloated fish, sand crabs, and sea hawks were exquisite examples of Seaside Art Nouveau. Some of this original ornamentation is on display at the top of the waterfall escalator at Bally's Park Place, A Hilton Casino Resort, as if in homage to a better constructed, more imaginative Atlantic City. The luxurious old-world charm of the Marlborough-Blenheim, hot-and-cold seawater running in the bathtub tap in the great rooms, the formal dining rooms, lounges, sun porches, and library, was destroyed in 1979. The Dennis Hotel, now incorporated into the Bally Park Place complex and featuring the Dennis Lounge, is one of the few remaining public "rooms" where you can experience the grandeur of old Atlantic City hotel life.

The massive Egyptian Deco-style Traymore Hotel, designed by William L. Price, was destroyed in 1972 by massive dynamiting. The memory loss of these hotels is not just a case of nostalgia or sentiment for what was old and beautiful; but for what was serviceable, natural, grand, and functional. Now there is no openness to the ocean and its breezes, and everything seems shut off from its geographic location in order to focus in on the gambling tables. One new hotel mistakenly used mirrored gold plastic on the ocean facade that attracted hordes of gnats, flies, and other large bugs blown in from the Atlantic City meadows. The Claridge (built in 1930) and Merv Griffin's Resorts Casino Hotel (the renovated Chalfonte-Haddon Hall Hotel) had the good common sense to incorporate the old into the new. All over Atlantic City today you will see a great deal of attention paid in photo murals and displays incorporating architectural details from old buildings to the memory-image of old Atlantic City.

Convention Hall, built in 1929, the year of the Wall Street crash, is another great monument to authentic old Atlantic City, and was the largest building of its kind to be built without posts or pillars. Political and corporate business conventions, gigantic antique shows, car shows, and the famous Atlantic City Miss America Pageant are still held in this vast architectural wonder. A built-in pipe organ—called the world's largest—has 32,913 pipes. The building's facade and the pillared porticos along the ocean side are beautifully decorated with cement friezes in the Art Deco style of dancing nymphs, sea maidens, and sea creatures.

When traveling from one end of the long Boardwalk to the other, the rolling wicker chairs were always favored. There were 2,500 of them in operation in 1925. Many of them have been salvaged and reinstituted, and are today pushed by college students. Jitney service (tiny little buses) still operates up and down Pacific Avenue and continues to give Atlantic City some of the flavor it once had as a "continental" city that attracted the great in show business, international society, and the business world. Today, with the focus on gambling, the atmosphere is filled with another kind of excitement.

Ocean City Day Trip

Driving south on Atlantic Avenue—the closest avenue to the ocean once you hit Ventnor (just south of Atlantic City)—is quite remarkable for its architectural beauty and simplicity. You will see single-family homes in large Georgian Colonials painted gleaming white as if they were the White House by the sea. Some have 1930s-style striped awnings, manicured lawns, and are surrounded by blue hydrangea bushes. Others are in the Hollywood Spanish Dolores del Rio hacienda-style and are painted sand color with iron gates and Mexican tiles incorporated into the design. On Ventnor Avenue, which is a main thoroughfare, there are some interesting shops, ice cream parlors, and seashore-antique shops as well as more homes and restaurants, each with their own unique atmosphere. Certainly, Ventnor is a posh suburb of Atlantic City.

Note: Atlantic Avenue, from the Atlantic City Lighthouse at Absecon Inlet (the northern tip of Atlantic City), south through Ventnor, Margate, and Longport, to the Great Egg Harbor Inlet, is part of **Ocean Drive** and is marked with signs featuring a flying seagull and the words FOLLOW THE FLIGHT OF THE GULL. Ocean Drive crosses Great Egg Harbor on the Ocean City–Longport Bridge, and continues on through Ocean City, Sea Isle City, Avalon, Stone Harbor, and Wildwood right on down to Cape May Point. It is a wonderfully scenic drive and is clearly marked; the distance from Absecon Inlet to Cape May Point is 44 miles.

Souvenir postcard booklet of Ocean City, circa 1940.

Lucy the Elephant. Two early postcard views of the only known elephant hotel in the world, now a major tourist attraction in Margate.

South of Ventnor, in Margate (once called South Atlantic City) on Atlantic Avenue (Ocean Drive) and Decatur Street, you will see what must be the most remarkable of all seashore architectural oddities. This is the great **Lucy the Margate Elephant** building, 65 feet tall, made of wood and sheet metal. Her legs are 20 feet high and 10 feet in diameter. Her head is 58 feet around, her ears 17 feet long, her tusks 22 feet and her tail 26 feet. The trunk is 36 feet long. Her belly contains a 60-foot domed room and there are 18 windows. Built in 1881, this "elephant hotel" first attracted tourists in 1887 as a tavern, then became a rental cottage with a "rear view" window under the pachyderm's "rear end" tail. James Lafferty, the Philadelphia entrepreneur-developer who built Lucy to draw real estate investors to the Atlantic City area, built another elephant called the "Elephantine Colossus," a 37-room hotel in Coney Island. Built in 1884, it burned down in 1896; a sister pachyderm built in Cape May, the "Light of Asia," suffered the same fate in 1900. Today Lucy stands alone by the sea in Margate as a museum, thanks to concerned citizens who raised money and had her declared a historic site by the State of New Jersey. Fortunately, this treasure did not go the way of the old hotels in Atlantic City. Lucy is open April through October. Call (609) 823-6473 for information.

Longport, south of Margate, is a charming beach community at the tip of Absecon Beach, Sculls Bay to the west, and Great Egg

Harbor Inlet to the south. From Longport you will be on Ocean Drive across the inlet on a series of bridges, passing through some beautiful marshland. It is a wonderful route to travel at dusk or dawn as you spot wild egret and other fowl flying across the harbor to and from the **Tuckahoe Corbin City Fish and Wildlife Management Area** nearby. There is a miminal toll on the last bridge as you enter Ocean City.

Ocean City is a gracious old seaside town that maintains much of the flavor and atmosphere of a turn-of-the-century resort. Its architecture is not Victorian in the way that Ocean Grove or Cape May are, but its fine old wood-frame houses are well maintained and intact. There are dozens of rooming houses, guest houses, and some fine genteel old-style hotels here. The **Bellevue Hotel** at 8th Street and Ocean Avenue, (609) 399-0110, is highly recommended. The sprawling boardwalk is high up off the surf and has some commanding scenic views of the oceanfront and the surrounding landscape. The air seems particularly fresh and clean, and the swimming and immaculate beaches are a delight. There is a sophisticated rather than a stuffy feeling here. The casual strollers on the boardwalk are Philadelphia-smart and well-dressed, many actually reading classic novels as they sun themselves on the beach. This is the place where Grace Kelly, as a young girl, came from Philadelphia with her parents each summer, and it is much like Spring Lake, another Jersey shore Irish-Catholic resort. This wholesome atmosphere is part of what will make you feel like you are in a resort town of yesteryear (no loud radios blasting here). The boardwalk has a number of inviting concessions, amusements, and rides. There is very good pizza at **Mack and Manco. Shriver's Saltwater Taffy Shop,** which has been on the boardwalk at 9th Street since 1898, is still here; and is now run as a division of the Dairy Maid Confectionery Company of Philadelphia. Their delicious taffy is made from sugar, corn syrup, molasses, peanut butter, cocoa butter, hydrogenated vegetable oils, nut meats, chocolate, natural and artificial flavors, and food colors. Ocean City has two boardwalk movie theaters (something to be missed in Atlantic City, which has none), the **Strand**—designed in the streamlined art moderne style of the 1930s complete with glass bricks and neon—and the **Moorlyn,** which is now twinned.

The wonderful Ocean City boardwalk music pier and auditorium was built out over the beach and ocean in 1928, and the folks still gather to hear live bands and singers perform light operetta-style music or Gay Nineties ballads in summer concerts next to the breaking waves. You will find a great deal of pleasure just taking a walk in Ocean City. The people are friendly and the entire place is set up for old-fashioned relaxation and enjoyment, the way Atlantic City had been in the beginning. A couple of restaurant tips

Grace Kelly, movie star and princess of Monaco, spent summers at the Kelly family home in Ocean City.

are: the **Chatterbox** at 9th Street and Central Avenue, (609) 399-0113, serving burgers, super-thick shakes, sandwiches, and seafood—open daily from 7 A.M. to 9 P.M. and the **Dockside Cafe** at 10th Street and the bay, (609) 398-0451, which has been called by restaurant critics one of the Jersey shore's outstanding restaurants, serving seafood, coquille St. Jacques, and other specialties. Call for seasonal hours and reservations.

The **Flanders Hotel**, which opened in 1923, is a landmark in Ocean City at 11th Street and the boardwalk. Looking out on the ocean, the white stucco, red-tile-roofed hotel was newly developed and refurbished in 1997, featuring one-bedroom suites with queen-sized beds, sofabeds in the sitting room, kitchens, and private baths—recommended for 4 to 5 people. Rates for the ocean suites are $299, and the others are $269. A 10 percent discount is offered to Triple A members. Check-in is at 4 P.M. and check-out is 11 A.M. Call (609) 399-1000 for reservations and low off-season rates. BYOB (remember, Ocean City is *dry*), try the miniature golf course, and of course the ocean is just steps away across the boardwalk. This may be the ideal place to spend a night or two if you are planning to go to Atlantic City casinos. Some of the feeling of Atlantic City's old Marlborough-Blenheim Hotel can be experienced at this fine hotel.

A very attractive 1950s-style place with a swimming pool right on the boardwalk is the **Beach Club Hotel** (formerly the Sting Ray). There are floor-to-ceiling windows with ocean views and balconies, and a restaurant called the **Spindrift.** The stucco walls are painted white with turquoise trim and the name of the place is spelled out in vivid red neon. Summer rates for two in a room with double beds, television, and bathroom are $165 to $240 per night. An extra person is $10 more. These rates have to do with city view or ocean view. The Beach Club Hotel is at 13th Street and the boardwalk. Check-in time is 2:30 P.M. and check-out is 11 A.M., but the Beach Club is thoughtful enough to offer their guests shower rooms with private lockers (for those who wish to stay and use the pool and other facilities after check-out time). Who wants to leave the beach at 11 A.M. on a hot summer day? Call (609) 399-8555 for reservations. Of course, off-season rates are lower,

"Colourpicture" linen postcard.

though the Beach Club Hotel closes in mid-October and doesn't reopen until the beginning of May.

An excellent bed-and-breakfast is the elegantly restored 1894 Victorian **Northwood Inn** at 401 Wesley Avenue, which won a 1990 beautification award from the Ocean City Chamber of Commerce. There are spacious guest rooms with private baths, and a hearty gourmet breakfast is served. The rates are $90 up to $160, all with full baths and television. A fun place to stay here is the tower room ($120). Weekly rates are good, with the seventh day free; but the midweek rates (any day from Sunday through Thursday) are especially attractive—with more of a chance for pick of room. Northwood Inn is run by Marge and John Loeper and is open year-round and features low off-season rates as well.

While in Ocean City be sure to stop by the **Ocean City Historical Museum** at 409 Wesley Avenue (on the same block as the Northwood Inn). Here you will see a Victorian dining room and bedroom as it was in Ocean City in the 19th century, as well as hundreds of pictures, maps, and books depicting life in this city more than 100 years ago. There is an excellent antique doll collection on view. The admission is free, with summer hours Monday through Saturday from 10 A.M. to 4 P.M.; winter hours are 1 to 4 P.M., Tuesday to Saturday, (609) 399-1801.

Corson's Inlet to Wildwood-by-the-Sea

The 35-mile section of Ocean Drive south of Ocean City, from Corson's Inlet Bridge at Strathmere toward Wildwood and Cape May, is always a very pleasant trip indeed. You will find many points of scenic interest along the way with a good number of antique shops for which this southern tip and cape is noted. The southern shore area includes many waterways, bays, and inlets, as well as the beautiful wide, white-sand seashore towns of Strathmere, Whale Beach, Sea Isle City, Townsend's Inlet, Avalon, and Stone Harbor, all noted vacation spots with motel units for an overnight, weekend, or week's lodging. Avalon has particularly high sand dunes, charming old homes, and is dedicated to a vacation style that is quiet and serene. The **Stone Harbor Bird Sanctuary,** a famous spot for heronry, is just south of Stone Harbor on Seven Mile Beach. Inland on Route 9 at Swainton, between Avalon and Sea Isle City Boulevards, is one of the most beautiful gardens in New Jersey, called the **Thomas Leaming Farm.** You can relive the days of the earliest settlers here as you tour the intact settler houses surrounded by tall pines and flowers. Open June through October daily from 9:30 A.M. to 5 P.M., (609) 465-5871 for further information.

The real hot spot seaside resort in the southern tip is Wildwood-by-the-Sea. To the north is North Wildwood, and to the south Wildwood Crest. The Wildwoods offer five miles of wide, safe beaches, and a three-mile-long boardwalk packed with amusements, rides, and games. There are motels every few feet, nightclubs, bars,

Greetings from Wildwood by-the-Sea, linen postcard.

*A "Funhouse" breeze-hole pinup,
on a penny arcade slot machine
postcard painted by Lugren.*

restaurants, movies, hotels, diners, and stores and concessions that jump day and night with excitement and activity. There are several amusement piers with every conceivable ride jutting out over the beach, which like Atlantic City's, is free. The many concessions and jumping joints on the boardwalk and on the spacious **Hunt's Pier** remind one of the good times going on in the Seaside Heights summer community. The city area proper has large five-and-dime stores and other merchants to accommodate all your vacation needs. Wildwood as a city is more together than the Atlantic City outside of the casino areas. If fun and pleasure or sun and surf is your goal—and you are single—Wildwood is the place to be wild and free. Though teenagers are probably not too keen about it, the **Wildwood Historical Museum** has exhibits that trace the history of Wildwood over the centuries. It is located at 4400 New Jersey Avenue, (609) 522-2444. The convention hall provides facilities for varied events and seats 4,000. Motels along Ocean and Atlantic Avenues feature lots of neon and exotic names, from the **Acropolis** and the **Aquarius** to the **Royal Hawaiian,** the **Singapore,** the **Tahiti,** and the **Waikiki Motor Inn. Ed Zaberer's Restaurant,** open from mid-May to mid-September at 400 Spruce Avenue in North Wildwood, (609) 522-1423, features reasonable family dinners, does its own baking, and has the "world's largest collection of Tiffany lamps."

The main attraction at Wildwood are the six piers featuring $10 million of the latest rides including the Zoom Phloom, a maze of waterfalls, rapids, caverns, and a watery roller coaster, a Sea Serpent, and the 150-foot giant wheel adorned with 16,000 light bulbs. The piers include **Morey's Pier, Mariner's Landing, Hunt's Pier** (which dates back to 1905) and features the extraordinary roaring rapids ride that imitates the sport of whitewater rafting, the **Nickel's Midway Pier** featuring the German ride "katapault" (the Nickel's Pier started out with a humble "guess-your-weight" concession years ago), the **Funchase Pier,** and the **Fun Pier,** which received a major overhauling and facelift not long ago.

Cape May Day Trip

B y contrast to Wildwood, Cape May, five miles south, at the southernmost tip of New Jersey, is a place relatively uncluttered by pizzeria stands, T-shirt emporiums, or hot dog-sausage concessions. This geographic point is also the only place in New Jersey where you can watch the sun both setting and rising over the ocean. The colors of the sky at various times of the day are magnificent, resembling those wonderful sky colors found at Provincetown, Massachusetts. Cape May is a historic landmark district where there are over 600 gingerbread Victorian homes, all within a 2-mile radius. Birdwatchers flock to **Cape May Point State Park,** as it is a temporary landing and rest spot for over 50 species of birds. The many old hotels, guest houses, and bed-and-breakfast inns offer turn-of-the-century-type accommodations to guests looking to get away from the flash of city living or from suburban shopping mall "tremors." Beachcombers enjoy finding semi-precious quartz stones called Cape May diamonds along Sunset Beach or near Cape May Point Lighthouse.

Just 150 miles south from New York City and readily accessible from Wilmington, Delaware, and Philadelphia, this enchanted seaside fantasy place has a town proper with a restored street filled with quaint shops, ice cream parlor–luncheonettes, restaurants, candy, clothing, and gift shops, many with a distinct feeling of old-time elegance. This restored Cape May street is now called the **Washington Street Mall** (open year-round) where you will also find Cape May "diamonds" for sale, and collectible dolls at the **Treasure Cove,** the "original" **Fudge Kitchen,** selling fudge, taffy, peanut brittle, almond crunch, cashew turtles, butterscotch, molasses sponge, macaroons, rock candy, and other seashore sweets (locations at 513 Washington Street Mall, 728 Beach Drive, and 2112 Boardwalk in North Wildwood), **McDowell's Gallery of**

Vacationers at Cape May at the turn of the century.

Gifts, a store set in an 1895 bank, selling craft gifts, jewelry, glassware, pottery items, and many antique emporiums. Look at the Cape May landmark, **Morrow's Nut House** on the promenade and the Washington Street Mall, where they make taffy from recipes handed down from a family tradition. The owners, Bill and Eleanor Morrow, met at the Philadelphia Sequicentennial Exposition in 1926, where they developed and sold their own delicious homemade sea foam fudge with nuts and other special ingredients. Call (609) 884-3300. An original Victorian bandstand in the town square offers summer concerts just as it has for more than 100 years. Cape May is one of those places where the old values integrate smoothly with the new.

Cape May is named after Cornelius Jacobsen Mey, the Dutch navigator who first explored this choice spot on the ocean and Delaware Bay in 1614. Cape May is divided into Cape May City (the hub of hotel life and the ocean boardwalk, and five-mile long swimming beach), Cape May Point (Cape May Point State Park), Sunset Beach, and the Cape May Migratory Bird Refuge where you can watch the migration of hawks in September and October from a special hawk-watch platform. **Cape May Point Lighthouse,** built in 1859, stands 170 feet high, has walls 8 feet thick, and its beacon of light is visible 19 miles out to sea. West Cape May is a part of this latter area, and the town called North Cape May (on the Delaware Bay) is also an interesting and beautiful spot.

The oldest Victorian guest hotel is the **Chalfonte Hotel** at Howard and Sewell Streets. It was built in 1876 by Colonel Henry Sawyer, who became the first exchange prisoner when he was traded in 1863 by the Confederacy for W. H. Fitzhugh Lee, the son of General Robert Lee, by order of an agreement overseen by Abe Lincoln. Rates at the large, gracious old hotel are from $120 to $190, tax and gratuity included as well as breakfast and dinner. Single rooms with sinks-only share hallway bathrooms. Many double rooms have private baths. For reservations call (609) 884-8409. The southern-style cooking is excellent at the **King Edward Lounge;** recommended are the deviled crabs and southern fried chicken with spoon bread and homemade biscuits.

Picturesque Cape May is not only renowned for being the oldest seashore resort in the United States, but as a place to view the largest collection of Victorian buildings in the country. Walking tours of these architectural treasures that are well maintained by proud owners who see them as functional historical monuments are frequent. What is most exciting to anyone with a sense of respect for their American heritage is to find such a town at this geographic point, a point that stretches 20 miles "out to sea." For an even further excursion out to sea take the Cape May–Lewes Ferry, which connects Cape May to Lewes, Delaware. The year-round service (call Cape May Terminal at [609] 886-2718 or the Lewes terminal at [302] 645-6313 for departure schedule) plying the broad ocean mouth of the Delaware Bay is performed by 5 vessels that hold 800 passengers and 100 cars each. Reservations can be made at least one day in advance by calling (800) 717-7245 daily from 7 A.M. to 8 P.M.

Victorian guest houses and bed-and-breakfast accommodations include: **The Mainstay Breakfast and Tea,** operated by preservationists Tom and Sue Caroll at 635 Columbia Avenue, (609) 884-8690, is a lavish and faithfully restored guest house, circa 1872.

The Victorian Rose at 715 Columbus Avenue, (609) 884-2497, features a wide veranda to sit and rock on or to lie in a hammock. The innkeepers are Bob and Linda Mullock.

The Brass Bed Inn, open all year at 719 Columbia Avenue, (609) 884-8075, has lots of wicker and rockers with original furniture. John and Donna Dunwoody provide a hearty breakfast.

The Abbey Bed & Breakfast, a Gothic revival villa at Columbia Avenue and Gurney Street, (609) 884-4506, features exceptional architecture and is also open to the public for tours. Call Jay and Marianne Schatz, innkeepers.

Two places, also open all year round, are the **Gingerbread House** at 28 Gurney Street, (609) 884-0211, a tastefully restored 1869 Victorian cottage run by Fred and Joan Echevarria, and the **Columbia House** at 26 Ocean Street, (609) 884-2789, which features spacious apartments and rooms with 19th-century antiques, run by Roger Crawford and Maggie Fenton.

Other year-round bed-and-breakfasts are: the **Queen Victoria,** the **Duke of Windsor Inn,** the **Dormer House Internationals,** **Captain Mey's Inn,** the **Hanson House,** and the **Seventh Sister.**

Oceanfront motels include **La Mer** at Beach and Pittsburgh Avenues, (609) 884-2200; **Colton Court,** 105 Beach Avenue, (609) 884-5384; **Colonial Hotel and Motor Lodge,** at Beach Drive and Ocean, (609) 884-3483; the **Montreal Inn,** 1028 Beach Avenue, (609) 884-7011; and the **Camelot Motel,** (609) 884-1500.

Dining out in Cape May is always a special experience, as there are a good number of fine restaurants in this wonderful old Victorian town.

The **Merion Inn** has been serving satisfied diners since 1885. Having celebrated its 117th year, this family-owned and -operated restaurant, with its candlelit tables with fresh flower centerpieces, has an antique bar serving cocktails; there is period artwork on the walls. In this relaxed atmosphere you can try some of their fresh seafood dishes like stuffed lobster tail. Hours are 4:30 to 10 P.M. daily; 106 Decatur Street, (609) 884-8363.

Maureen's at Beach Drive and Decatur Street has won national acclaim for its gourmet dinners, professional service, beautiful ocean views, and their charming cocktail lounge. Proper dress is required here, (609) 884-3774.

Casual seashore dining can be had at **McGlade's Mansion House,** family-owned and -operated, featuring seafood specialties like bluefish provençal, mussels fra diablo, homemade crab cakes, French fried lobster and a shrimp/crab "delight." Broadway and Sunset Boulevard, (609) 884-2429.

Rated "best in New Jersey" with four stars by *The New York Times* four years in a row is **The Mad Batter,** featuring international and nouvelle cuisine including crab margarita, duck à les amis, Chinese dim sum, pasta pesto Freddo, and other interesting dishes served in a European atmosphere on the oceanview veranda, in the skylighted Victorian dining room, or by the fountain on the garden terrace. 19 Jackson Street, (609) 884-5970.

The **Huntington House** buffet is the best place to hit if you're really hungry. Serving everything from soup to dessert nightly from 4:30 on, the buffet includes fruit salad, fisherman's chowder, 25 different salads and relishes, roast beef, country ham, fried shrimp, fried clams, chicken with Chinese vegetables and Chinese noodles, fish filets cooked in lemon butter and white wine, "Huntington corn pudding," seafood Newburgh with rice, scalloped potatoes, Italian sausage, baked stuffed peppers, and desserts that are out of this world, including cheesecake with cherry or blueberry topping, vanilla, chocolate, and butterscotch pudding parfaits, pumpkin pie, carrot cake, apple crisp, apple, cherry, and blueberry pie, all topped with homemade whipped cream that you can spoon yourself. There is also a complimentary beverage. Who needs seconds? Off Beach Drive on Grant Street, (609) 884-5868.

Special off-season events in Cape May include: The Tulip Festival, with thousands of tulips heralding Spring and Cape May's Dutch heritage; September Seafood Festival, memorializing fishermen lost at sea and celebrating Cape May's fishing heritage, with special seafood dishes being served in all the restaurants and hotels, and an outdoor restaurant festival featuring a seafood smorgasbord; Victorian Week, October, featuring tours of the historic

Columbia House in Cape May.

district by foot and trolley, fashion shows, slide and film presentations, an antique show, dinner dances, and individual house tours; the Christmas Ball and Community Ceremony, held in December, celebrates the Christmas spirit with tours of specially decorated houses and shops. A Christmas Ball, a tree lighting ceremony, and dancing to the big bands is part of the holiday festivities in Cape May.

Postscript—Travelers' Advisory

When the weary and satisfied traveler is back—safe and snug at home—we authors hope the followers of this Jersey guide will drop us a line and let us know just how their Jersey jaunt went. We sincerely welcome any interesting Jersey stories or travel tidbits (did you have a sighting, or an encounter with the Jersey Devil?). Any valid suggestions, thoughtful recommendations, or legitimate complaints may well wind up in future editions of *O' NEW JERSEY*. Vacations quickly and fondly become a memory; but today and tomorrow will hopefully find us again winding down that long road or trail.

Writer Gertrude Stein once told a friend that he may as well stay in the same place, not go anywhere. What for? While we are not advising staying in a stasis point, we have suggested all along that there is no need to travel thousands of airplane or railroad miles to have a good time. Looking at a vacation slide (on a home-viewing projection screen) of a group of friends, or the entire family standing in front of "Old Barney" lighthouse on Long Beach Island in New Jersey, may be just as vital as seeing this same group posing in front of the Eiffel Tower, the Pyramids of Egypt, or the Great Wall of China—and think of the money saved! Driving slowly in a leisurely manner down the old back roads and enjoying the passing scenery has been our basic credo. What's the hurry, anyway? If you are hungry, tired, or angry don't forget to take time off the road to enjoy a cruller and a cup of coffee—or maybe a malted milkshake at a Jersey diner. Many farmstands on the back road will offer a glass of free cider or a lump of maple sugar as a pick-me-up. If you are lost and you can't tell where you're at on the map—stop and ask for directions. Remember, most Jersey back roads will eventually lead you to a busy thoroughfare, a gas station, or a major highway. You may need to take a break from driving or even a nap if you can. Most major roads will have designated rest stops and encourage the taking of naps or coffee breaks. Watch for signs along the big highways that point to rest areas. Another option (if tired) is to exit the Parkway or Turnpike and check into a roadside motel somewhere.

Often it is desirable to have a specific destination in mind along with a travel plan; but there are those kind of Sunday drives where it is just fine to amble and wander without a destination in mind. Stop the car and get out and walk! To some this might seem like a radical idea. What, me walk! It is, of course, not a good idea to wander onto private property. What looks like an open field can

License plate attachment, enamel on metal, featuring the famous Mobil Oil Company red Pegassus.

sometimes turn out to be a farmer's bull pen. A number of beaches in the land of Jersey require day badges during the summer season, so there can be costs involved. This also means that to take a walk in certain state parks you must pay a fee. Beaches and parks require maintenance—and money is needed to maintain the ecological balance in these regions, so please don't complain too much about costs that continue to rise and fall. In the case of the Jersey beaches, fees have been reduced in recent years, making them more accessible to the greater populace, so sometimes costs can change for the better. Off-season, from September through the middle of June, the beaches are free.

Take notes of your jaunts on the following pages marked Journey Notes, and let us hear from you.

We also hope that drivers will take care not to hit deer and other animals who cross the highways, sometimes darting in front of a vehicle without warning. The title of one of Stevie Wonder's songs is "Don't Drive Drunk!" On the recording of this song there is the sound of a crash and of shattered glass. While we are not telling drivers not to have a cocktail, beer, or wine with dinner, we are advising them to **DRIVE SOBER!** And **DRIVE SAFELY.** Have fun!

Index

Abbey Bed & Breakfast, 203
Abesecon Light House, 188
Acorn Hall, 75
Adriatic, 141
advisory, travelers', 206–207
Alegria, Ramona, 89
Alegria, Ruth, 89
Allaire State Park, 135
Allamuchy State Park, 118, 122
Allen, Win, 173
Allen, Woody, 139
Allenhurst, 133
Allen's Clam House, 173
Amherst, The, 139
Angelo's Fairmount Tavern, 188
Anheuser-Busch brewery, 38
Appalachian Trail, 114, 120
Applegate Farms, 51
Argyle Restaurant, 22
Armstrong, Maitland, 36
Artie's "Club Elmour," 67
Asbury Park, 140–42
A. S. Hewitt State Forest, 120
Athens Diner, 30
Atlantic Bar & Grill, 157
Atlantic City, 7, 163
Atlantic City, 190
Atlantic City:
  casinos, 183–88
  day trip, 179–82
  old, 189–93
Atlantic City Art Center, 191
Atlantic City Historical Museum, 191
Atlantic Highlands, 131
Atsion Lake, 178
August Moon Chinese Restaurant, 74
Avalon, 199
Aztec Motel Bar, 158

Backstage Restaurant and Cabaret, 96
Baeder, John, 30
Bahrs, 131

Ballantine, John, 38
Ballantine House, 38
Bally's Grand Casino, 185, 186
Bally's Park Place, A Hilton Casino Resort, 184–85, 192–93
Bamberger's Department Store, L., 36
Bamboo Club, 154
Bandiera, Bobby, 140
Baremore, James, 174
Barnegat, 172
Barnegat Bay, 148–49, 156
Barnegat City, 170
Barnegat Inlet, 169
Barnegat Lighthouse, 156
Barnegat National Wildlife Refuge, 172
Bass River State Forest, 173
Batona campsite, 178
Batona Trail, 178
Batsto Lake, 177
Batsto Mansion, 177
Batsto Village, 177
Bay Avenue Diner, 173
Bay Head, 148, 149
Bay Head Sands, 149
Beach Club Hotel, 197–98
Beach Haven, 170
Beach House, 145, 146
Beans, 49, 50
Beauty of Civilization, The, 77
Bellevue Hotel, 196
Bellevue movie theater, 51
Bell Telephone Company, 36, 37
Belmar, 143–44
Belmont Tavern and Restaurant, 44
Bennet, F. H., 125
Benny, Jack, 7
Bergins, Annette, 145
Berkeley Carteret Hotel, 141
Berkeley Fish Market and Restaurant, 158
Berkeley Sweet and Taffy Shop, 154

Bernardsville, 84
Big Swartswood Lake, 118
Bitucci, John, 67
Black Bass Hotel, 97–98
Black Cat Tavern, 180
Black Horse Inn, 76
Black Horse Pub, 76
Black River, 76, 77
Black River and Western Railroad, 91–92, 95
Bloomfield, 40–46, 47
Blue Diamond, 33
Blue Moon, 69
Boardwalk Pavilion, 144
Boat Bar, 188
Bonaparte Park Garden House, 108
Boonton, 121
Bordentown, 108
Bossone, Dominic and Marguerite, 146
Boulton, Agnes, 146–47
Bozarth, William, 163
Bradley, Bill, 76, 98
Branch Brook Park, 38–39
Branchville, 123
Brass Bed Inn, 203
Brass Penny, 85
Brass Rail, 16–17
Bridgestreet House, 95–96
Bridgeton, 111
Brielle, 146
Brigantine National Wildlife Refuge, 173, 175
Brighton Bar, 141
Broad Street Church, 111
Broadway Bar, 147
Bucks County Playhouse, 96
Bum Rogers, 158
Buncher's hardware store, 58
Burlington, 107–108
Burlington County Prison Museum, 108
Bush, Barbara, 52
Bush, George, 52, 66
Butterfly Pond Fish and Wildlife Management Area, 166
Buttzville Hot Dog Johnny's, 116
Byram, Ebenezer, 76

Caesars Atlantic City, 184
Cafe-Grill Rotisserie, 68
Camden, 102–105, 170
Camelot Motel, 203
Campbell, 169–70
Campbell, James, 102
Campbell Museum, 104–105
Campbell's Soup, 102–105
Cape May, 201–205
Cape May-Lewes Ferry, 202–203
Cape May Point Lighthouse, 202
Cape May Point State Park, 201
Captain James Lawrence House, 107
Carlis, Tom, 29
Carlo's City Hall Bake Shop, 18
Carmelita's Café, 17–18
Caroll, Tom and Sue, 203
Carolyn Taylor, Inc.–Gallery of Vintage, 48–49
Carranza Memorial, 178
Carriage House Antique Center, 146
Carrington, Frank, 57
Cascade Trail, 56
Cassville, 167
Castelo's Restaurant, 39
Castle Point, 12, 13
Cathedral of the Sacred Heart, 40, 43
Central Arcade, Seaside Heights boardwalk, 153–54
Chalfonte-Haddon Hall Hotel, 184, 193
Chalfonte Hotel, 202
Chaplin, Charlie, 88
Chatsworth, 177
Chatterbox, 154, 197
cherry blossoms, 39
Chesapeake Bay Seafood Company, 78–79
Chester, 77–78
Churchill, Helen, 44
Circus, The, 142–43
Clam Broth House, 11
Clam Hut, 131
Clam Town Books, 173
Clara Barton School, 108
Claridge, 50
Claridge Casino Hotel, 186, 193

Clementon Amusement Park, 108–109

Clinton, 114–15

Clinton, Bill, 66

Clinton Historical Museum, 115

Clockedile, Kathy, 45

Club Miami, 130

Coast Guard, 169–70

Cohen, Ofer and Ronnie, 31–32

College of St. Elizabeth, 73

Collingwood Auction, 134

Colonial Hotel and Motor Lodge, 203

Colton Court, 203

Columbia House, 203, 205

Commini's, 101

Community Episcopal Trinity Church, 109

Connecticut Farms Presbyterian Church, 68

Conover's Bay Head Inn, 149

Convention Center, Atlantic City, 182

Convention Hall, Asbury Park, 140, 142

Convention Hall, Atlantic City, 182, 193

Cordova, The, 139

Costa, Mario, Jr., 28

County Seat restaurant, 122–23

Cowboy Steakhouse and Saloon, 168

Cowtown Rodeo, 112–13

Crab's Claw Inn, 159

Craigmeur Ski area, 119–20

cranberries, 167

Crawford, Roger, 203

Crazy Rhythms, 50

Cromwell, James, 83

Crowe, Tom and Jacqui, 77

Culver Gap, 123

Cunningham, John, 5, 147–48

Dairy Queen, 65

Darlington County Park, 120

Darrow, Charles, 183

Deal, 133

Delaware River, 93

Delaware Water Gap National Recreation Area, 114–15, 123

Delicious Apple Orchards, 135

DeNichilo, Sergio, 19

De Niro, Robert, 44

Dennis Hotel, 185, 192–93

Dentzel/Looff carousel, 150–51

DePalma, Nicholas, 19

DeVito, Danny, 141

Dexterity, 49

Dickie-Dee Pizza, 44

Difiglia, Joseph, 125

Dillon family, 85

diners, 23–26
  day trips, 27–34
  design of, 23–25
  list of, 33–34
  origin of, 23

Di Pietro Italian Specialty Foods, 68

DiTerlizzi, Leo, 19

Dockside Cafe, 197

Dock's Oyster House, 188

Dorance, Arthur, 102

Dorca's Ice Cream Parlor and Restaurant, 149

Doris and Ed's, 131

Down the Shore, 145

Down the Street, 141

Drayton, Grace Gebbie, 103

Drew University, 73

Dukakis, Olympia, 49

Duke, Doris, 81, 82, 83

Duke Farms, 83, 85

Duke Gardens, 80–82

Duke Island Park, 82

Dunwoody, John and Donna, 203

DuPont, E. I., 110

Eagle Rock Reservation, 54–55, 60

Ebby's Cafe Alfresco, 157

Ebby's Deli, 157

Echevarria, Fred and Joan, 203

Edison, Thomas, 7, 192

Ed Zaberer's Restaurant, 200

Ehman, Artie, 67

Einstein, Albert, 88

Eisenberg, Lee, 190

Elmdale, 55

El Taco Loco, 96

Elysian Fields, 16

Elysian Park, 12–13

Engelhard, Charles, 85

Engelhard, Jane, 85
Englishtown Auction Market, 135
Erie Lackawanna Train Terminal, 11, 14
Escargot Books, 146

facts about New Jersey, 7–9
Fairleigh Dickinson University Florham-Madison campus, 73
Fallon, Steve, 13, 16
Fantasy Island Amusement Park, 153, 170
Far Hills, 84–85
farms, 106–107, 126, 165
Farouk, King, 83
Farris, Diane, 50
Fast Lane II, 141
Faulkner, Virginia, 74
Fenton, Maggie, 203
Ferry House Tavern, 98
Figueroa, Eutiquio, 12
Finns Point National Cemetery, 110
Fiorino Ristorante, 67
Firestone Library, 87
firsts, New Jersey, 8–9
Fishermen's Pier, 141
5¢ & Dime, 95
"Five Points" intersection, 68
Five Star Diner, 123
Flanders Hotel, 197
flea markets, 134, 135
Flemington, 90–92
Flemington Cut Glass Company, 91
Forbes family, 85
Ford, Charlotte, 84
Forked River, 168
Fornos of Spain, 39
Fort Hancock, 129, 130
Fort Mott State Park, 110
Fralinger's Saltwater Taffy, 181, 192
Francis, Connie, 47, 52
Fran-Jay, 94–95
Franklin, Benjamin, 6
Franklin Lakes, 120
Franklin Museum, 120
Freddie's Pizza, 132
Freehold Raceway, 135
Frenchtown Inn, 98

Friends Meeting House, 108
Fudge Kitchen, 201
Funchase Pier, 200
Fun Pier, 200

Gaiser's Pork Store, 66
Gajdos, Robert, 95
Galatas, Sam, 29
Galloping Hill Inn, 68
Garden State Arts Center, 134
Garret Mountain Reservation, 20
Gateway National Recreation Area, 129
geography, 6–7
George Washington Slept Here, 7
Georgian Court, 164
Gibraltar Building, 36
Gifts by Tina, 138
Gilman, John, 228
Gingerbread Castle, 124, 125
Gingerbread House, 203
Gladstone, 84, 85
Glassboro, 109–10
Glen Ridge, 47
Gold, Al, 190
Golden, Richard, 95
Golden Age Books and Comics, 16
Golden Nugget Saloon, 118
Goshen Pond, 178
Gotsis, Louis "Tex," 168
Gould, George Jay, 164
Gourmet Wine and Cheese Shop, 123
Graves, Michael, 37
Great Adventure, 165–66
Great Auditorium, 137
Great Bay, 173
Great Bay Fish and Wildlife Area, 173
Great Falls, 21–22
Great Gorge Ski Area, 119
Great Swamp, 70–71
Great Swamp National Wildlife Refuge, 71
Green, Hetty, 15, 17
Greenhouse Restaurant, 88
Greenwich, 111
Greenwood Lake State Park, 120
Grob, Gary J., 158
Guggenheim Memorial Library, 133

Hacklebarney Farms, 76
Hacklebarney State Park, 76
Hague, "Boss," 6
Hamburg Mountain Wildlife
    Management Area, 121
Hamilton, Brian, 125
Hancock House, 111
Hand Mad, 16
Hans, Jim, 17
Hardyston, 121
Harrah's Casino Hotel, 185
Harris, Grant, 113
Harris Diner, 31, 32
Hauptmann, Anna, 90
Haymes, Dick, 190
Heath, Debbie, 45
Heide, Robert, 61–65, 228
Helmer's German Restaurant, 13
Hemlock Falls, 55
Hepburn, Katherine, 150
Hidden Valley, 119
High Button Shoe Antique Cen-
    ter, 90
"Highlands," 117–18
Highlawn Pavilion, 60
High Point, 124
High Point Monument, 124
High Point State Park, 117, 122
Hinck Building, 48, 50
Hindenburg, 167
Historical Society of Bloomfield,
    46
Historical Society of Princeton, 87
Historic registers, 38, 73, 94, 115,
    118, 139, 195
history, 7
Hoagland's Tavern, 108
Hoboken, 7, 15–19
    day trips, 10–14
Hoboken Bookstore, 16
Hoboken City Hall, 17
Hoboken Historical Society, 17
Hofbrauhaus, 131
Hoffer, Madeline, 136
Holiday Inn, 115
Holland, John P., 20
Holland Tunnel, 4
Holst, Hans, 18
Holsten's Brookdale Confec-
    tionery, 44–45
Hopatcong State Park, 118

Hopewell, 90
Hopewell Canning Company, 90
Hopewell Museum, 90
Horn, Martin L., 58, 59
Horn family, 59–60
Horseshoe Cove, 129
Hotel Grenville, 149
House By The Sea, The, 139
Houston, Whitney, 41
Hull, William, 48
Huntington House, 204
Hunt's Pier, 200
Hurricane House, 172
Hutton, Barbara, 180

Iberia Tavern and Restaurant, 39
Ichiban, 88–89
Immerso, Michael, 43
industrial belt, 6, 22
Inn at Lambertville Station, 95
In-Retro Vintage Clothing and
    Collectibles, 16
Ironbound District, 39
Irvington, 61–65
Island Beach, 156–60
Island Beach Motor Lodge, 157
Island Heights, 160
Island Park, 116
Israel Crane House, 50–51
Iu, Colan, 74
Ivanka's, 186

Jacob Ford House, 75
Jacobson family, 76
Jahn's, 67
James Fenimore Cooper House,
    107
James Wilson Marshall House, 94
Jenkinson's South Amusement
    Park, 147
Jenny Jump Forest, 118
Jersey City, 27–28
"Jersey Devil," 6, 161–63, 172,
    175, 177, 189
Jersey shore:
    Atlantic City, 179–93
    Cape May, 201–205
    Island Beach, 156–60
    Long Beach Island, 169–70
    North shore, 131–33, 140–60
    Ocean City, 194–98

Jersey shore (*cont.*)
   Ocean Grove, 136–39
   Sandy Hook, 129–30
   Seaside Heights, 150–55
   travel to, 126–28
   Wildwood, 199–200
J.J. Astor House, 17
Jockey Hollow, 72
Joe's Diamond diner, 23
Joe's Famous Pizzeria, 68
Johnny Rockets, 16
Johnson, Lyndon, 110
Johnson's Popcorn, 154
jokes, Jersey, 5–6
Jorgensen's Inn, 121
Journal Square, 27–28

K & K Spanish-American Restaurant, 30
Kanter, Fred, 121
Kanter Auto Products, 121
Keansburg, 130
Kearny, 22
Keeler, Ruby, 130
Kelly, Grace, 196
Kennedy, Caroline, 85
Ken's Landing, 147
Keyport, 129–30
Keyport Fisheries, 129–30
Killcohook National Wildlife Refuge, 110–11
King Edward Lounge, 202
Kirk's New Modern Diner, 25
Kitch & Kaboodle, 138
Klee's Bar, 152–53
Klein's Waterside Cafe, 143–44
Kless's Diner, 65
Knife & Fork Inn, 188
Knowles family, 60
Kohr's, 154, 155
Koppel, Ted, 104
Kosygin, Aleksey, 110
Kovalsky, John and Pat, 116
Kullman Industries, 25
Kuser, Colonel and Mrs. Anthony R., 124
Kutschera, Tony, 191

Laemmel's Pork Store, 18
Lafferty, James, 195
La Gondola, 101

Lagoon, 188
Lake Absegami, 173
Lake Girard, 121
Lake Hopatcong, 118
Lake Hopatcong State Park, 122
Lakehurst Naval Historical Society, 167
Lake Musconetcong State Park, 122
Lake Pohatcong, 173
Lake Rova, 166
Lakewood, 164–65
Lam, Henry, 74
Lambert Castle, 20
Lambertville, 93–98
Lambertville Antiques Flea Market, 97
Lambertville House, 94
Lambertville Railroad Station, 95
La Mer, 203
Landis, John K., 111
Land of Make Believe, The, 118
Lane, Nat, 141
Larison's Turkey Farm, 77–78
La Spina, Arnold, 16
Latino culture, 66
Le Dome, 53
Lee, W. H. Fitzhugh, 202
Leed, Aunt Millie, 190
"Leeds Devil," 161, 177
Leeds Point, 175
Left Bank Bookstore, 94
Lenape Trail, 43, 56
Leon, Joe, 157
Leo's Grandevous Restaurant, 18–19
Levi, Vicki Gold, 190, 191
Levine, Al, 46
Liberace, 59
Liberty Village, 91
Lido Diner, 82
Lindbergh, Charles, 90
Linder, Monsignor William J., 43
Little Egg Harbor, 173
"Little Italy," Newark, 43–44
Little Swartswood Lake, 118
Livingston Mall, 58
Loeper, Marge and John, 198
Loews of Jersey City, 28
Long Beach Island, 169–70
Long Branch, 132

Longport, 195–96
Longstreet Farm, 134
Long Valley, 78–79
Long Valley Inn, 78
Lorrimer Nature Center, 120
Los Dos Compadres Restaurant, 11–12
Lucy Evelyn, 170
Lucy the Margate Elephant, 195
Lueders, Norman, 13
Lumberville, Pennsylvania, 97
Lutz's Pork Store, 66

McCarter Theater, 87
McDowell's Gallery of Gifts, 202
McGlade's Mansion House, 204
McGuire Air Force Base, 167
Mack and Manco, 196
Maclean House, 87
McPhee, John, 5
Mad Batter, The, 204
Madison, 73
Madison Hotel, 73
Mahn, Patrick, 83
Mahwah Railroad Museum, 120
Mainstay Breakfast and Tea, 203
Main Street Antique Center, 91
Mall at Short Hills, The, 58
Manahawkin, 172–73
Manasquan, 146
Manasquan River, 164–65
Mandlebaum, Minnie, 49
Manor, the, 52–53
Manor Restaurant, 60
Mantoloking, 150
Maplewood, 68
Maplewood Cinema, 68
map of New Jersey, ix
Mardi Gras, 158–59
Margate, 195
Mariner's Landing, 200
Marlboro Inn, 51–52
Marlborough-Blenheim Hotel, 184, 190, 192
Marmaras, Bill, 31
Maruca's Pizza, 151–52
Maruca's Tomato Pies East, 152
Maruca's Tomato Pies West, 152
Mason, John L., 112
Mathis, J. Vaughan, 179
Matthews, Don, 158

Maureen's, 204
Max's Grill, 30
Maxwell's, 13–14
Mayfair Farms, 59
Meade, George Gordon, 169
Meisch, Bill, 138
Melrose Diner, 31
Mendham, 76
Menlo Park "lightbulb" memorial, x, 7
Merion Inn, 203–204
Merv Griffin's Resorts International Casino Hotel, 184, 193
Mexican Village, 89
Mexican Village II, 89
Mey, Cornelius Jacobsen, 202
Millburn, 55, 57–60
Miller, Beth, 138
Miller, Florence, 191
Minuteman Family Restaurant, 71
Miss America Diner, 29
Molly Pitcher Inn, 132
Mom's Kitchen, 142
Monmouth Battleground State Park, 134
Monmouth Beach, 132
Monmouth College, 132–33
Monmouth Park Racetrack, 134
Monopoly, 183
Montclair, 47–53
Montclair Art Museum, 51
Montclair Book Center, 49
Montclair Country Club, 52
Montreal Inn, 203
Moon Motel, 164
Moore, Bette, 73
Moorlyn, 196
Moravian Church, 109
Moreland, Dr. Floyd, 150–51
Morey's Pier, 200
Morris and Essex Line of New Jersey Transit, 84–85
Morris Canal, 118
Morristown, 74–76
Morristown National Guard, 75
Morristown National Historic Park, 75
Morrow, Bill and Eleanor, 202
Morrow, Tom, 48–49
Morrow's Nut House, 202

Mother's Restaurant, 96
Mount Holly, 108
Mount Mitchell, 130
Mount Zion Primitive Baptist
    Church, 64
Mullica Hill, 109
Mullica River wilderness camp-
    site, 178
Mullock, Bob and Linda, 203
Municipal Pool, 144
Murchison, Kenneth, 11
Museum of Early Crafts and
    Trades, 73
music, 13, 140–41
Myoptics, 16
Mystic Island, 173

Nail House Museum, 111
Nassau Hall, 87
Nassau Inn, 88
Nast, Thomas, 74
National Wilderness Preservation
    system, 71
Navesink Twin Lights, 131
Neptune, 142
Neshanic River, 92
Neshanic Station, 92
Newark, 2, 35–39
    Bloomfield, 40–46
    celebrated persons who lived
        in, 40
Newark Art Theater, 57
Newark Museum, 37–38
Newark Paramount Theater, 36
"New Community," 43
New Gretna, 173
New Hope, Pennsylvania, 96, 97
New Horizon Restaurant, 170
New Jersey Certified Farm Mar-
    kets, 107
New Jersey Performing Arts Cen-
    ter, 37
New Jersey Shakespeare Festival,
    73
New Jersey State Aquarium, 105
New Jersey State Library, 100
New Jersey State Museum, 100
New Jersey Symphony Orchestra,
    37
New Jersey Turnpike, 6
Newton, 122–23

Newton Fire Museum, 122
Nicholas, Bill, 31
Nicholson, Jack, 142
Nickel's Midway Pier, 200
Nickerson's, 130
Nixon, Richard, 52, 150
North Arlington Diner, 22, 30
North Beach Haven, 170
northern mountains and lakes,
    117–25
North Shore, 131–33, 140–60
Northwood Inn, 198
Nostalgic Nonsense, 144
Noyes, Fred and Ethel, 175
Noyes Museum, 174
Nunzio's, 132

Oakdale Trail, 56
Ocean Bay Diner, 147
Ocean City, 194–98
Ocean City Historical Museum,
    198
Ocean County Artists Guild, 160
Ocean County Historical Society,
    167–68
Ocean County Park, 164
Ocean Drive, 194
Ocean Grove, 136–39, 141
Ocean Plaza, 139
Of Rare Vintage, 138
Olaf, King of Sweden, 109
Old Barnegat Lighthouse, 169
Old Barracks, 100
Old Book Shop, 74–75
Old Clinton House, 115
Olde Union House, 132
Old Heidelburg Inn, 130
Old Homestead, 64–65
Olmstead, Frederick Law, 39, 54,
    73
Olympic Park, 61–64
Onassis, Jacqueline Kennedy, 84
O'Neill, Eugene, 146
On the Waterfront, 12, 15, 16
O' Poeta Bar and Restaurant, 39
Ort Farms, 78, 79
Owl Haven, 134
Oyster Creek Inn, 175

Page I Cafe, 49
Palley, Reese, 163

Pals Cabin, 58–60
Panko, Alex, Jr., 128
Papermill Playhouse, 57
Paramount Theater, 140
Park South Beauty Parlor, 50
Park View Hotel, 139
Passaic Township Grange, 70
Paterson, 20–22
Paterson Museum, 20
PATH (Port Authority Trans-
    Hudson) system, 11
Pat's Stand, 162
Peapack, 84, 85
Pearson House, 107
Pegasus, 77
Penn Station, 35
People's Store, 94
Pequest River, 116
performing arts, 57
Perzel, Bob and Nancy, 91
Pesci, Joe, 44
Pete and Elda's Tavern and Car-
    men's Pizzeria, 142
Peterpank Diner, 128
Peters, Stefan, 49, 50
Peter Skoko's Drive-In, 147
Peterson's Riviera Inn, 164–65
Phillips, Gary, 153–54, 170
Phillipsburg, 115
Phoenix Books, 94
Pierce, C. J., 67
Pier House, 158
Pine Barrens, 6, 7, 161–63, 167,
    172, 173, 176–78
Pineland National Reserve, 176
Pine Tree Inn, The, 139
Piscopo, Joe, 6
Pitcher, Molly, 134
Point Pleasant, 146–48
Point Pleasant Antique Empo-
    rium, 148
Pomegranate, 148
Pompton Lakes, 120
Popkorn Antiques, 91
Port Jervis, New York, 124
Potter's Tavern, 111
Powerhouse Tattoo, 50
Price, William L., 193
Princeton, 86–89
Princeton Chapel, 87
Princeton University, 86–88

Priory Restaurant, 40, 43
Prudential Insurance Company, 36
Prudential Museum, 36
Pulaski Skyway, 7
Pushkin Gardens, 166

Quarry, The, 119

Raccoon, 109
Rahway River, 55
Ramapo Mountain Forest, 121
Ramapo Valley County Reserva-
    tion, 120
Ram's Head Inn, 60
Rancocas State Park, 108
Raritan River, 92, 115
Rauschenberg, Robert, 104
Reagan, Nancy, 52
Reagan, Ronald, 52
Red Bank, 131–32
Red Bank Antiques Center, 132
Reservoir Pizzeria & Restaurant,
    56, 69
Resorts International Casino Ho-
    tel, 184
Ringwood Manor House, 121
Ringwood State Park, 120–21
Rispoli, Michael, 138
River Bank Park, 22
River Belle, 147
Roadside Diner, 143
roadside stands, 107, 126
Robin Hutchins Gallery, 68
rock-and-roll, 140–41
Rockaway Gorge, 121
Rockefeller, John D., 164
Rod's 1890s Ranch House, 73–74
Roebling, Mary, 150
Roosevelt, Eleanor, 57
Roque and Rebelo, 39
Round Valley State Park, 115
Rova Farm Bar and Restaurant,
    166
Rova Farms, 166–67
Rowan University, 109
Rowan University Library, 110
Rubirosa, Porfirio, 83
Rum Runners, 140–41

Sagres Restaurant, 39
St. Joseph's Plaza, 40, 43

St. Vladimir's Church, 166–67
Sale, Bion LeRoy, 58, 59
Salem, 110–11
Salem County Historical Society, 110
Salem Oak, 110
Sammy's Ye Old Cider Mill Inn, 76
Sampler Hotel, 138
Sampler Inn, 138
Sand Castle, 179–80
Sands Hotel and Casino, 185
Sandy Hook, 129–30
Sandy Hook Lighthouse, 129
Santa Maria House, 179
Sawmill Lake, 117
Sawyer, Colonel Henry, 202
Schatz, Jay and Marianne, 203
Schnackenbergs, 16
Schooley Mountain Park, 79
Schooley Mountains, 78
Schooner's Wharf, 170
Schuyler Hamilton House, 75
Schwarzkopf, H. Norman, 90
Scialla, Johnny, 132
Scudder, Antoinette, 57
Sea Bright, 131
Seabrook Farms, 112
Seagull's Nest, 129
Seaside Heights, 150–55, 158–60
Seaside Park, 157
Second Sun Energy Information Center, 111
Seton Hall University, 69
Seventh Heaven, 95
Sferrazza, Julie, 91
Shaller, Shirley, 49
Shark River, 144
Sheridan, Ann, 7
Shields, Brooke, 89
Ship Bottom, 170
Short Hills, 57, 58
Short Stop Diner, 30, 45–46
Showboat, 187
Shriver's Saltwater Taffy Shop, 196
Silver Lake Inn, 109
Sinatra, Frank, 11, 15–16, 17, 18
Sinbad, 169–70
Six Flags Great Adventure, 165–66

Skokos, Tina, 138
Skylands, 121
Smithville, 174–75
Smithville Inn, 175
Smithville Mansion, 108
Smithville Village, 108
Somerville, 83
South Mountain Reservation, 54–56
South Orange, 56, 69
Southwestern farm country, 106–13
Space Farms, 119
Spaeter's, 67
Spermaceti Cove, 129
Spike's Fish Market and Restaurant, 147
Spindrift, 197
Spirit of St. Louis, The, 20
Spring Lake, 144–46, 196
Spring Lake Christmas Bed and Breakfast Tour, 145
Springsteen, Bruce, 6, 140, 141, 143
Spruce Run River, 115
Spruce Run State Park, 79, 115
Squan Tavern, 146
Stanley Theater, 28
Stark, Rudy and Ron, 44
Starr, Jacob, 38
State Historic Register, 73, 94
Stations West Antiques, 49
Stegman, Steve, 95
Stein, Gertrude, 206
Stevens, Colonel John, 15
Stevens Gatehouse, 12
Stevens Institute of Technology, 12, 13, 15
Stevens Park, 12
Stewart Inn, 115
Stewart's Root Beer, 30, 173
Stewart's Root Beer Drive-In, 22, 33
Stewartsville, 115
Stokes State Forest, 114, 117, 123, 124
Stone Harbor Bird Sanctuary, 199
Stone Pony, 140, 141
Stony Lake, 117
Strand, 196
Studebaker Showroom, 179

Subject Was Roses, The, 144
Summit, 67
Summit Diner, 32
Surf City, 170
Sussex County Historical Society headquarters and Museum, 122
Swainton, 199
Swartswood State Park, 118, 123
Swedesboro, 109
Symphony Hall, 40

Taj Mahal, 187–88
T-Birds Cafe, 141
Tecza, Pat, 144
"Telling the Ocean Slant," 136
Tesauro's, 147
theater, state, 57
Thomas Leaming Farm, 199
Thomas Paine House, 108
Three Little Girls in Blue, 189
Tillman Ravine, 123
Timbuctoo, 108
Time After Time Clothing From the Past, 73
Tinton Falls, 134
Tiny Tim, 155
Tivoli Pier, 186
tomatoes, 107
Tomato Factory Antique Center, 90
Tony Da Caneca's, 39
Tony's Baltimore Grill, 181–82
Top of the Trop, 186
Top O' the Mast Restaurant, 157
Town Green Historic District, 46
Town Hall, Newton, 122
Town Hall Deli, 69
travelers' advisory, 206–207
Traymore Hotel, 193
Treasure Cove, 201
Treat, Captain Robert, 40
Trent, William, 100
Trenton, 99–101
Trenton Battle Monument, 100
Trenton City Museum, 100
Trenton state fair, 101
Trinity Apartment buildings, 50
Tri-State Rock, 124
Tropicana Casino and Resort, 186
Trump Castle, 187

Trump Plaza Hotel and Casino, 186
Trump World's Fair, 185
Tuckahoe Corbin City Fish and Wildlife Management Area, 196
Tuckerton, 173
Tuckerton Emporium, 173
Tunnel Diner, 34
Turtleback Zoo, 55–56
Tuzzio's, 132
Twombly, Florence Vanderbilt, 73

Union, 66–68
Union Center, 66–67
Union Cinema, 67
Union City, 66
Union Hotel, 92
Upper Montclair, 51
Urban, Joseph, 125

Valentine, Tom, 83
Valley General Store, 109
Varela, Evencio, 12
Vaughan, Sarah, 41
Ventnor, 194
Vernon Valley Action Park, 119
Vernon Valley/Great Gorge Ski Area, 119
Verona, 52
Verona Park, 52
Victorian Rose, 203
Vineland, 111–12
Vineland Historical Society, 111
Voorhees State Park, 79

Wall Township, 142–43
Wall Township "Demo Derby," 135
Walpack Center, 123
Walpack Inn, 123
Walt Whitman House, 105
Warhol, Andy, 102, 104
Warren Hotel, 144–45, 146
Warwick, Dionne, 41
Washington, 115–16
Washington, George, 7, 56, 68, 72, 74, 75, 98, 99–100
Washington Auto Graveyard, 115–16

Washington Crossing State Park, 98
Washington Rock, 56
Washington Street Mall, 201
Watchung Reservation, 55
Watchung ridge, 54, 60
Waterloo Festival of the Arts, 118
Waterloo Village, 118
Watson House, 100
Wawayanda State Park, 114, 120
Weiner, Richard, 146
Welch, T. B., 112
West Bloomfield, 47–48
West Long Branch, 132–33
Wharton, Joseph, 177–78
Wharton State Forest, 177
Whay, Betty, 51
Wheatley's Drugstore, 108
Wheel House Marina, 158
White, Stanford, 35, 73
White Circle System, 33
White Clock System, 23
White Diamond dinette, 25
White Diamonds, 33
White House Sub Station, 180–81
White Manna, 28, 31–32
White Rose System, 33
White Star Diners, 33

White Tower restaurants, 105
Whittingham Wildlife Management Area, 123
Wick, Tempe, 72
Wick House, 72
Wightman Farm, 71
Wilder, Thornton, 127
Wild West City, 118
Wildwood-by-the-Sea, 199–200
Wildwood Historical Museum, 200
Williams, Harrison A., 6
Williams, William Carlos, 20–21
William Trent House, 100
Wilson, Gladys A., 162–63
Windjammer Motor Inn, 158
Wolff, Chris, 75
Woodrow Wilson Hall, 133
Woodruff Indian Museum, 111
Woodstown, 112–13
Woolsey, Jim, 123
Worthington State Forest, 114, 116
Wyckoff, Bonny, 174

Yakety Yak Club, 154
Ye Cottage Inn, 129
Yellow Cottage, 123
Ye Olde Centerton Inn, 111
Yesterday Books and Records, 50

Journey Notes

The authors, John Gilman and Robert Heide

Write to the authors at: St. Martin's Press
175 Fifth Avenue
New York, NY 10010

Happy trails!

ROBERT HEIDE was born in Irvington, New Jersey.
JOHN GILMAN was born in Honolulu, Hawaii. They
are both residents of Manhattan who have spent
many years on the byways, backroads, and super-
highways of New Jersey, enjoying the small towns,
industrial areas, seaside resorts, diners, and interesting spots along the way. Both authors have written
extensively about the state of New Jersey for such periodicals as the *Village Voice* and the *Daily News*.
Gilman is a pop-culture archeological historian and
preservationist. Heide is a published playwright
whose plays have been performed in New York in
Greenwich Village at the Cherry Lane and Caffe
Cino and in the East Village at Cafe LaMama and
Theater for the New City. Two of his plays, *The Bed*
and *The Death of Lupe Velez* (starring Edie Sedg-
wick), were filmed by Andy Warhol.